# ARCHITECTURE

## A HISTORICAL PERSPECTIVE

jovis

**To Nora**

# ARCHITECTURE

## A HISTORICAL PERSPECTIVE

**PAVLOS LEFAS**

I am grateful to Michael Iliakis who carried the burden of the translation into English, to Sofia Bobou who helped in its initial stages, and to Inez Templeton who edited the text.

I want to thank the following colleagues who helped me avoid some mistakes and misconceptions. They are Hasan Badawi, Panayotis Evangelides, Panagiotes Ioannou, Lilian Karali, Nikos Karapidakis, Yannis Kokkinakis, Eleni Kondyli, Michael Kordosis, Martin Kreeb, Callirroe Palyvou, Stylianos Papalexandropoulos, Qiang Li, Eleni Sakellariou, Gebhard Selz, Panayiotis Tournikiotes, Jonathan Taylor, Dusanka Urem-Kotsou, Lorenzo Verderame.

At the end of each chapter, there are books and papers mentioned, which have directly influenced the author's point of view. A generic bibliography is not given, since it is constantly renewed and complemented with new, important contributions.

This book talks about architecture, about the concerns, the pursuits and the achievements of its people, and about how their work has been perceived.

Just as any other narrative, however, this account is by its very nature unfair—not only because Western architecture is overrepresented in it, but also because it leaves out of the picture thousands and thousands of buildings in which real people were born, brought up, lived, and died. Small jewels, monuments of vanity, or simply ordinary—all were the product of toil and the receptors of dreams; for that reason alone, they do not deserve the oblivion into which they are pushed deeper with each new reference to other, seemingly slightly better, slightly more important, or slightly more celebrated contemporary buildings.

With the unkindness and arrogance associated with our power to choose, to remember, and to forget, this book looks at the past through the lenses of someone who—in the chaotic complexity of the universe of edifices—seeks to understand why and how people build.

The past emerges unexpectedly in its proximity. This is probably the best vindication of those who devoted their time and efforts to create day by day, stone by stone, the environment in which we live today.

This book is a guide for reading architecture of yesterday with our eyes focused on tomorrow. It is written with the hope that it will spur the reader to search for other views and to complement his/her knowledge with further reading and the examination of other sources; and to look around him/her once more at the magic of the world surrounding us.

# ARE THERE ARCHETYPES IN ARCHITECTURE?

## The Terra Amata Huts

Unlike clothes, buildings cannot be squeezed into the back of our closet or taken to the local charity shop when no longer in fashion; they are meant to stay. Not having the chance to design new ones for the upcoming season, architects would like their buildings to withstand the test of time and not be seen as obsolete the day after; owners who pay good money to have the buildings erected expect their investments to have value for as long as possible; and users insist that certain things be done the way they "should" be done, no matter how fascinated by innovative ideas they might be. This is why the question "are there archetypes in architecture?" has been central to architectural theory throughout the ages, and still retains, to some extent, its validity. An archetype in architecture is a form that we keep reproducing, more or less deliberately, acknowledging therein an irrefutable wisdom and an appeal that may never perish. "Form" is used here in the original sense of the term: as the structure, organization or essential character of something, rather than merely its appearance. An archetype, then, is a paradigm that incorporates what is important and perennial, and as such one that can adapt to specific contemporary requirements over changing times, while maintaining all its primary qualities.

Watching children drawing pictures of their dream homes in the almost stereotypical shape of a small house complete with roof and smoking chimney, one feels as though he/she is witnessing an archetype in architecture. This might well be so. In the remote past, humans evidently used to build huts fairly similar to our own perception of an essential dwelling: the simplest imaginable shelter with a smoking chimney.

In the nineteen-sixties, a team led by Henry de Lumley discovered at the site of Terra Amata in Nice, southern France, vestiges of large huts erected 400,000 years ago—although other scholars doubt his interpretations completely or date the finds tens of thousands of years later; 400,000 years is a long time. The human species, to which the individuals

Hut, Terra Amata, France, circa 400,000 years before today; reconstruction by Henri Puech/Musée de Terra Amata/Ville de Nice

who built the huts belonged, was extinct long ago. Modern humans came to Europe from Africa about 40,000 years ago. The Parthenon was built 2,500 years ago; Leonardo da Vinci conceived his flying machines 500 years ago; and the first underground railway line began operating in London 150 years ago.

De Lumley's excavations revealed that several meters beneath the current surface of the ground, earth and sand were thinner in texture in some places. He interpreted this as dirt accumulated in holes born by tree branches pinned to the ground; the wood disintegrated over time, but left traces on the walls of the holes, providing further evidence to support his assumptions. The holes, clustered in several groups, were not perpendicular, indicating that the branches converged together forming real roofs. The huts, erected along what would have been the seaside at that time—to offer temporary shelter to humans coming to the area to hunt or fish—were oblong, measuring approximately eight to twelve by four to five meters. At the center of each hut, traces of fire were found; probably at the top an opening was left to let the smoke out. Also uncovered here and there were clusters of similar objects—fragments of stone, animal bones, food remains, etc.—suggesting that the space inside each hut had been organized so that different activities (preparing and cooking food, tool making, sleep, etc.) should take place in distinct zones, similarly to modern dwellings.

Traces of a more recent but still very early dwelling—150,000 years old—were discovered inside a cave only a few kilometers away from Terra Amata. At Grotte du Lazaret, a number of large stones circumscribed an area about 11 meters in length and 3.5 meters in width. While outside this area, finds of human activity are scarce, inside they are abundant: numerous bones, stone tools, and stone fragments have been found, as well as two circular charcoal concentrations that researchers have identified as hearths. This suggests that the stones had supported branches propped up against the wall of the cave, and were layered with animal skins, forming a shelter. Fire residue shows that the proportion of slow- to quick-burning logs was considerably higher there than within a radius of several kilometers around the cave.

**Cave hut, Grotte du Lazaret, France, circa 150,000 years before today; reconstruction drawing CNRS**

Its occupants had obviously fairly advanced know-how: they knew that such logs would keep the fire burning low and for longer, making it suitable for keeping the shelter warm. Some finds suggest that the cave was occupied only during the coldest season of the year, when temperatures would fall considerably, particularly at night. Large concentrations of small seashells were uncovered around the hearths. It seems that the occupants of the cave would gather seaweed from the shore, bring it by the fire, and make bedding to sleep more comfortably.

Numerous traces of early human shelters have been unearthed at sites around the globe. Evidently, early humans would often opt for a survival strategy involving what anthropology terms "base camps," settling temporarily at specific locations. This is where the more vulnerable members of the group would be sheltered during the daytime from rain or scorching sun and predatory animals, while the more vigorous members would go hunting or set out for other endeavors. This is where a fire would be lit; it would keep them warm and they would use it to cook the meat to make it healthier to consume and easier to digest. This is also where they would make most of their tools and where they would sleep at night. The location would be near a source of fresh water and preferably in an area rich in raw materials: stones to make tools, deadwood to build a fire, and fruit and prey to secure food. Ideally, it would also allow dwellers to survey the surrounding grounds. This would make them less vulnerable to surprise attacks and on occasion, it would offer the additional advantage of responding more easily to an attacker, who would have to overcome the difficulty of climbing uphill. Perhaps our inherent affinity for a beautiful view and an open horizon goes back to a self-preservation instinct that we have learned to satisfy by choosing dwellings on elevated locations.

Human building activity enhanced the advantages of favorable geo-logical formations: our ancestors realized that it was worthwhile to spend their energies improving the shelters provided by nature or, if necessary, constructing better ones from scratch.

This activity kept on for ages as we can see, for example, in the case of the huts unearthed in Mezhirich, Ukraine, dated barely 15,000 years ago. Built to protect their inhabitants from the cold winter winds, they were made from a frame of mammoth mandibles, tusks, and other bones, and were probably layered with fur. Erecting them required materi-als weighing several tons and several days of teamwork. However, they were quite large in order to accommodate sizable groups, whose members obviously worked together to hunt down the mammoths.

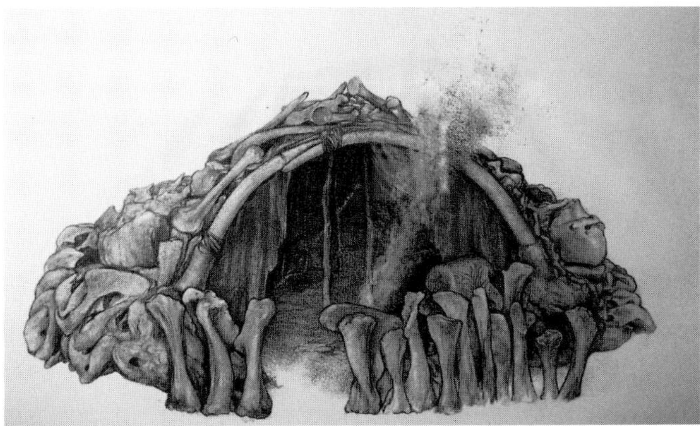

**Mammoth bones hut, Mezhirich, Ukraine, circa 15,000 BCE (fur and skin covering partly omitted); reconstruction drawing Pavel Dvorský**

As humans had probably been doing for hundreds of thousands of years—and have continued doing since—the people who built the Mezhirich huts made clever use of local materials. Nothing substantial has changed since the huts of Terra Amata or the shelter in Grotte du Lazaret. Neither the concept, nor the overall configuration, nor the allocation of ac-

tivities to specific spots inside or in the vicinity of the huts is substantially
different. In this respect, one can suggest that for at least 400,000 years,
and possibly many more—as the 1.75-million-year-old finds unearthed in
Olduvai Gorge in northern Tanzania seem to indicate—there were no crucial changes in the way we used to build our dwellings.

By contrast, progress has been colossal in other fields of human
activity. The sharp follicles and the sharp-edged "axes" manufactured for a
variety of uses 2.5 million years ago have gradually given way to more sophisticated tools. Humans were able to produce a wide range of extremely
specialized tools made of stone and animal bone—from needles and hooks
to javelin spears and knives—250,000 years before our time (that is, long
before Mezhirich).

Ritual disposal of the dead marks another turning point in human
history, since it is a strong (but neither sufficient nor necessary) indication
of a developed self-consciousness and concern with metaphysical questions: what are we, what happens when we die, etc. The earliest burials
possibly date back to at least 100,000 BCE and were practiced in parallel
by both anatomically modern humans and the Neanderthals, who coexisted with the former for a period of time.

Then there is the development of art. Musical instruments date
back at least 35,000 years. Depictions of the real or some fictitious world
also date back tens of thousands of years ago. Such items of craftsmanship were not used in tasks directly associated with securing food, keeping the fire alight, or building dwellings, so in some sense they were
redundant; the evidence though suggest that they were nevertheless
indispensable for the highly sociable Homo sapiens sapiens species: in the
modern world, there is not one known community of people, not one tribe
or group who do not spend vast amounts of their energy to create such
"not-of-direct-use" artifacts.

Early art is largely found deep inside caves at relatively inaccessible areas, hardly ideal for a comfortable viewing. Art such as the
15,000-year-old cave paintings of Lascaux, southern France, may be
labeled as secretive and its purpose may well have been to control nature with methods nowadays considered as witchcraft; however, it was
the product of extremely skilled labor. Additionally, there were probably
also art forms directly involving all community members, as suggested
by today's widely spread practice of body ornamentation, which is
performed mainly for ritualistic purposes, to express the established
social order, or to indicate and confirm a tribal identity. Decoration of the
temporary dwellings humans used to build—which is marginal to proper
architecture—may have been also practiced, although no evidence
thereof has surfaced so far.

Evidently, all of these non-utilitarian artifacts were not useless altogether. They helped to maintain social coherence, to encourage individual
development, and to enhance the awareness of belonging to an organized,
productive, and creative group or community. This would certainly have

made the group or the community stronger and would offer it an advantage in the increasingly competitive world they inhabited.

Arguably more than any other living being, humans do not just adapt to their environment; they also constantly try to change it to their advantage. By improving natural shelters and building huts, humans established themselves in areas that until then had been off limits—a major contribution of "architecture" (if we may call it that) in shaping the world as we know it. Such constructions offered rudimentarily controlled environmental conditions, plus some security; and may have also been good enough to be imbued, when such need emerged, with some kind of symbolism associated with both their form and use of space within or around them, as we can deduce from archaeological or ethnographic parallels—i.e., comparable contemporary cultures—as is the ritual segregation of space in modern-day yurts. This meant that they offered their occupants relief from hardship and would help them increase their chances of survival; they may also have provided them with an additional psychological advantage—peace of mind. Evidently, humans need a roof over their heads, unlike other primates. Gorillas and chimpanzees build their nests on trees every night anew: they bend a few branches, they entwine them with other smaller twigs, they stamp on them with the outer part of their extremities to make the surface smoother, and within a few minutes time, they have built a cradle-like shelter.

While humans developed tools, rites presumably associated with heightened self-consciousness, and, more recently, art, they did not improve their dwellings. There might have been attempts to do so, but they were evidently not worthwhile enough to be followed. The extra effort and energy required to invest in improving dwellings was to no avail: the concluding result did not offer the occupants an advantage strong enough to offset the losses that such investment inflicted. Evolution-wise, any development in "architecture" seems to have been of no use to humans. For years and years, the human need for a shelter was met in most parts of the globe by temporary structures with a frame made of rigid materials and layered with vegetable matter or animal skins, or variations thereof.

All finds suggest that this went on until humans started to settle down in specific locations, which only happened in the very recent past. This is when things changed. This is when investing in dwellings considerably more solid and secure than those that had been built for hundreds of thousands of years began to pay out. Shelters became more permanent and were made of new materials. They controlled climate conditions in their interior more effectively and offered better security against intruders; moreover, they symbolized the appropriation claims made by the settled communities of the land they had built on in a way that everyone could understand. This was a complete package.

New materials began to be used, which were rather inadequate for the temporary shelters humans were building up to that time. Of those, clay was the most popular, a soil rich in argil. Mixed with water, it was easy to mold, whereas left out to dry in the sun it became rigid. Usually reinforced with vegetable matter such as straw and mixed with sand, clay was used in a variety of construction techniques: to cover and waterproof "walls" made of shoots, thin bamboo, and straw that filled in the gaps between the load-bearing branches of a typical frame construction; ladled on stone foundations in successive layers; in the form of sun-dried bricks; and many more variations. Timber, in the form of whole tree trunks and wooden poles, was also used increasingly. The new building techniques changed the configuration of dwellings: walls became vertical, which created more space in the interior. However, the basic concept remained unchanged, as suggested by a 7,000-year-old small clay model of a dwelling found in Thessaly, central Greece: a roof over the heads of people; usually pitched, more rarely flat.

**Clay model, Krannon, Greece,
circa 5000 BCE**



A few thousand years after the new form of dwelling—permanently built shelters—was well established, another chapter in cultural history opened: the object and role of building changed radically. Human communities became, relatively suddenly, much more complex than they had been for hundreds of thousands of years. These communities started to devise increasingly refined vehicles to achieve coherence. One of these vehicles was the construction of non-utilitarian, monumental edifices. Thus, the answer to the question "are there archetypes in architecture?" must be sibylline.

If architecture denotes the purposeful and conscious act of changing our environment by constructing shelters that serve for the immediate survival of humans, as individuals and as a species (Oscar Wilde points out that "if nature had been comfortable, mankind would never have invented architecture"[1]), then the archetypal building is a hut like that of Terra Amata: a construct that, in the first place, offered them a roof over their heads; and onto which, from some point onward, they could also project their world view. Huts have been built since time immemorial, and are still being built today. Tellingly, huts have captured the imagination and have had a crucial part in the folk traditions and religious ceremonies of different peoples—some of whom had developed meanwhile extremely advanced architecture, including the Egyptians, the Greeks, and the Japanese—and have been architecture's sacred cow since Vitruvius, the forefather of our discipline's theoreticians.

If architecture primarily denotes the construction of edifices whose role is ultimately very similar, in terms of evolution, to that of art—i.e., that of a vehicle for enhancing social coherence, and that's what architecture has evolved into in the past few thousand years—then it is hard to single out an archetypal building, only various crude models that stand out locally or regionally for limited time. As we will see, the means architecture uses to respond to its duties have changed again and again over time to such extent that no form has managed to claim a secure place in our consciousness and in our unconsciousness. Religious edifices and tombs, residences and palaces have all assumed every possible shape; they were made tall as well as flat, serene as well as impressive, excessively decorated as well as solemn.

The only building that has retained its archetypical form for hundreds of thousands of years—despite its diversity through the ages and across the globe—is the primordial dwelling, the hut. Nonetheless, it would not be far off the point to claim that the basic features of this archetypical construct partake in every edifice we erect, that they are being reproduced each and every time we begin to build. The bottom line is that the hut is an archetype we keep imitating in its essence without even intending to do so …

### Notes

1 Wilde, Oscar: "The Decay of Lying." In: *Intentions.* The Nottingham Society, New York 1909, 4.


### Selected Bibliography

de Lumley, Henry: *Terra Amata.* editions CNRS 2008.
Ingold, Tim: "Building, Dwelling, Living." In: M. Strathern (ed.): *Shifting Contexts.* Routledge 1995.
Leakey, Mary: *Olduvai Gorge, Vol. 3.* Cambridge University Press 1971.
Pidoplichko, Ivan Hryhorovych: *Upper Palaeolithic Dwellings of Mammoth Bones in the Ukraine.* BAR, International Series, 712.
Rykwert, Joseph: *On Adam's House in Paradise: The Idea of the Primitive Hut in Architectural History.* MIT Press 1981.
Villa, Paola: *Terra Amata and the Middle Pleistocene Archaeological Record of Southern France.* University of California Press 1983.

# ARCHITECTURE AND PLACE

## Mesopotamia:
## The Oval Temple

Without humans settling down more or less permanently at specific locations, the erection of large and complex edifices would have been an unimaginable feat; the toil required would probably have been pointless, if people would not occupy them for many years and had to abandon them before their completion. Moreover, without permanent settlement in situ and involved with construction only occasionally, it is doubtful whether people would accomplish even that. Nomads never built pyramids, stadiums, skyscrapers, or theaters. Nomads have no need for architects—for better or for worse.

Nothing, therefore, contributed to the development of architecture in the long run more than the invention of agriculture, a technological achievement that radically changed the fate of the human species. The cultivation of land is an investment that yields returns after several months of hard work. Moreover, because plants have roots and cannot travel, people become attached to their land along with their crops. It is estimated that modern hunter-gatherer societies spend about three to four hours daily to secure their food supplies and a total of five to six hours daily on all tasks required to sustain their living standards. They are constantly on the move following their food sources. Unable or unwilling to store more than a minimal food surplus lest they compromise their mobility, they make do with little material wealth, but, unlike the overwhelming majority of modern people, they gain considerable spare time. Admittedly, nowadays these societies are using technologies and knowledge developed by farmer societies they usually associate with. Still, the required amount of work to meet their needs in the past, before people learned how to cultivate land, must not have been all that different, at least while there was no overpopulation and climatic conditions were favorable.

Agriculture was most probably invented independently in at least five or six separate regions worldwide, when local human populations had risen to such levels that naturally renewable food sources were no longer sufficient. Thus, they were forced to find other ways to increase food production. Possibly after other survival strategies—such as increased mobility or decreased population density—proved ineffective, or were unattainable or not employed for reasons we are not aware of, they opted for a radical innovation. Evidence suggests that for the first time, about 11,000 years ago, in the region known as the Fertile Crescent (an area extending from modern Israel to north Syria and from southeast Turkey to modern Iraq), humans discovered that they could grow plants bearing edible fruit. Almost simultaneously, people (initially more often in mountainous terrains) started breeding goats for meat and much later for milk and skin; and used dogs—an animal species that had just emerged—for herding as well as for hunting.

Slowly but steadily, the cultivation of land expanded into increasingly remote areas exercising its dramatic charm to the greater part of the planet. Up to that point, people used to live in small groups (called clans) of usually twenty to fifty individuals based on kinship. These clans formed part of bands and tribes and moved from one place to another, securing their food supply, which was not difficult while the land was thinly populated. They were able, however, to settle down permanently in areas rich in sources of food, water, and abundant in raw materials.

While not imposing permanent settlement, the invention of agriculture (a "delayed return" activity) strengthened the tendencies for it—some groups probably still moved to nearby areas once a productive crop cycle was completed. Settled communities tended to be quite populous. Complex power balances were formed, which seem to have allowed for or directly led to the establishment of some kind of social stratification. By 5000 BCE in arguably one of the most developed areas of the world, the southeast part of the Fertile Crescent in modern Iraq—an area known by its Greek name, Mesopotamia, the land between rivers Tigris and Euphrates—the need to organize production, irrigate farming land, and transport its fruit became more pressing. It was now possible to accumulate surplus. The possibility to control and manage this surplus as a defense mechanism against poor harvests ensued; writing, which was invented much later, around 3000 BCE, arguably the most important tool in spreading the benefits of civilization, was perhaps born out of the need for systematic record keeping. The need for specialized labor began to multiply. Tasks were probably no longer differentiated by gender alone, as seems to have been the case in much less complex societies, in which—based on modern ethnographic data—all men and all women had the knowledge and skills to perform most required actions for their own and their families' subsistence. Specialization increased productivity, but also intensified interdependencies.

Humans now lived in large permanent settlements (cities) with rules on cohabitation, which everyone accepted or was subjected to. The allocation of different roles in these complex societies allowed differentiation in power, authority, and prestige between its members and systematically undermined the relatively egalitarian relations inherited from the past.

Administration was handled in an increasingly less collective way; elite classes were formed. The inhabitants of cities—more likely craftsmen, merchants, and administrators than farmers—acquired considerably more privileges than the inhabitants of rural areas had.

Cults, developed in response to metaphysical questions, were codified into religions—though these may have originated in the more distant past, before the advent of agriculture. Priesthoods increasingly monopolized intermediation between the divine and mankind. Mechanisms were put into place and arguments were devised to organize societies more efficiently and strictly. Having developed a rather holistic worldview, the Sumerians—the most advanced people of the region—seem to have believed that people are complex entities. Gilgamesh, the hero of the first known epic, was two-thirds god and one-third human[1]; and ordinary people had in some sense a part common to all members of their family: this part was often identified with the family god who guarded and guided them. Everybody was thus embedded in a stable and eternal world order and his/her office and his/her position and function within the society defined for a large part his/her identity; even the gods were deified functions rather than individuals, as the ancient Greek deities were later meant to be.

By the early fourth millennium BCE, some of the cities had developed imperialistic aspirations. Powerful men secured leading positions in their communities. These men gradually usurped leadership and, indispensable as they were in protecting their city in times of need or peril, they expanded their authority at the expense of others. Hereditary transfer of social status and the privileges that came with it became general practice. Administration became more authoritarian and used force—on which it acquired more or less a monopoly—at an unprecedented scale. The states were born.

The new leaders were not the only beneficiaries; an entire cast serving the institutions legitimizing authority saw their privileges augment. Of those institutions, the most important was religion. As it transpired in the following millennia, one of its most effective tools was architecture.

Groups tend to claim rights over the land that provides them with the means for their subsistence—albeit through hard work—initially without physical means. They develop beliefs and myths associated with it; soon, though, they also resort to matter. The first states that were established thousands of years ago had to devise means to denote that they had appropriated swaths of land; and to denote that they were structured in a way that enabled them to protect their perceived rights under firm leaderships. Tangible symbols have probably had a crucial role in signifying, as well as in maintaining those two basic pillars of the new order: the territory of the state and its hierarchical structure. Monumental architecture has played a major role in this enterprise. The immobility of materials weighing thousands of tons, from which edifices representing authority were made, was alone a blatant statement of a bond to the territory as strong as the bond between farmers and their land. Immobility in space, however, also denoted immobility in time; as such, it sanctioned the status quo—a status quo favorable to the leader and the ruling class.

Temple, Göbekli Tepe, Anatolia, Turkey, circa 9000 BCE

In modern southern Turkey, in Göbekli Tepe, a building complex was recently unearthed, which (if it is correctly dated) seemingly refutes our conviction that highly sophisticated edifices are the brainchild of the aforementioned era. It is an 11,000-year-old sanctuary, consisting of several megalithic structures, geometrical in shape and with a quite composite ground plan—comparable to Stonehenge, which is 6,000 years younger. The people who built it, or some of them at least, were probably permanently settled in the area and subsisted on hunting and foraging. In any case, they had given up one of those traits of nomadism: the lack of any artifact that could not be packed and carried with them as they migrated from one place to another, or one that could be constructed easily at their next temporary settlement. We do not yet know the degree to which their society was stratified. What is difficult for one to imagine is that the construction of the complex was not assigned to some members of the community who were relieved from the burden of performing all necessary tasks to sustain their families and themselves. It may well have been the need to feed those working in its construction, or the worshippers who gathered there, that encouraged the transition from food gathering to agriculture; the latter could ensure sufficient food supply at a point of time known beforehand.

It seems that the sanctuary—the largest of its kind in the whole region and unique in many aspects—became the pivotal point of an extended area practically as well as symbolically, by being a place where people from local communities gathered, and by responding to their metaphysical concerns. In this context, one should note that Vittorio Gregotti's claim that the origins of architecture lie not in the primitive hut but in placing a stone on the ground to recognize a place in the midst of an uncharted territory and an unknown universe, acquires a tangible foundation.[2]

The apparent discontinuation of comparable building activity, however, may suggest that such an endeavor could have added an unbearable burden to the community, and that the investment in effort and time needed to accomplish such a feat was not sustainable. In other words, it was not worthwhile, and that's why it was not repeated. The function of architecture to visualize in monumental terms the practical as well as the symbolical center of community life seems to have faded and sunk into oblivion for millennia, only to reemerge in Mesopotamia and independently in various other regions around the globe from 4000 BCE on. Thus, monumental architecture was "reinvented" in order to serve first and foremost the further strengthening of social cohesion, which was gradually under way, albeit at the cost of equality and justice.

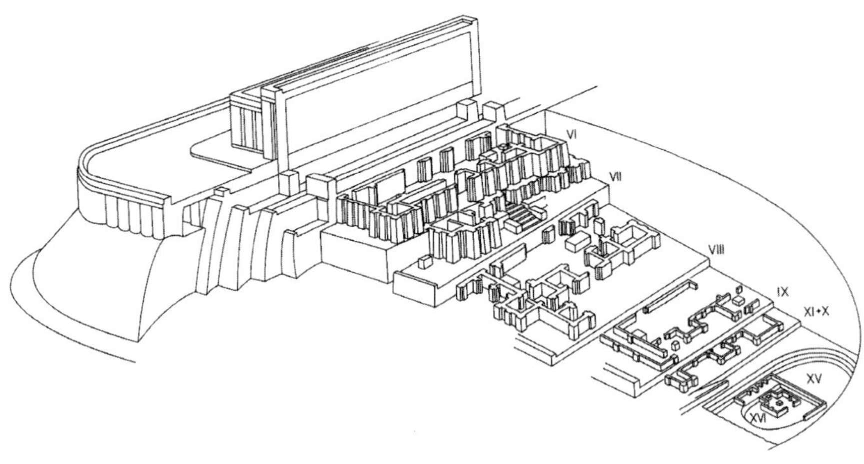


**20**

Enki temple, Eridu, south Iraq, phases XVI (circa 4900 BCE) – I (circa 3000 BCE); reconstruction drawing E. Heinrich & U. Seidl, DAInst.

It is in Eridu, a city founded around 5400 BCE, where we can clearly trace architecture's steady steps toward monumentality. The temple of Enki, built before 5000 BCE, was initially just a small room made of mud bricks, measuring approximately three by three meters. A few years later, this early building gave way to a newer one, of similar dimensions, but with a niche on the wall opposite the entrance where the statue of the god was placed. Although not spectacular, the differences between the two temples were significant: the ground plan of the new temple had become more complex in order to emphasize the importance of the god. On the remains of that temple, a larger and more complex one was built, and on its ruins a still larger one. Enki's temple has seventeen discernible phases spanning 2,000 years, developing unambiguously in one direction. It became increasingly detached from the ground and the access to it became increasingly difficult.

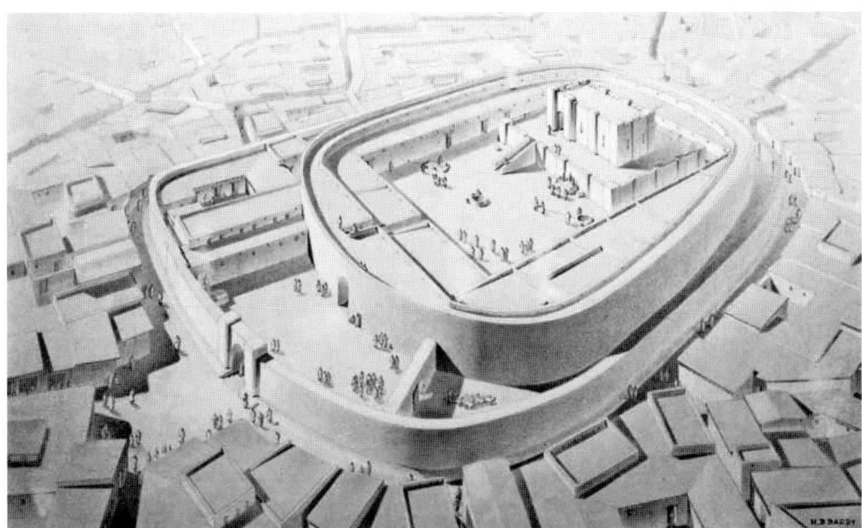

The Oval Temple, Tutub (modern Khafajah), central Iraq, circa 2700 BCE; reconstruction drawing P. Delougaz, Oriental institute, University of Chicago

There is probably no more eloquent example of this new role—or was it the very birth?—of architecture in Mesopotamia than the so-called Oval Temple. Built around 2700 BCE in the city of Tutub (modern Khafajah in Iraq), this building complex expanded over a surface of nearly 8,000 square meters; large temples were not rare at that time and they coexisted alongside the dozens or hundreds domestic sanctuaries and small neighborhood temples that dotted the cities.

The Oval Temple, enclosed by two rather irregular oval-shaped outer walls, looked like a fortress. Its distinctive shape may have been intended to mark the temple proper as the most significant element of the enclosure without having to situate it at its geometric center. The oval shape allowed a longitudinal axis pass through successive gateways and courtyards; at its end the main temple was built on an elevated platform. Grain was accumulated in storerooms around the central, ceremonial courtyard to be rationed by the priesthood. They performed a very important service redistributing the surplus and managing crises, which only heightened their already strong authority; by that time temples were power centers competing with palaces and large estates for control over important resources.

The temple was located at the eastern end of the city, near one of the gates of the outer wall. That area had been inhabited for centuries, and at the time was densely populated and had narrow streets. To build the temple, dwellings were demolished and graves were removed. The entire surface was dug to a depth of eight meters to the water level. Small bones and twigs, old building materials and food waste were removed. The pit was then filled with pure, sifted sand. The symbolism was clear: the site designated for the temple was purged of all things human, perishable—of all things reminding people that time goes by, and that things change.

The temple was supposed to secure human contact with the heavens and the gods, and also the underworld and the deities who lived there. Its erection illustrates the view of Martin Heidegger, the controversial twentieth-century German philosopher, who argued that building *creates* a place; buildings do not occupy already existing places.[3] A place, argued Heidegger, becomes what it is by the very construction of the edifice, by the nurture and care in its construction and by the bonding generated between human beings and earth through the labor of building.

As years went by, *ziggurats*, those geometrically shaped, tiered stacks of brick, rose in the plains throughout Mesopotamia, presumably based on the shape of mountains. Rain was born on the mountains giving life to land and humans. Ziggurats are the places where gods would descend to meet humans or, to be more precise, to meet their emissaries—high-ranking priests.



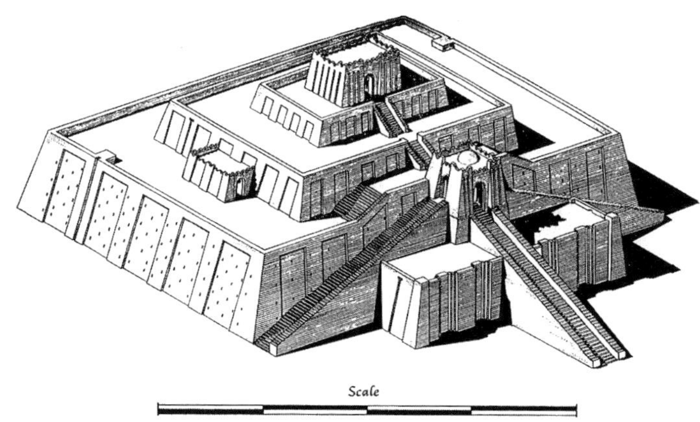



**The ziggurat of king Ur-Nammu, Ur, south Iraq, circa 2000 BCE; reconstruction L. Wooley, University of Pennsylvania Museum of Archaeology and Anthropology & British Museum**

The main temples, the shrines, were rather small edifices at the top of the ziggurats. Unlike Christian churches, mosques, or synagogues, they were not intended for admitting the congregation of the faithful. From there, the priesthood observed the stars in order to prepare detailed tables useful for making calendars and predicting the future; astrology was highly developed in that part of the world. This imbued ziggurats with immense moral authority. Their prominence within cities remained unchallenged for centuries. However, circumstances changed and thus 2,000 years later, ziggurats were reduced to mere appendices of palaces of extremely powerful kings, who monopolized power in the cities and states they ruled.

In the Oval Temple, people nominated one of their artifacts as an indispensable intermediary between them and their deities. This artifact was placed in a specific location and cleansed of all traces of previous activities. The relationship between people and their gods no longer took place solely in the realm of the imaginary, in their minds and souls. With buildings like the Oval Temple, this relationship acquired a visible form. Thus, it was meant to become more credible and univocal, as well as thoroughly controlled in dogmatic terms and, as such, a force unifying the community. In the clearer terms, it had been established that the gods were not directly accessible to everyone. Contact with them required rituals that only a select few had been initiated into (the priesthood), and was only possible in certain circumstances (at the top of a huge building); it was a contact possible only in conditions of spatial and temporal stability. Architecture helped to consolidate the respective (religious in our case) "rule" and the given social order. Inextricably bound to the place, its product—the sacred edifice—expressed and helped perpetuate authority.

No building would be what it is, had it not been erected where it is. No place would be what it is, had an edifice not been built there. In Jerusalem, the Dome of the Rock stands on a hill where, as Muslims believe, Muhammad set his ladder to ascend to the heavens. It is the hill where Jews believe—probably for good reason—the second Temple of Solomon once stood, and where they kept their most revered heirlooms. The Romans demolished this temple and built a temple dedicated to one of their gods, driving the Jewish people into exile two thousand years ago. It is a hill for which blood and tears have been shed for millennia; a hill for which world peace and stability are in peril still to this day; a hill more important than any other nearby.

Historically, architecture has assisted societies and communities in building identities intertwined with certain locations. This contribution has two sides. On the one hand, it offers a sense of belonging. On the other hand, it gives people the certainty that the place where they are settled belongs to them forever. For this reason, they have the right to exclude others that might also have a claim on it. Normally, this does not contribute to building peaceful, open, and tolerant societies with an eye toward the future, but societies chained voluntarily to conflicts of the past.

Could it be that architecture is condemned to bind people to the land where they happen to be at a specific moment? Or is there an architecture conceivable detached from place? In the first decades of the twenty-first century, anything we still build renews the fundamental question raised by the construction of the Oval Temple of Khafajah 5,000 years ago and the answer that it received with the excavation of its foundations …

**Notes**

1  George, Andrew: *The Babylonian Gilgamesh Epic—Introduction, Critical Edition and Cuneiform Texts*. Oxford University Press 2003, I,ii.
2  Gregotti, Vittorio: "Territory and Architecture" (1966). In: *Architectural Design Profile 59*, no. 5–6, 1985, 28–34.
3  Heidegger, Martin: "Building Dwelling Thinking" (1951). In: David Farrell Krell (ed): *Basic Writings From Being and Time (1929) to The Task of Thinking (1964)*. Routledge & Kegan Paul Ltd 1978.

**Selected Bibliography**

Crawford, Harriet: *Sumer and the Sumerians*. Cambridge University Press 2004.
Delougaz, Pinhas: *The Temple Oval at Kafajah*.
University of Chicago Press 1940.
Gowdy, John (ed.): *Limited Wants, Unlimited Means: A Reader on Hunter-Gatherer Economics and the Environment*. Island Press 1998.
Safar, Fuad/Mustafa, Mohammad Ali/Lloyd, Seton: *Eridu*. Iraq, Ministry of Culture and Information, State Organization of Antiquities and Heritage 1981.
Selz, Gebhardt: "Composite Beings: Of Individualization and Objectification in Third Millennium Mesopotamia." In: *Archiv Orientální*, 72, 2004, 33ff.
Verderame, Lorenzo/Capomacchia A.M.G.: *Some Considerations about Demons in Mesopotamia*. SMSR - Studi e materiali di storia delle religioni 77/2 (2011), 291 ff.

# CONCEPT AND MATTER

## The Giza Pyramids

Most likely responding initially to practical needs—such as restoring landmarks destroyed by the Nile's annual flooding, estimating the volume of a stone block, or recording of the position of the stars—the ancient Egyptians (like the Sumerians) developed a system of calculations: the predecessor of *geometry*, Greek for earth measuring. Although drawn from and referring to material objects—rocks, man-made edifices, stars—these objects and their relative positions were regarded as more or less simple conceptual shapes and more or less simple conceptual relationships: points, volumes, straight lines, triangles. Shifting from objects as physical entities to abstract concepts is, no doubt, a basic function of the human brain, language being its typical, most precious product. Once codified and rigorously organized in an efficient way, this shift was to become a cornerstone of contemporary civilization; to become the foundation of science as we know it today (which reduces complex natural phenomena into quantifiable entities), and of monetary economics (where everything is measured by the amount of money one needs to acquire it). Mesopotamia and Egypt were probably the first to witness the early steps toward this systematization, manifested in the development both of early mathematics and of writing: cuneiform in Mesopotamia and hieroglyphics in Egypt. And yet, as we shall see, in the land of the river Nile, the shift from objects as physical entities toward abstract concepts, epitomized by geometry, was associated in the field we are interested in with the worship of matter—literally and figuratively—rendering matter into the very prerequisite for every attempt to rise beyond it.

Early in their history, the Egyptians opted for a simple geometric shape as the most suitable for their most important buildings. In Giza, an area about fifteen kilometers from the center of Cairo and about twenty kilometers north of the then capital city Memphis, pyramids were the dominant features of burial complexes built to accommodate three of the most prominent Pharaohs in the afterlife: they were the deified kings of Egypt, Khufu, Khafre, and Menkaure, until recently known by their Hellenized names Cheops, Chephren, and Mycerinus. The people who labored to build them were more likely "free citizens" than slaves, who were probably charged with a type of *corvée*, as was often the case in many preindustrial societies; no matter how harsh their working conditions were, they must have taken great pride in their work, as indicated by graffiti found in their communal lodgings.

**The pyramids of Khufu in the foreground circa 2530 BCE, Khafre, circa 2510 BCE, and Menkaure, circa 2485 BCE, Giza, Cairo**

The first, the pyramid of Khufu, was built within twenty years around 2530 BCE. This period is known as the Old Kingdom—i.e., the first period of unified Egypt, lasting from the twenty-seventh to the twenty-second century BCE (experts disagree on the exact dates of key incidents in Egyptian history). Similar to the other two, its base is oriented with great precision to the four cardinal directions, a fact among many suggesting that designing the pyramid relied partly on the vast, remarkably advanced insights of Egyptian priesthood into astronomy.

Astronomical phenomena were taken seriously into account in the design of monumental buildings, already from earlier on in Mesopotamia, and would continue to do so for many years across the globe. They included both phenomena that were intrinsically important as markers of crucial turning points (such as the summer solstice and the movement of the point of the horizon where the sun rises or sets as the days become longer or shorter), or were attributed rather arbitrarily great importance (such as the appearance in the night sky of a constellation, a group of seemingly neighboring stars billions of kilometers apart). The great rock-cut temple of Abu-Simbel (built around 1265 BCE), for instance, was configured so that twice a year, on significant dates, rays of sun would penetrate the inner sanctum at dawn to shine on all the statues at the far end of the temple except that of Ptah, god of the Underworld. Similar but independently developed astronomical considerations are attested at the Temple of the Sun in Machu-Picchu, Peru, and at the Fatehpur Sikri Jami in India, both built more than 2,500 years later; and Christian churches built even today normally conform to the rule that requires them to be oriented to the east— i.e., the point in the horizon where the sun rises on the equinoxes.

The pyramid of Khufu was built of large stone blocks, and measured 2.5 million cubic meters in total mass and 5.9 million tons in weight. Its height was approximately 146 meters and the length of each side of its square base was 230 meters. Its surfaces were polished and its apex shone under the rays of the sun. Its external proportions and those of the chambers—height to length of side, etc.—conform to special geometric relations. Typically, in a cross section, the proportions of the pyramid of Khufu correspond with what is known as the golden ratio; those of the pyramid of Khafre generate a 3:4:5 Pythagorean triangle, whose properties were known to the Egyptians.

The Egyptians manifested their affection for geometry in almost every edifice of importance they built. They were not the only people to do so. Regular geometrical shapes have often been used in architecture in the course of history, far and wide. From medieval cities in India, such as Madurai, to Renaissance towns in the West, such as Palmanova; from ziggurats in Mesopotamia to the seventeenth-century gardens of Versailles; from the Revolutionary Architecture of E. L. Boullée to the Neo-Rationalism of A. Rossi in the nineteen-eighties, easily recognizable, regular, shapes have been employed to indicate that the form before us is the result of deliberate choices aimed at conveying complex meanings and sophisticated

**The "bent pyramid" of pharaoh Sneferu, Dahshur, Egypt, circa 2570 BCE**

symbolisms and not the outcome of inconsistent, random actions carried out by a large set of active agents.

And yet, it was only during a few periods in their history that the Egyptians opted for elementary geometric shapes to configure their monumental buildings. The earliest such case was the burial monuments of Giza, although experimenting with pyramidal shapes had been going on for some time. But the reign of pyramids as the prominent feature of royal tombs did not last forever.

The "broken pyramid" of pharaoh Huni, Meidum, Egypt, circa 2580 BCE

Already before 2000 BCE—i.e., just five centuries after the Pyramids of Giza—a large burial complex for a pharaoh was built, which was not dominated by a pyramid. It was the mortuary complex of Mentuhotep II, founder of what is known as the Middle Kingdom—the second period during which Egypt was under unified rule, from the twenty-first to the seventeenth century BCE—in Deir el Bahri across from Luxor, ancient Thebes, about 600 kilometers south of Cairo. The complex may have included a pyramid, but a rather small-sized one, if at all, possibly symbolizing the mountaintop where the sun was thought to be reborn every day. The mortuary complexes of some of the later pharaohs assumed the Old Kingdom tradition and had a pyramid as their prominent feature. However, from the eighteenth century on, this practice was gradually abandoned. The last significant pyramid was built by Pharaoh Ahmose, the founder of what is known as the New Kingdom—the period from the sixteenth to the eleventh century BCE—around 1550 BCE and served as his cenotaph. Later mortuary complexes employed different architectural forms to replicate, as did earlier ones, in some idealized way the environment in which the deified king used to live before his death.

Even in the afterlife, the dead king was expected to act for the sake of all his subjects. Assigning a specific architectural form to his last residence constituted the architectural concept; the buildings themselves show that this would change over time. The architectural concept of the three great burial complexes of Giza was the same; their designs varied slightly. By contrast, the concept of the tomb of Mentuhotep II differed considerably; the rock-cut tombs in the Valley of the Kings even more. In the burial complexes of Giza, the focus was on the astronomical/theological symbolisms of the pyramid. In the tomb of Mentuhotep II, half a millennium later, the emphasis was probably placed on providing a setting that would make the ritual performed there every year as majestic as possible. In the rock-cut tombs of the Valley of the Kings, several centuries later, the concern was primarily to hide the burial chamber to prevent desecration; undoubtedly, security had also been a priority in the Giza pyramids. We know that the entrance to the corridors that led to the burial chambers was very well hidden and the obstacles met in gaining access to them were virtually insurmountable.

What remained unchanged was the priesthood's intention to appropriately accommodate the deceased pharaoh's afterlife. The person to assume the responsibility for materializing this intention was arguably the priest in charge of the rites, i.e., the High Priest; as a consequence, he also assumed the role of architect. Two thousand years later in Classical Greece, the architect was in charge of the laborers building the structure.

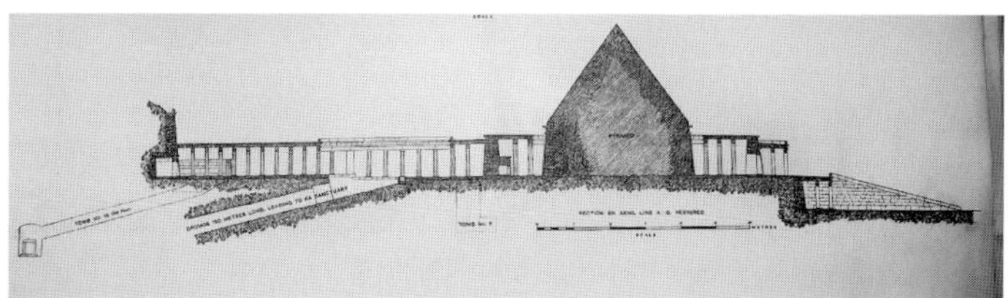

**Mentuhotep's II mortuary complex, Deir el Bahri, ancient Thebes, south Egypt, circa 2040 BCE, aerial view (top), and section (down); the pyramid is hypothetical; section drawing E. Naville**

His task was to convert into a physical object the guidelines laid out by the person or the body assigning the project. The range of initiatives that an architect could take, as well as his status and responsibilities, varied considerably from society to society.

About 5,000 years before our time, the Egyptians had evidently grasped the principal act of architecture: to render the product of the mind from whatever "paper" to "stone"; that materializing a concept is the action par excellence through which architecture acquires its identity. The very fact that at some point they chose an elementary geometric shape for their most important buildings not only speaks of their advanced mathematical knowledge; it underlines how clearly they had appreciated that every architectural idea would be in limbo, and it would be outside the scope of architecture if matter was not used as a means of its realization—in the case of pyramids, quite a lot of matter actually.

To them, the immortality of the soul relied on preserving the perishable dead body. Likewise, the Giza pyramids suggest that the validity of a product of the mind relied on its actualization with durable materials. Matter was worshiped—literally in the former and metaphorically in the latter case—as the vehicle for keeping the incorporeal alive. To appreciate how radically different architecture is from drafting the same geometric shape on paper, and from materializing the same concept and the same idea using different material means, let us consider what the pyramids of Giza would be if, rather than 146 meters, they were five meters tall. If architecture differs from other "creative" arts, it is primarily in that it shapes matter to conform to the idea conceived in the human mind.

Nothing corroborates more clearly the Egyptians' preoccupation with the materialization (in the literal sense of the word) of the respective concept than the pyramid of Pharaoh Djoser, built in Saqqara, close to Memphis probably around 2630–2610 BCE—i.e., a few decades before the pyramid of Khufu.

The mortuary complex was unprecedented in size: at its final stage it measured approximately 150,000 square meters. The main burial monument was shaped initially as a rectangular "mastaba"—a low, truncated pyramid measuring approximately fifty-seven meters by fifty-seven meters and eight meters in height, quite typical at the time. This structure clearly conformed to the (early, at least) symbolic and ritual requirements probably laid down in great detail. Besides, the entire building process followed a very strict ritual, as everything we know about the foundation ceremonies of similar, later complexes suggests: at night, under a starlit sky, the high priests defined the four corners of the complex; they stretched a cord from one corner to the next and then let it drop onto the ground; using a wooden shovel they dug out the foundations forming an offering pit, etc. Rituals also determined many key features of these structures. In the burial complex of Djoser, the walls featured fourteen carved "gates," which served as portals through which the *ka*, the pharaoh's spirit, could come and go. The, presumably few, mere mortals who were allowed access to the interior of the complex had to use the one and only true entrance to it. Chambers and rooms without functional, but with only symbolic, entrances were also intended for the dead king's use. As per custom, the burial chamber was in the ground under the truncated pyramid, but a shaft allowed the pharaoh's ka to communicate with the outside world.

**Pharaoh Djoser's mortuary complex, Saqqara, south of Cairo, circa 2610 BCE**

However, the truncated pyramid built for Djoser's tomb most likely failed to meet the special requirements of architecture as an activity that converts a conception of the human mind into tangible object. Successive extensions gave it increasingly greater volume, increasingly greater mass. The initial extension on all sides was followed by an addition to one side only, and then again by a substantial addition, which transformed it into a stepped pyramid of four horizontal tiers. This construction was extended in width and height to produce in its final form a six-tiered stepped pyramid measuring 62 meters in height and approximately 109 meters long and 125 meters wide, visible now from the Nile.

Some Egyptologists argue that the changes in the design of the central building, which transformed it from a mastaba into a stepped pyramid, were due to changes in the intended symbolism or the burial rituals—yet it is strange that this occurred five times in a few years. In matters of doctrine, however, what we may perceive as a slight differentiation, the parties involved may perceive as huge. In any case, if the symbolic and ritual requirements had indeed changed, it is likely that this also had to do with whether the structure that gradually came into being could accom-

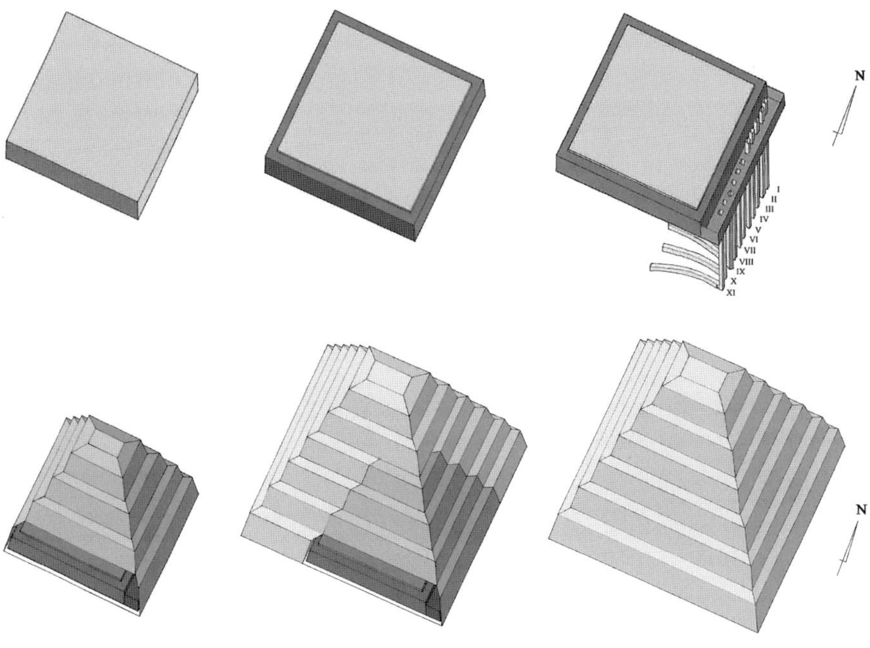

**The successive construction phases of Djoser's pyramid, Saqqara, south of Cairo, circa 2610 BCE; drawing F. Monnier**

modate them. In contrast to several art forms, particularly to contemporary art, in architecture the end result—the final form of the building—is infinitely more significant than the steps followed to achieve it. A stairway to the heavens (assuming that this was the new intended symbolism) had to be as tall as a modern twenty-story building; clearly, the initial eight-meter structure fell short of enabling even a pharaoh to reach the North Star. An abstract idea gained the desired status, and became convincing and esteemed when it was transubstantiated into an accumulation of matter in thousands upon thousands of tons.

The person who had the foresight to realize the building's inability to meet its purpose four times in a row and to insist on a new extension is arguably justly regarded as the forefather of all architects. His official capacity was High Priest; his name was Imhotep and he was bestowed an exceptional honor, albeit two millennia after his death: he was deified, an honor enviable even to holders of the Pritzker Prize. The fact that he was deified as a doctor and healer raises no doubts about his accomplishments as architect: the name of Imhotep became associated with that of Ma'at, the goddess who personified justice and cosmic order out of chaos. Order was fundamental to both architecture and medicine, considering that in the ancient world, disease was often attributed to a disturbance of the order sustaining the body and disturbing the balance of its parts. Besides, was not Claude Perrault, the trusted architect of Colbert and of Louis XIV, who designed the famous east wing of the Louvre and translated Vitruvius into French, a doctor, and in that capacity one of the first members of the French Academy of Sciences?

In the great pyramids of Giza, architecture revealed with utmost clarity its dual nature: the ethereal, completely detached from anything that belongs to the material world, conception of an edifice, and its earthly materialization fully dependent on physical things. Without doubt, in the last 5,000 years, when people have talked about the "form" of a building, they have meant not only its geometric features, but also its size and mass. "The ship on which Theseus sailed with the youths and returned in safety, the thirty-oared galley, was preserved by the Athenians down to the time of Demetrius Phalereus. They took away the old timbers from time to time, and put new and sound ones in their places, so that the vessel became standing illustration for the philosophers … some declaring that it remained the same, others that it was not the same vessel," mentions Plutarch.[1] Since the time of Imhotep, architects have known that both concept and matter are equally important components of buildings.

**Notes**
1  Plutarch: *Thes.* 23.

**Selected Bibliography**
Arnold, Dieter: *The Encyclopaedia of Ancient Egyptian Architecture.* Princeton University Press 2003.
David, Rosalie: *The Pyramid Builders of Ancient Egypt: A Modern Investigation of Pharaoh's Workforce.* Routledge 1996.
Lehner, Mark: "Of Gangs and Graffiti: How Ancient Egyptians Organized their Labor Force." In: *AERAGRAM*, 7 (1), 11 ff.
Lehner, Mark: *The Complete Pyramids.* Thames & Hudson 1997.
Robins, Gay: *The Art of Ancient Egypt.* Harvard University Press 2000.
Spencer, A. J.: *Early Egypt: The Rise of Civilization in the Nile Valley.* British Museum Press 1993.

# THE MAGIC OF THE CITY

## Ur: Igmil-Sins's House

Today, one in two people live in cities in a world shaped by the civilization created within them. Most probably, all readers of this book know that in order to cross a highway safely they have to use the pedestrian overpass. They know how to complete their tax return statement with its hundreds of boxes. They have developed criteria to choose between fifty different types of pasta in the neighborhood supermarket. And they can calculate with relative precision what time they will arrive in a location 100 or 1,000 kilometers away from their homes. It is doubtful, though, whether they can survive more than a few days, if they find themselves alone in a forest or on the beach for which they are longing so much during their daily routine.

Since when do people feel more comfortable in cities than away from them? Since when do they become so familiar with the man-made environment that they project it in their hopes for a good life? Since when do their fears derive from it?

The answer could be very simple: probably since specialization and the division of labor led people to develop only some skills and knowledge, enabling them to live in complex social environments but not in nature. Although, as we saw in Chapter 2, specialization existed long before the creation of cities, it was in the complex and stratified urban societies in which it was developed in the fullest extent. According to all indications in southern Mesopotamia, urbanization began about 7,000 years ago. Within a few hundred years, a new way of life, and eventually a new civilization was created.

The *Epic of Gilgamesh* speaks with admiration about Uruk, whose walls in the third millennium BCE had a length of nine kilometers.[1] *The Sumerian Temple Hymns*, probably composed shortly before 2200 BCE, refer to thirty-five cities of south Mesopotamia. If Eridu was the oldest—the first city in the world according to the *Sumerian King List*[2]—Ur was probably the most famous. Its population according to Sir Leonard Woolley, the most prominent excavator of the site, reached 200,000 people or maybe half a million around 1900 BCE, and this despite its destruction a few decades earlier and its subsequent subordination to neighboring Larsa. Only with difficulty can we realize today how great this number is for a city without cars and metro railway systems, phones, and the Internet. However, we can surely imagine that the problem that all these people had to face was not how to protect themselves from wild beasts or how to trap a boar for its meat and skin as their ancestors did several hundred years ago. They were probably preoccupied with how and at what cost they would be supplied with food every day and how they would dispose of their garbage; and if they were artisans or craftsmen, how they could acquire raw materials and where they could sell their products.

**Residential quarter of the Larsa period, Ur, south Iraq, circa 1900 BCE; courtesy of the University of Pennsylvania**

It was a colossal change in the daily lives of people, in the most fundamental characteristics of their self-image; in the way they perceived themselves. Possibly some may have realized, as we do today, that life in the cities enabled them to live in them, and only in them, and that the urban environment was their new natural habitat. It is no coincidence, therefore, that the city foundation occupies such a large part of the literary production of the people of Mesopotamia, but also of their art, even three millennia after the first cities emerged.

The material remains of this great change have not yet been erased. These are the ruins brought into light by persistent archaeological research. The cities and the buildings themselves talk to us about the people who lived in them; about their daily lives, about their brave new world, our world.

Only a fraction, about one-sixth, of 1900 BCE Ur's inhabitants lived in its walled section, the "old city," as the research team who conducted the excavation called it. Equally densely populated areas also existed outside the walls, even one mile away from them. Further away—up to almost six miles—were more thinly populated areas, "suburbs," stretching along important roads, and satellite cities. And most certainly, there were also simpler houses, makeshift constructions from reeds and other materials that leave no traces.

The houses in the "old city" were built next to one another and formed large irregular building blocks. The city had grown "organically," apparently without a predetermined plan, as Classical Athens and Republican Rome one-and-a-half millennia later. The roads were very narrow and almost never straight. Although the wheel—initially the potter's wheel and then the wheel for transportation—was invented in this region of the world, carriages were not able to pass through them and traffic and transportation were conducted on foot, using porters or with pack animals. It was very common for masonry at street corners to be rounded so that passers-by did not graze themselves on sharp brickwork, and in some places a low flight of brick steps was located—two three steps above the road level—apparently as a "mounting block for the convenience of riders."[3] Most roads were not paved and were filled with mud when it rained, but they did not have the open drains along them that are still common today in many parts of the world. It seems that the residents threw the—little in comparison to ours—garbage, dust and dirt from cleaning their houses and rubble resulting from minor repairs outside their doors. Unbuilt "plots" and the land around the city were also used as garbage pits. As a result, the street level rose over time, ending up higher than the thresholds; consequently muddy water entered the houses when it rained. The solution was to build a new threshold one step higher, and then another, and so on. There are cases that one had to descend five or six steps to enter the house. Eventually, of course, further elevation was impossible, because with each added step the door became lower since its lintel remained stable. Then the whole house had to be demolished to the level of the lintel and rebuilt using the "buried" walls as foundations.

Although each house was different, their layouts were roughly the same; the prevailing paradigm was adapted to different circumstances, even if the overall shape of the house was destined to be completely irregular. To this standardization of houses contributed a tradition codified in the so-called house omens. These were a group of oracles (of the type if/then), some of which referred to houses and cities. According to one of them, for example, "if the foundation of a house encroaches onto a street,

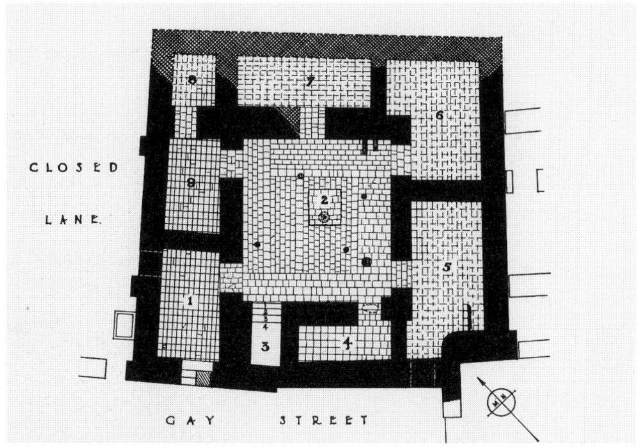
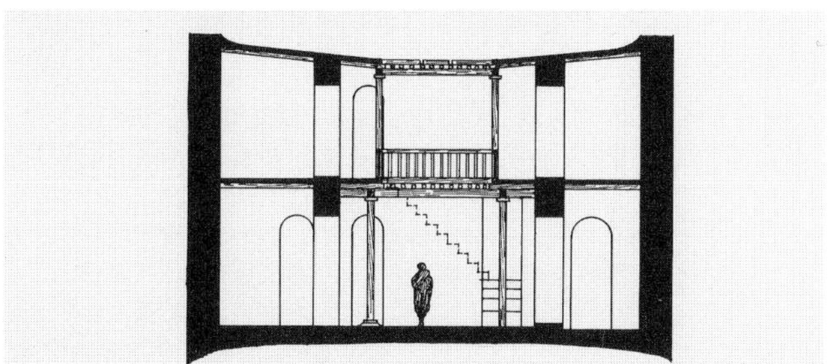


**House in Gay Street no. 3, Ur, south Iraq, circa 1900 BCE, ground plan and cross section; drawing L. Woolley, courtesy of the University of Pennsylvania**

that house will be abandoned and its owners will repeatedly change."[4] In order to preserve the stability of the family hearth, everyone preferred to respect the already formed building line and to maintain the width of the road in front of his property. According to another, more colorful omen, "if a house's doorways open toward its front, the man's wife will cause her spouse trouble,"[5] something that surely many would like to avoid at all costs. What choice did they have other than to make the door of their houses open inwards? Passers-by could be certain that a door opening suddenly would not hit them in the face.

The outer door of the house was usually small and led to an anteroom. From there, crossing a second, interior door, one entered into the paved courtyard, which—at least in some cases—might have had a flat elevated roof letting light and air to enter perimetrically. All of the rooms were arranged around it: the reception room, elongated and of small depth, where visitors sat during the day, and mattresses were set for them to stay overnight. Further away were a small lavatory and a storeroom. Then there was the kitchen and next to it the room where the household slaves slept; societies without washing machines, microwave ovens, and vacuum cleaners often resorted to forced labor to meet the urban household's

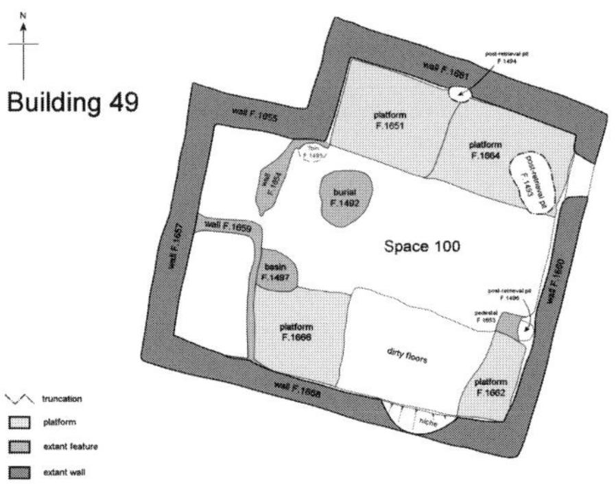

**Building 49, Çatalhöyük, Anatolia, Turkey, circa 7000 BCE, ground plan; drawing J. Swogger, Çatalhöyük Research Project**

**Building 56, Çatalhöyük, Anatolia, Turkey, circa 7000 BCE, interior; drawing J. Swogger, Çatalhöyük Research Project**

demands. A built staircase leading upwards occupied the space of what could have been a room. The excavators assume that the houses usually had two floors (since a wooden mobile ladder would suffice for climbing on the roof of a one-story house); if that is the case, the private rooms of the owner and his family would have been in the upper floor and accessible by a wooden corridor built around the courtyard.

The building material was baked (therefore quite durable) bricks up to a certain height and unbaked bricks from that level and above. The construction quality of a house was a matter of concern for the neighborhood since any poor workmanship and possible collapse endangered passers-by and the adjacent homes. A bit later, in the eighteenth century BCE, the so-called Code of Hammurabi was implemented in this part of the world; it included the oldest known regulations for building activity, awarding penalties for improper or negligent construction by contractors.

The houses of Ur attest to the full development of the new culture, which clearly distinguished urban dwellers from those of the countryside. The houses of Ur didn't follow the model of the Terra Amata huts. They were not "man-made caves" whose interior was insulated in the best possible way from the surrounding nature—such man-made caves always exist with reference to the "outside"—a paradigm that dominated the construction of shelter and lodgings of all kinds until about the middle of the third millennium BCE.

The houses in the eighth- and seventh-millennium BCE settlement unearthed in Çatalhöyük near Konya in Turkey were also a kind of man-made cave. Built next to each other, a few centimeters apart or sharing walls, without roads between them, they formed compact habitation islets. People walked on the roofs from which they entered their houses. Any gaps resulting from the desolation or collapse of houses were used as outdoor living spaces for the adjacent houses or as garbage dumps. Each house consisted of a rather large, usually roughly rectangular, room measuring up to five or six meters (sometimes with one or two elongated storage rooms attached to it) and covered with a flat roof constructed on wooden beams. The walls were plastered and sometimes adorned with frescoes and bullhorns. According to a rather widespread practice of this period, the dead were buried under the floors in various parts of the houses—normally, the children separate from the adults. There were no public buildings, or if there were, they were no different from ordinary houses. The variation of building forms according to function had yet to emerge: what we now consider normal—that a church or a theater is quite distinct from an apartment block—was at the time out of people's horizon of expectations, with few exceptions as we have seen in Chapter 2. The compact structure of the Çatalhöyük settlement is, in a sense, a transfer to a larger scale of the individual lodging's paradigm. Each house may seem to have stood on its own—isolated from its surroundings—but it fully depended on it, since its inhabitants had to occasionally venture outside, where they came into visual, at least, contact with their neighbors.

And this was also the case with the houses in Mesopotamian cities since their emergence. By the fifth millennium BCE, urban dwellings seem to have consisted of an elongated central room and smaller rooms adjacent to it. They had few small windows in the street, or in a vacant

**Çatalhöyük, Anatolia, south Turkey, circa 7000 BCE, hypothetical view of the settlement; drawing J. Swogger, Çatalhöyük Research Project**

plot, or in the garden if there was one, and were built next to one another, without always forming a continuous web.

It was in the middle of the third millennium that the new house model emerged—a fully developed example of which is preserved in 1900 BCE Ur atrium houses. Its fundamental difference from the previous paradigm is that an open, relatively spacious courtyard replaced the elongated central room. The houses could now provide its inhabitants with the opportunity to remain inside for long periods without having to venture outdoors and expose themselves to natural elements or to the public view. Their introverted layout turned them to oases of calm in the middle of the noisy gathering of people—i.e., the urban environment. They did not have to open up to the street—they opened up to the sky. Nature did not frighten the inhabitants of these houses, since it was no longer hostile; the skies brought only the beneficial sun and the relieving rain, the basic ingredients for life. What the city dwellers had to protect themselves from was probably gossip. They did not need to leave their houses to survey the surrounding area out for fear of unknown attackers. The city's walls and its armed forces ensured their safety. Support from neighbors was no longer so vital for their security that they had to sacrifice their privacy. What could be a better proof for the change—as we surmised in the beginning of the chapter—that had taken place in daily life and self-image of people from the very form of their houses?

In some cases, the houses of Ur underwent rather radical modifications as is evident in Broad Street no. 1 (the name given by the archaeologists who conducted the excavation). The doorways of the ground floor rooms opening onto the court had been bricked up. Hence, the yard itself, the reception room, and the lavatory were completely cut off from the rest of the house and the only means of communication was a small opening. Simultaneously, a new doorway was opened in the yard's north wall leading directly to the street. The approximately two thousand clay tablets found scattered in situ leave little doubt of what had happened. The house's owner was a priest named Igmil-Sin as deduced from several letters which were all addressed to the same recipient. Igmil-Sin modified a section of his house to function as a private school. Several tablets similar to modern school notebooks were unearthed, and were probably used by students for exercises in writing and mathematics. Other tablets contained history and religious texts, probably used for dictation and memorization; others contained the principles of geometry and multiplication tables. Igmil-Sin's students apparently received all the necessary skills to staff an increasingly complex administration and an increasingly complex economy necessary for an increasingly complex city. Further down the street, a house was converted—according to available evidence—into the neighborhood cookhouse, with one of its rooms serving as a dining hall.

Modifications like those visible in the houses of Ur demonstrate that people felt quite comfortable in the built environment. By then, living in houses—i.e., in relatively controlled climatic conditions, and the security

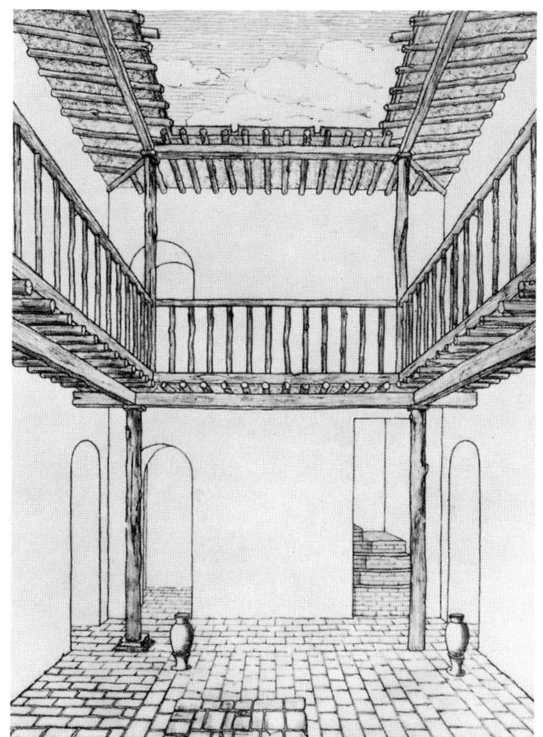

**House in Gay Street no. 3, Ur, modern south Iraq, circa 1900 BCE, court; hypothetical reconstruction according to L. Woolley, courtesy of the University of Pennsylvania**

provided by a roof—was common practice since millennia. Evidently, in 1900 BCE Ur the house was not owed respect for securing the survival of its inhabitants in an inhospitable environment; it was no longer a sacred arc. The house had lost its magic. It had become a tool. It had become more or less *une machine à habiter*, as Le Corbusier, the great theorist of modern architecture, wanted for the twentieth-century house.

Albeit somewhat simplistically, we can argue that people evaluate the products of architecture—and have done so since the distant past—according to three criteria: a) the physical characteristics of the buildings, i.e., they judge them as material objects—how well they serve their purpose, how beautiful they are, etc; b) the embedded ideas, i.e., they judge them as the vehicles of their creators' intentions; c) the extent to which they reflect the value system of their cultural environment, i.e., they judge them as symbolic objects. The relative *gravitas* of each of these criteria changes from society to society, era to era and, most importantly, from person to person and moment to moment. We have all probably found ourselves in a sudden downpour when standing before a nice building, and all of us have realized that we all but forget its beautiful proportions and the noble intentions of its maker, and we stop contemplating their sophisticated symbolisms until we find a shelter.

We treat buildings according to this complex, more or less three-part evaluation; we take care or abandon them, we maintain or demolish them. Converting them in order to serve us better is a step further. This step arguably occurred for the first time with clarity and confidence in the environment of the first Mesopotamian cities. Of course, people always modify their houses; in Çatalhöyük, there are many traces of conversions made 8,000 years ago. What is particularly interesting, though, is that in many cases, the reason behind the changes in Ur houses was none other than a response to the constantly evolving demands of the inhabitants' daily lives in a complex urban environment.

I believe that it can be suggested, even somewhat schematically, that the cities are where people became completely familiar with buildings. In cities, the built environment became the given context of human life. In cities, buildings became routine and ceased to be awe-aspiring achievements. In cities, buildings became dispensable.

The revolutionary changes in people's way of living, which took place for the first time in Mesopotamia 5,000 years ago, decisively changed the real world because they changed the world of our imagination. Everything else that followed was just a matter of time.

## Notes

1 George, Andrew: *The Babylonian Gilgamesh Epic: Introduction, Critical Edition and Cuneiform Texts*. Oxford University Press 2003, I, i.
2 Jacobsen, Thorkild: *The Sumerian King List*. Oriental Institute, Assyriological Studies 11, University of Chicago Press 1939.
3 Woolley, Leonard: *Ur Excavations, Vol. VII: The Old Babylonian Period*. British Museum Publications 1976, 16.
4 Freedman, Sally M: *If a City is Set on a Height*. Samuel Noah Kramer Fund, the University of Pennsylvania Museum 1998, Chapter 5, Omen 22.
5 *Ibid*: Omen 75.

## Selected Bibliography

Adams, Robert McCormick: *Heartland of Cities*.
University of Chicago Press 1981.
*Çatalhöyük Archive Reports*, esp. 2006 &2008. Çatalhöyük Research Project.
Liverani, Mario: *Uruk: the First City*. Equinox Publishing/ 2006.
Pollock, Susan: *Ancient Mesopotamia, The Eden That Never Was*. Cambridge University Press 1999.
Postgate, J.N.: *Early Mesopotamia*. Taylor & Francis 1992.
Woolley, Leonard: *Excavations at Ur: A Record of Twelve Years' Work*. Apollo 1965.

# ARCHITECTURE AND IDENTITY

## The Temple of Amun at Karnak

Would it be an exaggeration to allege that people recognize architecture as one of the most characteristic, if not one of the most important, creations of societies? We often use buildings to illustrate our references to a country and its inhabitants: the Eiffel Tower for France and the French; Big Ben for England and the English. On many occasions, architecture indeed disproportionally influences our general impression about a society—especially one from the past. This should not come as a surprise, since it seems that to a certain extent, this has always been the case. Thucydides, the ancient Greek historian, wrote in approximately 400 BC: "I think that if the city of the Spartans should be deserted and nothing should be left of it but its temples and the foundations of its other buildings, posterity would after a long lapse of time be very loath to believe that their power was as great as their renown."[1] He was referring to the Spartans' complete lack of interest regarding architecture and the absence of important buildings in the settlements comprising their city.

Many rulers, autocratic sovereigns, and elected state leaders alike were keen to erect impressive buildings with vivid symbolic character. Napoleon ordered the construction of a large triumphal arch of Roman inspiration opposite the Louvre, l'Arc de Triomphe; and nearly two centuries later François Mitterrand commissioned its modern version, the Grande Arche, in the same axis five kilometers away. Besides, all of us generally consider that edifices are our representatives of sorts in the city and the landscape. To the extent that we can, we shape our house according to our taste, and we choose our apartment not least, because of the external appearance of the building in which it is located. We do not seem to consider seriously the fact that we do not see it while we are inside it; we know what it looks like, and this suffices—as indeed happens with the clothes we wear. On the other hand, it is clear that the potential choices even absolute lords and rulers have are ultimately limited, and so anything constructed bears the seal of the society within the context of which it was created. Consequently, the question of whether the building is a vehicle of collective choices and therefore represents each society as a whole (and the ruling class in particular), or whether it is a vehicle of personal choices and therefore represents the person, resurfaces each time a foundation stone is laid.

We saw in Chapter 3 the great importance attributed by ancient Egyptians in preserving the bodies of the dead pharaohs, and what they were willing to do in order to ensure the best conditions for their afterlife. However, even that was not enough. Although the pharaohs' souls were hovering between their luxurious tombs and the skies, they were still supposed to be constantly present among their former subjects, even if the latter lived crammed together in two- and three-story mud-brick residential buildings in the cities, or in huts made of mud and straw in the fields—i.e., in places that probably the pharaohs had never visited. The dead kings should not be forgotten. Oblivion was tantamount to actual death and if that occurred, the preservation of their bodies would somehow lose its meaning. Clearly, the Egyptians had to use any means possible to prevent this from happening. Architecture was called to play its part in this effort.

From early on, the Egyptians built the pharaohs' tombs—which represented the dead kings in their godly status—to be as visible as possible. A key feature of the Great Pyramids was that ordinary people could see them from afar. Thus far away, but forever etched in the memory of those who set their eyes on them; the more the better. From this point of view, a location near a large urban center was ideal. This made certain that the impression would pass down by word of mouth to an even larger audience and would ensure the pharaohs' presence among the living. Let us remember that in the case of Djoser's mortuary complex Imhotep made his Pharaoh's tomb visible from the Nile, and similar considerations evidently prevailed throughout the Old Kingdom.

Nevertheless, even in Egypt times changed. Gradually, the pharaohs' main concern became preventing the looting of their tombs. In the New Kingdom, and after two periods of dissolution of central authority, the tombs were built underground, cut inside the rock, guarding in the bowels of the earth the precious remains of the deified kings. Ineni, the confident of Tuthmose II, regarded as his badge of honor that he arranged the digging of his king's tomb with absolute secrecy—"no one seeing, no one hearing"—in a modern rendition of the hieroglyphics inscribed in his own tomb.[2] This ongoing pursuit for secrecy created a shortcoming in the public image of the pharaoh, which had to be compensated. This could not be done through erecting particularly impressive palaces, as would happen later in other parts of the world, since the pharaohs did not have to be remembered necessarily as living beings. As a result, it seems that they invested in these kind of earthly projects as much money and as much human energy necessary to ensure simply their comfortable stay. Typically, the Egyptian palaces built mainly with bricks, not granite, are rather poorly preserved, and in most cases, only their foundations remain. It was the construction of temples that could counterbalance the shortcoming in pharaoh's public image.

The first temples of Egypt are at least as old as the first royal tombs, and some of them were of considerable dimensions; but it was in the New Kingdom when temple building peaked, which may also reflect a shift of power in Egyptian society. We know that pharaoh Akhenaten clashed with the priesthood when he attempted to introduce a new religion in the middle of the fourteenth century BCE, and that he was defeated. That the personal promotion of the pharaohs was not conducted with the construction of huge personal burial monuments, but eventually with the erection, renovation, and expansion of temples on a scale never before seen in Egypt, and with the building of mortuary temples completely detached from their graves, may be seen as a visualization of the power-sharing between the two most prominent institutions of state authority.

Things do not always proceed in linear sequence. The top priority of Ahmose I, the founder of the New Kingdom in the middle of the sixteenth century BCE, was the restoration of the throne's prestige. Ahmose's military successes had brought about the unification of Egypt and had filled the treasuries of the state, a prerequisite of every ambitious building program. Ahmose proceeded in a highly symbolical political act accomplished through architecture: he reconstructed several ruined royal tombs and pyramids. After over 150 years of polyarchy and the expulsion of the Hyksos conquerors, Egypt was again under the scepter of an absolute ruler, and the continuity of authority was demonstrated with the most visible way. Ahmose himself appeared as the heir and successor of a glorious past; assuming the old tradition he built a pyramid, albeit as his cenotaph. Perhaps the best indication that his efforts were not in vain is that princes and senior state officials began to visit Giza more often to pay homage to the deified pharaohs of the Old Kingdom, and to admire their monuments.

**The entrance to the temple of Amun, Karnak, ancient Thebes, south Egypt, mainly 1500 BCE–380 BCE**

Central authority apparently did not perceive this early religious tourism as a challenge to Ahmose's legitimacy, but rather as a factual recognition that Ahmose was linked directly with his predecessors and, like themselves, with the gods.

Ahmose's successor Amenhotep I, and the subsequent pharaohs, threw their weight in the renovation and expansion of temples in both Upper and Lower (i.e., the south and north respectively) Egypt, and mainly in the temple of Amun at Karnak in the then capital Thebes. The temple was part of a complex that would evolve into one of the largest religious compounds ever built.

Its original core, built long before the New Kingdom, was rather small. In about 2040 BCE, Mentuhotep II oriented the axis of his burial complex—which was at the other side of the Nile, at Deir el-Bahri, about five kilometers away—toward it. Mentuhotep II was the founder of the Middle Kingdom, who reunited Egypt after a period of dissolution of central authority. The benefit obtained by this architectural gesture was mutual. Mentuhotep II stood almost equal to Amun, a god symbolizing creation; and the god acquired prestige as the protector of a powerful regime that revitalized Egypt (a boost to his image that he most probably welcomed: even gods compete against each other and no one's position is secure in people's minds and souls). Thus, the investment of the pharaohs of the New Kingdom in the temple of the mighty god made sense: with each new wing, each new outbuilding, the bond between the god of creation and the earthly ruler became stronger in the eyes of his subjects—provided that each new building could be attributed to its founder.

In the stones of the new buildings, the name of each Pharaoh was engraved who had added something to the complex, as well as scenes from his life and his accomplishments. In addition, in each new edifice, a foundation deposit—a pit with offerings—was incorporated protecting the

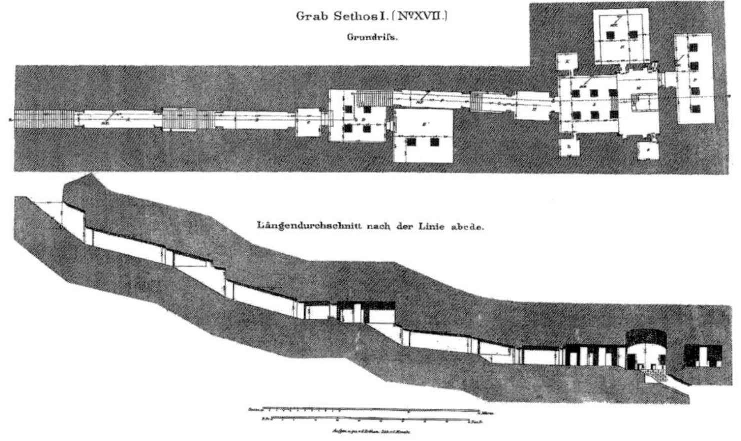


**The underground tomb of pharaoh Seti I, Valley of the Kings, ancient Thebes, south Egypt, circa 1290 BC; drawing K. R. Lepsius**

memory of the pharaoh from the attrition caused by time. With this dual initiative, a part of which addressed people—contemporary and subsequent—and the other the gods, the pharaoh could hope that he would not be easily forgotten. His credentials would endure forever, some of them visible and the rest known from stories. The immediate target audience was the priesthood, which had access to the temple's interior and would attest the deceased pharaoh's greatness to the wider audience, the generations to come.

Carving the name on a stone is a rather unsophisticated way of perpetuating the founder's name. It is, however, effective: the range of means that architecture (even good architecture) uses extends from the most noble and elaborate to the most mundane and unrefined.

In some cases, the next pharaoh attempted to erase the traces of one of his predecessors; history is full of similar incidents: the Romans often erased the name of the depicted person in marble busts and statues and replaced it with the name of the new official to be honored. This is practically what happened with queen Hatshepsut's buildings.

Hatshepsut was the daughter of pharaoh Tuthmose I and his primary wife Ahmes; and the wife, as it was customary, of her half-brother Tuthmose II. When Tuthmose II died in 1479 BCE, his son from a secondary wife was proclaimed pharaoh under the name Tuthmose III, and Hatshepsut was named coregent. Soon Hatshepsut proclaimed herself pharaoh and pushed aside or overshadowed Tuthmose III who was still a child. She skillfully bolstered Egypt's international commerce and the country flourished economically. A large portion of the state's resources was devoted to Hatshepsut's extensive building program, which included works in the Karnak complex.

The mortuary temple of Mentuhotep II (in the back), circa 2040 BCE, and Hatshepsut (in front), circa 1479 BCE. In-between, high up the slope, the traces of Tuthmose III's mortuary temple are visible, circa 1458 BCE, Deir el-Bahri, ancient Thebes, south Egypt.

Tuthmose III succeeded Hatshepsut as sole pharaoh in 1458 BCE under obscure circumstances. He was devoted initially to military operations in the north to obtain glory for Egypt and himself. Toward the end of his reign and presumably when his son Tuthmose IV was his coregent, he began a systematic effort to limit Hatshepsut's traces. This would bring into acceptable proportions, the radiance of a queen who as a woman was still rather an exception than the norm in statesmanship.

Her name, carved in hieroglyphics on stone, along with her image was chiseled from the most prominent locations of the buildings. The two obelisks she erected in front of Pylon V were incorporated in the new hypostyle hall built by Tuthmose III and were built perimetrically so that they were no longer visible. The shrine of red quartzite that Hatshepsut had erected in the heart of the temple was replaced by a new one made of pink granite. Moreover, on the other side of the Nile at Deir el-Bahri, Tuthmose III built his mortuary temple (not his grave, which was rock-cut and located in the Valley of the Kings several kilometers away) directly next to that of Hatshepsut. In fact, the term "directly next" does not convey reality adequately. Hatshepsut had erected her mortuary temple a few dozen meters from that of the founder of New Kingdom Mentuhotep II—and indeed in almost the same shape. Mentuhotep II had reunited and strengthened Egypt and had established the connection of his name with Amun. By building next to the mortuary temple of Mentuhotep II and using similar architecture, Hatshepsut wanted to show that she continued his work. However, Tuthmose III—or whoever saw to his mortuary temple—was determined to disrupt the symbolic links the queen attempted to establish. His mortuary temple was literally squeezed between those of Hatshepsut and Mentuhotep II, with its ramp partly obstructing their visual contact. The battle for posthumous fame was transferred to a fight with architecture as its epicenter.

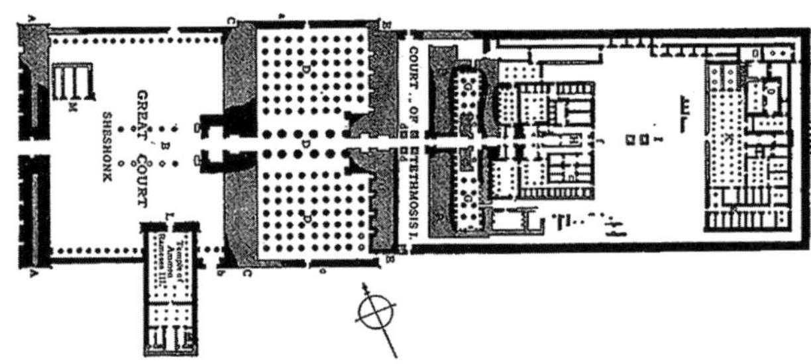

**Temple of Amun, Karnak, ancient Thebes, south Egypt, mostly 1500 BCE–380 BCE; *Encyclopedia Britannica*, 1911**



Despite several extensions, the temple complex of Karnak retains the character of a more or less unified whole. The road with sphinxes leading to the temple, the successive impressive pylons, the outdoor courtyards and the hypostyles halls do not give the impression of a clutter of disparate components. This was certainly helped by the relative uniformity of the architectural members and the sculptures; key features of Egyptian art and architecture changed very little over time. The huge papyrus- and lotus-shaped columns, the epistyles (i.e., the horizontal beams) with the characteristically simple outline, the curved cornices at the upper part of the compact walls, the frameless openings, the richly decorated pure geometric forms, the stylized statues of supernatural dimensions with their calm grandeur—all of these evolved little in 2,000 years. On the other hand, the persistence on preserving and strengthening the central longitudinal axis, the creation of a succession of pylons, courtyards and halls leading into the interior of the temple—which with each new extension became increasingly inaccessible—contribute to the impression of unity of the whole. This means that each new pylon that was built in front of the previous ones should preferably have been larger. The last pylon constructed—which has been recorded as Pylon I because it is the first one encountered when entering the complex—was built in 380 BCE, and if completed would have a height of over 40 meters, a length of 110 meters, and would be 13 meters thick. The next pylon, Pylon II, was built 1,000 years earlier in 1323 BCE as the outer pylon of the already huge complex. This pylon is located approximately fifty meters west of the next pylon, Pylon III, which was built as the outer pillar of the complex about seventy years before Pylon II. When around 1492 BCE Tuthmose III decided to build a pylon in order to make the entrance to his Hall of Records—located in the heart of the complex—more formal, he made it smaller than the

The hypostyle hall of Seti I, temple of Amun, Karnak, ancient Thebes, south Egypt, circa 1290 BCE

pylon that the visitor meets immediately before his own, even though this pylon existed previously.

In 1294 BCE, pharaoh Seti I transformed the outdoor courtyard between Pylons II and III into a hypostyle hall measuring 100 meters by 50 meters. Its roof was supported by 134 massive columns, eighteen meters in height (and twenty-two meters those in the colonnades forming its central axis). The temple was also expanded to the east—i.e., behind its initial core. Courtyards and ceremonial halls and walls were created there, which enclosed the shrine with successive layers of constructs enhancing the sense that it constituted the de facto center of a uniformed, hierarchically structured whole. The unique longitudinal axis along which the huge temple complex of Karnak is laid out is rivaled by a second axis running perpendicular to it. This second axis initially began at the courtyard of the temple of Amun (the main temple of Karnak) and connected it with the temple of Mut, a few hundred meters to its south. However, as the temple of Karnak expanded to the west, the perpendicular axis now began from its middle. This "defect" might have been addressed in a future expansion of the temple, which never occurred. With what, undoubtedly genius, method this would have happened, we will never know.

The fact that the individual elements that compose the temple—and which can be attributed to each founder separately—form a unified large whole makes the temple of Karnak a real masterpiece. Obviously, the pharaohs and their architects realized that their "building within a building" had to be both distinct and imperceptible, both unique and part of a harmonious whole; on the one hand, in order to represent each pharaoh in the future, and on the other, to display him as member of a series of kings whose strength and wealth were unprecedented.

Architecture has been deliberately used as a powerful tool for expressing or creating individual as well as collective identities since at least the first large extensions of the temple of Karnak 3,500 years ago.

### Notes

1 Thucydides: *Hist.* I.10.2.
2 Breasted, J. H.: *Ancient Records of Egypt, Vol II.* University of Chicago Press 1906-7, 106.


### Selected Bibliography

Arnold, Dieter: *The Temple of Mentuhotep at Deir el-Bahari.* Metropolitan Museum of Art 1979.
Arnold, Dieter et al. (eds.): *Temples of Ancient Egypt.* Cornell University Press 1997.
Cline, Eric/O'Connor, David (eds.): *Thutmose III: A New Biography.* University of Michigan Press 2006.
David, Rosalie: *Life in Ancient Egypt.* Oxford University Press 1998.
Dodson, Aidan/Hilton, Dyan: *The Complete Royal Families of Ancient Egypt.* Thames & Hudson 2004.
Strudwick, Nigel/Strudwick, Helen: *Thebes in Egypt.* Cornell University Press 1999.

# NEW IDEAS OR CHANGING PREFERENCES?

## The Acropolis of Athens

The early ancient Greek temples were hardly like the grand Egyptian ones. They were mud huts and small edifices with thatched or flat roofs. In other words, they looked more like the dwellings of contemporary Greeks—the eighth-century BCE temple of Apollo Daphnephoros in Eretria is a typical example. Humanlike in form, the gods would reside in abodes similar to those of normal people. Indeed, some of these early temples had been the residences of prominent citizens; then their descendants bestowed them to the community, thus maintaining their family's leading status.

After 700 BCE, against a backdrop of growing population and the increase of available means, larger temples started being erected. The most prominent among them were the peripteral temples. They typically consisted of an ordinary, often elongated chamber, the *cella*, surrounded

**The precinct of Apollo Daphnephoros, Eretria, Greece, circa 770 BCE; courtesy of the Swiss School of Archaeology in Greece**

by a colonnade (*pteron*)—i.e., a portico with wooden posts similar to modern-day porches, which are meant to offer protection from the rain or sun. This type of temple would be an idealized version of the small hut, a form that would persist even in the grand marble temples built centuries later. Only the statue of the god or goddess—the embodiment of the temple's resident—belonged in the cella, which was the size of a large room. It is only natural then, that during rituals, the congregation of the faithful would gather outside the temple and not inside.

Temples would gradually become more massive, which might have been because of interaction with Egypt. The thin wooden posts, which until then were the norm, were replaced by monumentally sized wooden columns about seventy centimeters thick, like those at the Temple of Poseidon at Isthmia. The architrave, the principal beam resting on the columns, and the frieze above it, were also massive. Roof tiles came to replace reed- and straw-thatched roofs.

Around 600 BCE, timber gradually began to give way to stone as the main building material for temples and public edifices: the Temple of Athena Pronaia at Marmaria had stone columns and wooden entablatures (architraves, friezes, and the cornices above them), and the Temple of Artemis in Corfu, built shortly after, had columns as well as entablatures made of stone.

Stone temples retained many of the formal features of heavy wooden structures, even though these had only just become established: the monumental edifices featuring mud-brick walls and superstructure and massive columns made of timber were a short-lived seventh-century BCE novelty. *Triglyphs*, for example, the architectural elements alternating with the *metopes* on the frieze, had emerged from the decorative ends of the transverse roof beams; and capitals, the uppermost part of the columns, were a variation of the bolster block meant to distribute over a larger surface the load of the architrave where it rested on the wooden posts. To begin with, this kind of imitation is often encountered in comparable cases. Built some 2,000 years earlier than the Greek stone temples, many of the outbuildings at the mortuary complex of Pharaoh Djoser were made of stone carved in a way vividly suggestive of papyrus cane structures; columns inspired by local flora, papyrus and lotus, persisted in Egyptian architecture for millennia. Some 5,500 years later, the first cars looked like carriages, the main concern of their inventors being to replace the power of horses with engines, not to design a new vehicle from scratch. Several years had to pass before cars would take on their distinctive form.

The Greeks chose to continue reproducing these formal features on their stone edifices, which strongly resembled structures made of mud brick and timber. Wood (Greek *hyle*, Latin *materia*) was a readily available material used to make many useful things: from buildings and ships, to equipment, such as cranes and wheels. Aristotle would later use this very word to describe what all tangible things had in common, the "substratum" of every individual object, as Stoics would put it. The nascent concept of matter appropriated the word used up to that point for a raw material for practically every construction: wood. The choice of timber as building material added a primeval quality to temples.

The concept of ongoing progress had started to advance among Greeks, despite the fact that their ancient poets maintained a circular view of history, rather than a linear one. In a world moving constantly toward uncharted territories, the old was familiar, tried and tested through time; to resort to it was soothing. Several early temples were carefully preserved for centuries. Despite being quite primitive, they were no less respected in the fifth century BCE than Classical temples—such as the Parthenon and the Erechteion—which were infinitely more important in terms of architecture. By the same token, the old wooden statues—for which imagination was required to distinguish any human features—were no less respected than the masterpieces of Classical sculpture, so finely rendering the body and face of humanlike deities. Architecture cannot meet all the expectations of the society—not even all the expectations of a single person—since, in many cases, fulfilling one expectation often means failing to fulfill another. Shifting from hut-temples and house-temples to the glorious stone temples of the pre-Classical and Classical eras meant the loss of qualities inherent to the unassuming and simple older structures. The ancient Greeks may have attempted to offset this loss by reproducing features of the earlier buildings, and by doing so alluded to the humble beginnings of monumental temples.

By preserving in stone the details of wooden structures and maintaining forms resembling, albeit vaguely, the ancestral hut-temples, the ancient Greeks proclaimed that their monumental stone temples were perfect and everlasting versions of primeval buildings; that these were rooted in the distant past, yet at the same time destined for an existence that surpassed the life of humans; and that they were therefore, in a way, self-sufficient and self-reliant entities.

This view might have provided the grounds for the so-called optical refinements, introduced no later than 550 BCE—i.e., shortly after the first stone-built temples emerged. The term refers to a set of deliberate deviations from strict geometry; evidently, these deviations were intended to visualize a building's inner coherence and to breathe life into it. Indeed, in a way, extremely orderly buildings look as if they have been built cumulatively, by repetitively placing one column next to the other at equal distances, then the beams over the columns, then the roof over the beams. Clearly, the ancient Greeks meant to avoid this. The fact that the Athenians appointed the famous sculptor Phidias as head of the Parthenon's erection shows how they attempted to do it. The erection of the Parthenon raised great artistic and political expectations, and was seen as an opportunity for the Athenian democracy to display its superiority. Phidias had developed a sculptural style that, no more than a century earlier, had veered from the Egyptian pattern of depicting humans in a strict, ceremonial pose, to an exploration of how to render the natural movement and vibrancy of the body. This very vibrancy was what the Athenians sought to convey in their most monumental edifice. This might account for the anthropomorphism of ancient Greek architecture—i.e., the impression that the observer gets of standing before a living entity, a human being in particular, rather than an edifice made of inanimate materials; an impression that seems to have been widely held in antiquity, too. About 400 years after the Parthenon was erected, Vitruvius attributed it to the fact that both the Doric and the Ionic columns (i.e., the two main "orders" of columns in ancient Greek architecture) were inspired by the human body, whose proportions were transferred to temples.[1]

**Athens' Acropolis in late fifth century BCE; Parthenon (center), Erechteion (left), Propylaea (right); reconstruction M. Korres**

Phidias and his team, architects Ictinus and Callicrates, saw the Parthenon almost as a piece of sculpture and drew on all the experience gained in the previous 100 years—construction on the Parthenon began in 447 BCE. This great temple of the Athenian Acropolis hardly has any straight lines, but rather very gentle curves; and its surfaces are scarcely ever level, or entirely vertical or horizontal.

Vitruvius takes note of how the column shaft becomes narrower, like naturally grown tree trunks.[2] However, this narrowing is not smooth; as the columns rise, it becomes sharper. This creates the *entasis* (Greek for tension), a convexity or swelling of the column shaft at about one-third of its height in relation to the hypothetically steadily decreasing diameter. In the Parthenon, the 9.5-meter-tall columns have an entasis of no more than two centimeters, which is a ratio of about 550/1: only slight, but nonetheless among the largest ever applied. The purpose of the entasis might have been to create the impression that the column was bulging under the weight of a load, exactly like with human muscles. In earlier temples, statues and supports depicting human figures had been used occasionally instead of columns, so people were likely to draw such parallels.

The floor of the temple is not flat: there is an elevation that fades smoothly toward the outer corners. Compared to other temples, this curvature is again more pronounced in the Parthenon: about six centimeters along the narrow sides, which are about thirty-one meters in length, and around eleven centimeters along the long sides, which are about seventy meters in length. A similar curvature is also evident in the architraves, which makes them not completely horizontal, but arched along their length.

Moreover, the columns are not vertical, but tilted toward the inside with about the same gradient. Extended upwards, the vertical axes of the columns on the long sides intersect at a height of around 2,000 meters, and the vertical axes of those on the narrow sides intersect at a height of around 4,800 meters. Since the floor on which the columns rest tilts outward, both along and across, the vertical axes of the columns are not at right angles to the resting surface: the latter tilt outward and the column shafts inward. The *abaci*—the rectangular blocks that form the uppermost member of the capital—tilt outward. The outer surfaces of the epistyles resting on the abaci, and the friezes above them, tilt inward. Above the frieze, the cornices bear metopes, which in turn tilt outward.

This successive counter-balancing of tilts toward one or the other side strongly resembles the natural posture of the human body when the

**The northern colonnade of the Parthenon, Athens' Acropolis, 447 BCE, with the visible curvature of the *stylobates***

weight falls on one leg, a posture studied by the sculptors of that era. The *Doryphorus* (Spear-bearer), a statue by sculptor Polycleitus dating back to 450 BCE, rests firmly on its right leg, while the left is merely used to maintain balance. The right hip of *Doryphorus* is higher than the left. The exact opposite occurs with the shoulders: the right shoulder "falls" lower than the left. Polycleitus' work was widely known; his theories on art and the numerical ratios that existed between the members of the body were topics of discussion. The architecture of this period obviously quite consciously adopted the principles with which the *Doryphorus* was created.

A range of other features also keeps the eye of the observer focused on the Parthenon. Each column is an architectural member linear in shape (a property highlighted by the fluting, i.e., the streaks along its shaft), positioned vertically. In the colonnades, however, the individuality of each column disappears, and the image emerges of a horizontal array of similar elements. The corner columns are four centimeters thicker than the rest, which makes their lower diameter 1.93 meters instead of 1.89 meters. Although the columns are generally placed at equal distances, specifically at 2.36 meters, the four corners appear denser, as the corner columns are only 1.74 meters apart. The result of these violations of the geometric regularity is that the corners of the Parthenon are clearly defined and the horizontality is limited decisively by vertical elements—the reinforced corner columns positioned too close to the columns adjacent to them. This "dynamic" balance between horizontality and verticality, between the unit and the whole, makes the Parthenon more than an accumulation of architectural elements: a body with inner tension and cohesion.

This large temple rests partially on a filling that is eight meters high in places. The top of the uneven hill was converted to approach the ideal flat surface. The sculptures of the Parthenon depict the city's foundation myths—an idealized version of its "history." A few meters away lay the (contrived) relics of these myths: the point where water gushed out when Poseidon struck the ground with his trident while fighting Athena for the patronage of the city; the olive tree planted by Athena; the burial site of the first king of the city. A few years later, a smaller temple, the Erechteion addressed the circumstances: it was built in an irregular shape, which appears to have resulted from the juxtaposition of separate halls housing the randomly scattered (but conveniently adjacent) relics. Located opposite, the perfect, balanced Parthenon was clearly the antithesis of the Erechteion, the product of the transfer into matter of a pure mental concept free of any circumstantial limitation.

Once the construction of Parthenon was well under way, construction began on the new Propylaea of the Acropolis in 437 BCE. This was the gateway to the complex of temples, monuments, and public buildings on the hill overlooking Athens, the Parthenon being the most renowned among them. The Propylaea is a distinct, elaborate structure. First, it is a building with no interior space in the conventional sense. Visitors to the Acropolis coming through its long covered passageway, which is open

**The Parthenon, Athens' Acropolis, 447 BCE**

**Erechteion, Athens' Acropolis, 421 BCE**



on both ends, would nonetheless get the impression of walking along an enclosed space. The two front sides of the Propylaea—the western facing outward to the city and the eastern facing inward to the Acropolis—look very much like the narrow sides of the Parthenon, complete with Doric columns, architraves, friezes, and pediments, similar in size and proportions with those of the great temple. Still, two smaller side wings at its entrance, parallel to the axis of the incoming visitors to the Acropolis, render the Propylaea virtually inconspicuous at first glance. In this respect, the Propylaea seem to be in breach of the Classical tradition of making edifices immediately and easily perceptible. This design imposes what was later called an "experiential" relationship between the visitors and the building,

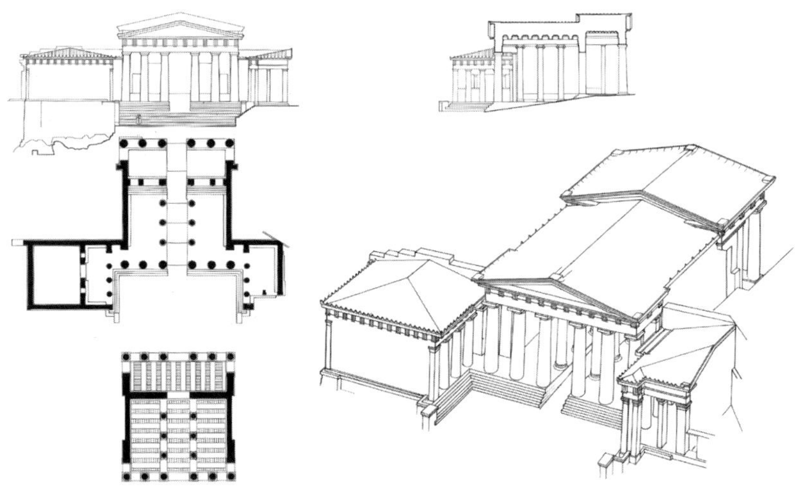

**Propylaea, Athens' Acropolis, 437–432 BCE; drawing Tasos Tanoulas, YSMA**

as opposed to a detached relationship of the observer with an object lying in front of him.

While very similar to that of the eastern front side portico of the Propylaea in all other respects, the western front side portico is twenty-eight centimeters taller. As it protrudes high up in the distance, visitors coming up the steep slope of the Acropolis must raise their glance to see it. The principle behind this design is clear: the columns do not all share the same—considered ideal—proportions, but the higher they stand in relation to the observer, the more slender they need to be.

Evidently, Mnesicles, the architect of the Propylaea, introduced a groundbreaking concept: structures were not built just for the sake of people in abstract; their design would have to take into account the conditions under which people came into contact with them. Lysippos, a Greek sculptor of the fourth century BCE, summarized this concept, claiming that the great sculptors of the Classical era of fifth century BCE (such as Polycleitus and Phidias) depicted people as they were, whereas he depicted them as they appeared.[3] Mnesicles did not belong to the circle of Phidias and the Parthenon architects who represented the Classical view that the building and artwork in general should be structured only according to the supposedly eternal rules of right proportions and beauty. According to Mnesicles, the work was directly accountable to the public and it should therefore be adapted to the specific constraints of where and when it was perceived. Monumental architecture had been completely demystified. The familiarization of people with the artificial environment, which first began in the cities of Mesopotamia thousands of years ago, had passed into a new stage.

Plato may have had these "subversive" views in mind a few decades after the Propylaea was completed, when he argued passionately against art that distorted reality. Such was the art of *skiagraphy*—i.e., illusionary painting aiming to trick the eye to create the impression of depth—a failed feat nonetheless, considering that "scientific" perspective was conceived during the Renaissance 2,000 years later. Colossal statues imposed unfavorable viewing terms and led to the need for altering their proportions to prevent them looking deformed: for example, located several meters high, the head appeared small in relation to the thigh, to the observer who would be standing closer to the latter. To make the statue look normal, one solution was to make the head bigger. Many thought that the generalization of this practice was completely unacceptable. For Plato, to depict "only the proportions that appear beautiful"[4]—known then as symmetries—rather than the actual proportions of the human body was to abandon altogether every effort to reach the truth: the gravest of human mistakes. Plato generally appreciated the works of Phidias,[5] not only because they did not distort the "actual" proportions of the human body, but also because he probably believed they were no mere replicates of tangible reality. In Plato's view, tangible reality is what we perceive through our senses, which are deceptive by nature. According to the theory that was formulated later at the Academy, the School of philosophy founded by Plato, art could reveal ideas, the true essence of things, without having to imitate tangible reality. Art which, for the sake of the eye, consciously distorted what the mind could perceive as absolute truth had no place in the ideal Republic.

Surely a twenty-eight-centimeter difference in height between the porticoes of the western and eastern sides of the Propylaea is tiny; today it goes unnoticed—as it probably did in antiquity, too. And yet, this tiny difference reflects a huge dissent of views, felt still to this day. On the one hand were the masterminds of the Parthenon's erection who sought the perfect proportions and then they tried to breathe life into their building, by denying it absolute regularity and rigid symmetry that cannot be found in nature. They did this in an effort to create the perfect work of art that would give rise to something eternal, something independent of the circumstances in which the public would perceive it—as was the case with the architects of the great pyramids of Giza. On the other hand were Mnesicles and his contemporary artists who claimed that a work of art should adapt to the individual circumstances of its perception by the public. To Mnesicles there was no such thing as indisputable and eternal perfection. What mattered was the impression the building had on the audience. As it was soon to become evident, though, this impression depends not only on the angle under which a three-dimensional work of art is viewed, but also on a variety of factors—not least of which being how exciting it seems to a public simply tired of the old. With the Propylaea, the change in preferences became legitimate. The evolution of architecture was no longer driven only by the (eternal) endeavor to find a fitting solution to the problem at hand, but also by the need to devise a different solution that would satisfy the constantly changing desires of the public, shaped under constantly changing circumstances.

Over the next few centuries, Hellenistic architecture—the architecture of the Greek World after Alexander the Great—preserved the fundamental features of Classical architecture, albeit increasingly slender and less bulky. The sense of accumulation of mass that the Parthenon invoked began to give way in favor of an increasingly understated elegance. Columns became more slender, and distances between them became larger. This trend of making columns increasingly thinner was by no means a novelty: the columns of the Doric temples of Sicily, dating back to 550 BCE, are significantly more massive than those of the Parthenon, built a century later. The trend remained unchanged for many centuries, during which time the prevalent views about art changed radically.

New ideas, new ideologies, and new value systems create the conditions for evolution in architecture. Nevertheless, tangible results, more pronounced differences, and visible progress often emerge from a simple change in the preferences of people and architects who work to satisfy them.

### Notes

1  Vitruvius: *De Architectura* V.1.3.
2  Vitruvius: *De Architectura* III.1.4.
3  Plinius: *NH* 34.65.
4  Plato: *Sophist* 235E.
5  Plato: *Meno* 91D.

### Selected Bibliography

Coulton, J.J.: *Ancient Greek architects at Work*. Cornell University Press 1982.
Gruben, Gottfried: *Die Tempel der Griechen*. Hirmer 2001.
Haselberger, Lothar: "Bending the Truth; Curvature and other Refinements of the Parthenon." In: Neils, Jenifer (ed.): *The Parthenon: From Antiquity to the Present*. Cambridge University Press 2005, 101 ff.
Korres, Manolis: "Der Plan des Parthenon." In: *Mitteilungen des deutschen archäologischen Instituts, Athenische Abteilung*, 109, 1994, 53 ff.
Neils, Jenifer: "'With the Noblest Images on all Sides': The Ionic frieze of the Parthenon." In Neils, Jenifer (ed.): *The Parthenon: From Antiquity to the Present*. Cambridge University Press 2005, 199 ff.
Pollitt, J.J.: *The Ancient View of Greek Art*. Yale University Press 1974.

# SINE QUA NON

## The Great Roman Aqueducts

In September 1960, in a period of intense competition between the Western and the Soviet bloc, Nikita Khrushchev, leader of USSR, visited the United States. President Eisenhower did not show to him missiles nor did he invite him to a military parade, like the ones taking place each year on May Day in Red Square; instead he took Khrushchev on a helicopter tour and showed him the highways leading to the suburbs of Washington during the afternoon rush hour.

I do not think that we can even imagine the image of our cities without cables, without traffic signs and traffic lights, without railway lines, without airports, harbors, and power plants. Infrastructure is now ubiquitous. One quarter of the surface of modern cities is devoted to automobile traffic or is accessible to them. We come across landscapes without power lines, highways or rural roads, and canals only in exceptionally sparsely populated areas of the planet.

It was not always like this. As we saw in the first chapter of this book, the diffusion of mankind into every corner of the planet became possible with the construction of shelters that protected their occupants from predators and made "their winters warm and their summers cool."[1] Permanent settlement, however, required infrastructure that would make life comfortable and safe; no site can offer everything in sufficient quantity that even a modest-sized community needs to survive and prosper.

The commodity that humans need the most is water. And, since springs or clean rivers cannot be found everywhere, wells are quite often the first infrastructure works built. Since procuring water from wells is tiring and their capacity is limited, transferring water from places with constant supply was considered at some point to be a worthwhile investment. The simplest way to achieve this is by getting water, usually from a point in a river at a higher altitude, and channeling it to flow by gravity in open earthen channels running on the ground surface—a method still widely used in irrigation.

Bringing water to villages and towns was more difficult, because the open earthen conduits are easily damaged when passing through inhabited areas. Aqueducts were devised to ensure minimal losses during water transportation, making it possible for people to live in high densities and allowing the development of cities, as we know them—a crucial condition for the creation of civilization. It was in Imperial Rome that the construction of aqueducts reached its peak.

Rome brought the extra grain necessary to feed its population from Egypt. It brought the required water from mountain springs and from rivers via fourteen aqueducts from a distance up to nearly a hundred kilometers away. At its peak—i.e., the first and second century CE—water consumption was several hundred thousand cubic meters per day; this is a huge amount, equivalent per capita to that of New York today. Water was channeled into public fountains, palaces, baths, and houses of wealthy and powerful citizens for a wide range of uses: from the most essential to those supporting lavish lifestyles, such as supplying the pods in Hadrian's Villa in Tivoli, a large complex thirty kilometers from Rome, where the emperor often retired.

**Artificial lake, Hadrian's Villa, Tivoli, outskirts of Rome, circa 120 CE**



The first aqueduct of Rome, Aqua Appia, was built shortly before 300 BCE, at the time when Alexander's Successors divided his kingdom. It brought around 73,000 cubic meters of water to the city per day, a quantity that increased fivefold with the other aqueducts built during the Republic until 27 BCE. The construction of more aqueducts continued at high pace in the following years, culminating in the middle of the first century CE when Aqua Claudia and Anio Novus were built. Combined, they supplied Rome with over 380,000 cubic meters of water per day.

In every aqueduct, a sedimentation tank was built near the site of water uptake, where foreign bodies—mud, small rocks, etc.—settled.

Afterwards the water was channeled, usually with covered conduits, into the city in the distribution tank. From there, it was distributed in various sectors; it reached its final consumption through lead pipes that were connected to each other with components similar to those used until the twenthieth century.

For decades, some historians attributed the collapse of Rome partly to lead poisoning of the ruling class—a far-fetched theory. It is true that traces of the substance—which affects, among others, brain functions causing intense mental and psychological disorders—were detected in the bones of people who lived at that period. Though larger intake probably occurred through wine consumption, since lead was added as a preservative. In any case, the pipe-related lead poisoning points out bitterly that the buildings' mechanical installations are much more important than they usually appear to be. The Parthenon did not have mechanical shafts. Behind the rectangular stones that formed the architrave was another row of stones and not some stainless abutment adjusted on a steel frame, as in modern buildings, in order to make room for pipes and wires. Attempting to achieve the structural honesty of stone buildings at Beaubourg in the nineteen-seventies, Renzo Piano and Richard Rogers did not conceal the mechanical installations necessary for the building to function properly. The truth's cost was great: the side toward Beaubourg Street is dominated by dozens of brightly painted pipes that prevent visual contact between the functional space of the building and the street.

The aqueducts' operating principle between the sedimentation and distribution tanks was simple: water flowed freely from high to low. In order to achieve this, however, the most advanced technology had to be used. Many of the aqueducts have sectors with a gradient below 0.1 percent, an elevation difference of less than ten centimeters in one hundred meters. The Romans invented simple but very accurate leveling instruments. They mainly used a five-meter-long beam with a groove along its length, which was filled with water, so they could place the beam completely horizontally and sight along it. A minimal settlement of the ground due to inappropriate foundation, or a subsidence of the conduit for some other reason was enough to render the aqueduct unusable and to require discontinuing the water supply until the damage was repaired. Despite that, malfunctions were rare, with the exception of Aqua Claudia, which was probably put into operation prematurely. The regular and systematic maintenance by the special services that numbered several hundred workers appears to have been the key for this success. Easy maintenance is vital for the very sustainability of a project, though not always compatible with an otherwise good design: in 2009, Boris Johnson, the mayor of London, slammed the Greater London Authority building designed by Sir Norman Foster because it is extremely difficult to clean its windows.[2] In the very same ceremony, he awarded the annual prize of Royal Town Planning Institute to the contributors of the construction of the complex, to which this building belongs.

In order to cross a valley, the water was sometimes driven into
pipes to descend a steep slope, tread a short distance horizontally, and
then climb the opposite slope—a method not commonly used after the
middle of the first century CE, since the inverted siphon's maintenance
was particularly difficult. When the terrain rose between the spring and
the city, a large part of the route was underground. This required surface
digging, an ancient version of the cut and cover method that is often used
today for constructing metro lines; in mountains and hills, this method was
not feasible, and they had to be pierced. The most striking feature of the
aqueducts, however, is the elevated water conduits. Around Rome, the
arches of ancient aqueducts are still visible for miles and miles. Where the
conduits crossed deep valleys or ravines, bridges had to be constructed:
twenty-nine meters high in Segovia, Spain; and close to fifty meters in Pont
du Gard, in southern France.

**Pont du Gard, southern France, circa 40 CE**



Pont du Gard, built in the mid-first century CE, is remarkable
because it is an immense structure. Stones weighing a total of 50,000
tons—utilized in the most efficient manner—form three rows, one above
the other, of arches passing over a relatively small but turbulent river. The
largest of them has a twenty-five-meter span and is nineteen meters high,
and all to support at the desired height a conduit—1.25 meters wide and
1.85 meters deep—which supplied an insignificant town in a province of
the huge empire with water.

Pont du Gard summarized the Roman way of thinking. Under
their rule in the period of Pax Romana, the peace they imposed in a geographical area extending from Scotland to Persia, the world changed. Not
by new ideas, not by new scientific advances, but by the systematic and

widespread application of the existing technology. With pragmatism, the Romans set as their ultimate goal the proper and effective function of the state, which treated its subjects with old-style paternal affection and severity. The improvement of the daily life for the denizens of the empire was, therefore, a source of pride for state officials. The aqueducts gave the world a commodity much less questionable than the entertainment offered by gladiator fights in large arenas built for this purpose. Sextus Julius Frontinus, Water Commissioner of Rome in 97 CE, urged the readers of his book: "With such an array of indispensable structures carrying so much water, compare, if you will, the idle Pyramids or the useless, though famous, works of the Greeks!"[3]

**Via Appia in Minturno, Lazio, Italy**

The work of architects and engineers was the key to achieving this goal. There were few obstacles considered insurmountable. Drainage works improved the hygienic conditions. Roads, partly wide enough to allow at least the passage of two carriages, traversed the empire from one end to the other, crossing through mountains and over rivers. Military forces could be moved quickly to any province needed, and the transportation of people, goods, and ideas was facilitated. The quality of construction was so good that many of the bridges of the Roman road network were in use until recently. Harbors and canals completed an infrastructure network of unprecedented scale.

For the construction of several of these projects, a material was used without which their financial cost would be probably prohibitive. Roman concrete was a mixture of volcanic sand, lime, and irregularly shaped stones, which when mixed with water and then left to dry became solid—*opus caementicium*. The Romans began to use this material systematically in the first century BCE. Initially, they usually built the irregularly shaped stones as if they were building with squared stones or bricks—i.e., placing them one by one by hand, but using plenty of mortar. Simultaneously, they erected both wall fronts with uniform, prismatic shaped stones or bricks. At regular intervals in height, they created horizontal belts of regularly built large bricks, reaching from one façade to the other, binding the construction together. Over the openings, they created relief arches made of bricks so that the vertical forces were driven on either side. As years passed by, the stones' placement became less and less diligent, since it became obvious that the wall's strength was due to the mortar and not to the structure's geometrical regularity.

The Romans developed a very sophisticated foundation method below the water surface in rivers or the sea, similar to the one that John Augustus Roebling and his son Washington applied in the construction of the Brooklyn Bridge in the late eighteen-sixties: piles were driven to the bottom to the point where each pedestal would be erected, one next to another in two rows, until a cofferdam with double walls was formed. The piles were driven into the river or seabed by a pile-driver. Mounted on a raft that was anchored in place over the pile, the pile driver itself was a large heavy stone suspended from a derrick by a rope. The stone was lifted to its highest point, usually by slave labor, and then left to fall onto the top of the pile, driving the pile deeper and deeper into the bottom of the river or seabed. The gaps between the two walls were filled with sacks or baskets made of grass grown in swamps, filled with clay, and packed down so that the box was made watertight. Then the water was pumped, sludge was removed, and the bottom was excavated until stable ground was reached where the pedestals could be properly founded. Wherever possible hydraulic mortar was used—i.e., mortar containing volcanic ash and congealing below water.

The Romans, having mastered the appropriate technology to overcome the occasional difficulties, proceeded to establish a series of cities. As a rule, these cities were planned with a rectangular street grid, paved with stones, and equipped with markets, theaters, amphitheaters and sta-

**Private apartments buildings (insulae), Ostia, outskirts of Rome, first century CE; upper floors missing**

**Public lavatories, Ostia, outskirts of Rome, first century CE**

diums, gymnasiums, public fountains, and public lavatories. Since the cities' safety was guaranteed by the legions and not their natural setting, the choice of location was made primarily according to the particularities of the commercial and financial networks. This alone was enough to determine the future of urban development in Europe in the next millennia: many of the cities of the then less developed part of the empire, such as Paris and London, were founded by the Romans.

A city's population was the measure of its power, and large cities would be unthinkable without multistory buildings. The idea of placing a floor over another was revolutionary—a revolution that took hold over a period of several millennia. To climb to the rooftop of your house, as in 7000 BCE Çatalhöyük, is one step. Building two-story houses in a walled city was probably based on the idea of utilizing the walls of the ground floor to hold another floor for the family's exclusive use. By 2000 BCE, three-story buildings existed in walled cities in Mesopotamia as well as in Egypt; each housed more than one family. Large five- and six-story buildings—each housing a large number of families—were rare in an unfortified city; though they abounded in Imperial Rome, the first having been built in Republican times. Each one was a small but densely populated building bloc—an *insula*.

The insulae were considered to be something completely different from the typical detached house, the *domus*, and I believe this allows us to regard them as infrastructure works. Indeed, the home of each citizen was in a way the reflection of his presence in the city. A narrow strip of unbuilt land, the *ambitus*, surrounded (in theory) every house detaching it completely from the neighboring one: the very idea of the ancient Greco-Roman city rested on the individuality of its citizens. This was not possible, however, with the insulae in the city.

The continuous population increases in the major urban centers during a period with no mass transportation, left little choice. The "conventional" one- and two-story houses of the lower classes, built one next to another, underwent constant additions and extensions in order to meet the housing needs of the families. Larger houses were dissected, and shops and workshops were installed on the ground floor toward the roadside. Often, the homesteads expanded to adjacent properties. As a result, the building blocks were transformed gradually into a chaotic jumble of constructs of all kinds—initially the word insula denoted a group of individual, but not clearly distinct properties—with low housing capacity. A society that wanted to be called rational, a society addicted to standardization—how else could this large and multitudinous dominion be administered?—came up with a radical solution to the housing problem.

Many wealthy Romans invested in urban properties and in the erection of insulae. Although the quality of construction was usually poor and the sanitary conditions bad as a result of overcrowding, there were also better-built insulae containing spacious apartments for the upper class.

More than 1,500 years had to pass for this region to experience such an organized and systematic construction of infrastructure works—roads, harbors, and canals. It was manifested in the country where the concentration of power had advanced the most: in the France of Louis XIV and Jean Baptiste Colbert, Superintendent of Finances, in the second half of the seventeenth century. Two hundred years thereafter the railroads would decisively defeat the mud, which had held down the transportations in the European plains—until 1850, 6,000 kilometers of railway tracks had been laid in England alone—and after another hundred years, power lines would cross over mountains and plains to illuminate the nights in the cities and power our televisions and factories.

An environment without infrastructure belongs to the region that now we call the wilderness—39 percent of the planet's surface, of which about one-third is permanently covered with ice. On the rest of Earth's surface, the works that allow mankind to survive beyond the capacity of its immediate environment are now ubiquitous. Among them, the aqueducts always stand out as monuments of the human ability to respond to every challenge using their minds and their hands.

**68**

### Notes
1 Vitruvius: *De Architectura* II.1.5.
2 Willoughby, Michael: "Mayor Slams Foster's GLA building—Then Hands over an Award." *building.co.uk*, February 25, 2009.
3 Frontinus: *De Aquis* 1.16.

### Selected Bibliography
Hodge, A.T.: *Roman Aqueducts & Water Supply.* Duckworth 2001.
Humphrey, John: *Greek and Roman Technology: A Sourcebook.* Taylor & Francis 1997.
Laurence, Ray: *The Roads of Roman Italy: Mobility and Cultural Change.* Routledge 1999.
Mays, Larry (ed.): *Ancient Water Technologies.* Springer 2010.
O'Connor, Colin: *Roman Bridges.* Cambridge University Press 1993.
Van der Bergh, Rena: "The plight of the poor urban tenant." In: *Revue Internationale des droits de l'Antiquité*, 2003, 443 ff.

# ARCHITECTURE TAKES CONTROL

## Inventing Interior Space

At the beginning of the nineteenth century, panoramas were particularly popular in large European cities. Panoramas were specially built circular halls, which received their name from the huge paintings—measuring up to ten meters in height and one hundred meters in length—created specifically to hang inside. These paintings usually depicted a famous city, a significant historical event, or a beautiful landscape, and were often the work of an artist or a young architect with limited professional opportunities; Karl Friedrich Schinkel, one of the major architects of classicism, painted panoramas at the beginnings of his career. The audience, typically several dozen people, sat or stood at the center of the hall and was surrounded by an impressive 360-degree image.

The basic idea behind the panoramas was similar to the basic idea behind the eighteenth- and nineteenth-century opera houses, and is similar to the basic idea behind twenty-first-century multiplex halls with Dolby surround sound systems: any other sensory stimulus is excluded so that the audience could immerse itself undisturbed in the offered spectacle.

Today, we are fully reconciled with the idea that architecture is trying in its own way to materialize an equivalent concept, to create fully controlled environments; environments in which almost all of the visual stimuli that people receive are prearranged. But this was not feasible in the remote past: it would not be off the point to argue that this was achieved for the first time in ancient Rome with the construction of large dimensions interior space. Indeed, if one would want to summarize in one sentence the evolution of architecture in the 900 years between the Parthenon and the final collapse of the Western ancient world one could only mention this achievement. These were spaces in which the attendees surrendered gladly in a guided sensory game. Seneca recounted in the middle of the first century CE that, "in this bath of Scipio's there are tiny chinks—you cannot call them windows—cut out of the stone wall in such a way as to admit light … nowadays, however, people regard baths as fit only for moths if they have not been so arranged that they receive the sun all day long through the widest of windows, if men cannot bathe and get a coat of tan at the same time, and if they cannot look out from their bathtubs over stretches of land and sea."[1] New horizons of manipulating peoples' everyday experiences were opened in architecture.

This did not come as a thunderbolt in a clear sky. From the time when people constructed their first huts, they were familiar with enclosed spaces. At that time, they were protected from cold, rain, and intruders, but they probably did not have the illusion that they were in a self-contained world. With some exceptions: let us recall, for example, that in Ur, introvert houses—arranged around atriums that opened to the sky—offered their inhabitants the possibility of retiring into their family life. Generally speaking, however, the interior space was so small that it existed almost always in reference to the "outside," usually opposed to it.

In the Greco-Roman world, the situation was similar. The temples did not host the faithful in their interior. The most prominent profane buildings, the porticoes (*stoas* in Greek), were initially simple shelters that protected visitors from the rain and the sun. The other large public buildings were basically outdoor structures: gymnasiums, theaters, stadiums. As time passed, the porticoes were made larger. Their length often exceeded one hundred meters and their depth was such that those who stood there were protected quite effectively from air, rain, and to some extent from cold. Therefore, porticoes became suitable for accommodating a multitude of activities such as trade, health care, administration, etc.

**Colosseum, Rome, circa 70 CE**



The theaters' configuration changed significantly over time as well, as seen in the case of Dionysus' theater on the south slope of the Athenian Acropolis hill. At a spot where the slope was not steep, the first *cavea* of the theater in rectangular shape was formed with minimum earthworks just before 490 BCE. There was wooden seating, but most spectators probably sat on the ground or lay down to watch the performances. At the end of the fifth or the beginning of the fourth centuries BCE, the cavea was shaped like an arc, with wooden seating. A few decades later, the wooden seats were replaced with marble ones and expanded upward—a part of these tiers survives today. The body posture of the spectators was now defined univocally; the sitting position may have been comfortable, but it was their only option: everyone had to look straight ahead, toward the stage. At the time of the wooden seating, the stage was simply a single-story shack. It expanded over time, but it never gained more than two stories and a limited length. The audience was able to see above or at the side of the stage the landscape stretching to the sea, or to turn its gaze to the sky and see it changing colors as dusk approached. The performances were held during the day and for many years, the spectators received an allowance in order to watch them.

The trend in theater building was clear. Gradually, the cavea's slope steepened; the stage was extended from one end to the other and became multistory, its height exceeding the last seat rows. In order to see the sky, spectators had to lift their heads very high—a body posture not at all natural. But soon even that ceased to be an option. Large, textile sun blinds were spread out over the cavea to protect them from the sun. Theaters were now constructed on level ground, not on hillsides. Nature, as morphology of the terrain, was no longer necessary; it was substituted by the massive stone structures that supported the stands. Nature, as background in front of which the stage action evolved, was also no longer necessary; it was substituted by the huge stages decorated with columns and pediments. Architecture had claimed and had imposed its sovereignty in the eyes and the mind of the spectators.

Machines were devised, which were intended to amaze the viewers—Heron of Alexandria's *automata* were the most renowned among them. Doors opening with the lighting of a fire on an altar moved with complex hydraulic systems; sounds resembling thunder announced the arrival of a god produced by bronze balls falling on horizontal metal flaps. These were some of the imaginative means often used in theatrical sets—but not exclusively there. In his palace at the Palatine Hill in Rome, Nero had a circular banquet hall with a continuously rotating floor. The guests would see a different picture each time they lifted their eyes from the plates of rich food to admire the ceiling depicting the night sky; and five or six centuries later, it seems that various automata were incorporated in the audience hall of the Byzantine emperors in their Palatium Magnum in Constantinople in order to impress foreign emissaries.

The open public spaces of the cities also changed. As the years passed, the buildings multiplied, the street walls became higher and more solid, and the view was increasingly restricted by man-made artifacts. The agora—i.e., the public space par excellence, the central square—of sixth-century BCE Athens was nothing but an unbuilt area whose boundaries were marked by sixty-centimeter-high stone signs and two to three small buildings. Slowly, larger and larger buildings began to line its boundaries and to create the impression of an enclosed public space.

By the first century CE, the Imperial Fora of Rome were large rectangular courtyards surrounded by majestic arcades decorated with Corinthian columns with such a height that in order to see the sky one had to lift his eyes high, and each dominated by a temple. In the Forum of Augustus, the temple of Mars the Avenger, Mars Ultor was built. It was placed on a high pedestal and was accessible through a large staircase extending the entire length of its magnificent façade. However, the back of the temple was merged with the back wall of the forum. Visitors could not circumambulate the temple, but moved in the space in front of it. Their gaze was directed, no doubt, toward it.

Rarely do we witness a trend so unremitting and unwavering, as the one that prevailed during the thousand years of the Greco-Roman world: the densification of the urban fabric and the gradual transformation of the open-air public space in more and more visually enclosed space; and the erection of buildings with ever larger and more impressive interiors.

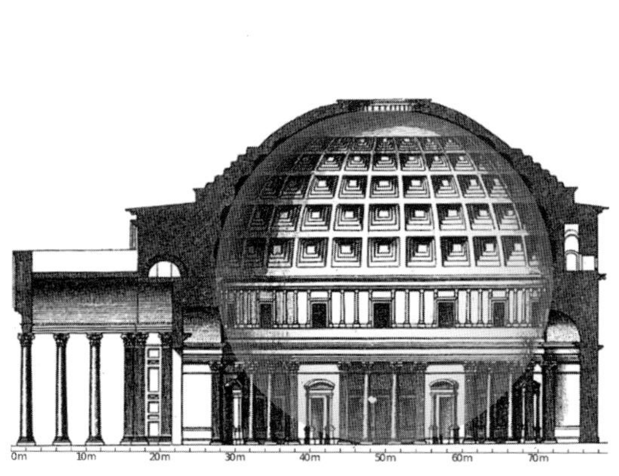
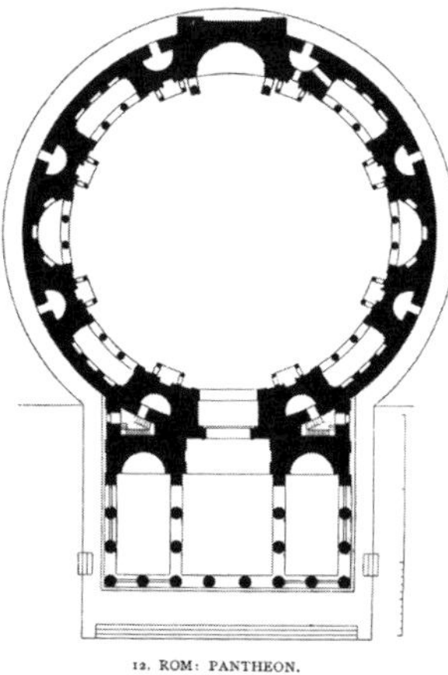


**Pantheon, Rome, circa 110 CE; drawings Dehio&Bezold and Cmglee/Meyers Konversationslexikon**



The Pantheon stands out among them. The original temple was built at what was then the outskirts of Rome and dedicated in 27 BCE, but it was almost completely destroyed in a fire; it was rebuilt about 150 years later—probably during the reign of Emperor Hadrian in the beginning of the second century CE. While the front portico is rather conventional, the cella deviated drastically from what used to be the norm: it is a circular hall covered by a hemispherical dome 43.3 meters in diameter, the largest in the world until the construction of octagonal dome of Florence's Cathedral, Santa Maria del Fiore, by Filippo Brunelleschi in the fifteenth century, which was a few centimeters larger. Substantially larger spans occurred for the first time in nineteenth century cast-iron architecture. The Pantheon's interior height is also 43.3 meters, which means that in this large space, a sphere of the same diameter can fit exactly; or, one could say, the internal shape of the building emerged from a sphere whose lower half is replaced by a cylinder.

This cylinder has a wall thickness of about eight meters, in order to support the dome's weight and to take on the side thrusts created. Eight deep niches have been formed in this wall decorated with large Corinthian columns; one of the niches is the entrance and pierces its entire thickness. These give the impression that they are porticos of small temples. So the great hall acquires the character of "outside," the character of the public space in which buildings open up, like the nineteenth-century panoramas: there, the audience inside the hall was surrounded by a picture that can actually be seen from outside. This reversal—i.e., the creating of the impression even momentarily, that "in" is "out"—is an essential feature of this new architecture, the architecture of interior space.

The niches are approximately as wide as the wall between them; one cannot be certain if there are cavities created on a solid wall, or protrusions of wall into the large hall. They substantially reduced the weight of the cylinder and relieved the foundation—usually the buildings' weakest point, especially for those built on unstable terrain such as the Pantheon.

The large hemispherical dome is mounted on this cylinder, also shaped in such a way that the observer cannot be certain whether any material was removed for coffers to be formed or whether the dome was reinforced with ribs. It opens up to the sky, because a hole is left at its top, an oculus six meters in diameter; the structure is stable because the perimeter edge of the oculus functions as a compression ring.

Although there are no windows, sufficient light enters the Pantheon: normally those inside do not see a light source, so the pupils of their eyes dilate. The relatively few hours of the year that the sun shines high enough, a beam six meters in diameter falls on the cylindrical wall creating a stark contrast with the rest of the interior, which is illuminated only by reflection. The atmosphere in both cases is quite mystical although the layout of the building is extremely simple and easy to read—a major achievement. The mystical atmosphere is enhanced when it rains and the raindrops fall in the hall, probably diffused by the rising hot air current created by the visitors' body heat; in any case, the largest part of the floor remains dry. The surface of the oculus is fifty times smaller than that of the floor.

From the outside, the shape of the building looks quite different from the shape one perceives once inside. Although the cylinder is clearly visible, the hemispherical dome is not, and that is because its thickness is reduced from more than six meters at its base to less than 1.50 meters at the top, gradually decreasing its weight as it rises in height. Successive counterweights of sorts prevent it from collapsing inwards, and form seven hoops receiving the outward thrusts that tend to break the dome: in later medieval cathedrals such thrusts are received by the elaborate flying but-

**Pantheon, Rome, circa 110 CE; drawing G. B. Piranesi**

tresses characteristic of Gothic architecture. Appearing over the last hoop, which is visible only from the outside, is a slightly curved surface—the upper part of the dome.

The cylindrical wall, as well as the dome itself, consist of zones with successively lighter aggregate stones placed irregularly in rich mortar of volcanic sand and lime; on the uppermost part of the vault, small clay pots and porous volcanic slag were used instead of pieces of rock.

The consequences of sanctioning Roman concrete as appropriate material for the empire's most prominent buildings, such as the Pantheon, became visible in the long run. Columns, epistyles, and pediments lost their structural character and became decorative elements: the weight was now carried by thick walls, and the openings were usually spanned with barrel vaults. The principal change, however, was that many of the functions of the city's public space were covered with a roof—in the literal sense of the word. The shift of a significant part of political and social life from the Fora in the baths and in the basilicas (rectangular halls of imposing size) was only feasible when appropriate buildings were erected. Such were the Baths of Caracalla: built at the beginning of the third century CE, they measured 228 by 116 meters and included pools with hot, cold, and lukewarm water in halls with heights of up to forty meters—equal to that of a modern twelve-story building.

The architects were almost indifferent about how the buildings of this new genre would look from the outside; they focused their attention solely on the majestic spaces that they could now create—spaces the likes of which people have never seen. At the beginning of the era of interiors, the old world of the buildings as sculptural forms could be ostentatiously ignored.

In less than a century, this new era crossed one more milestone. Classical art, which had known repeated revivals until then, was removed from the limelight. The new tastes were satisfied by colorful marbles and mosaics and not by balanced proportions; and by sculptural forms that ignored realistic representation in favor of expressiveness, paving the way for medieval art. We find the theoretical substantiation of this mentality already in the writings of Flavius Philostratus, who belonged to the circle of Julia Domna—wife of Emperor Septimus Severus—in the beginning of the third century CE. The creative force was no longer the Aristotelian imitation—i.e., the reproduction of the essential characteristics of reality—but imagination based on transcendent insight. The art of the late Roman period called for exhilarating communion in a made up world.

**Hagia Sophia, Constantinople (now Istanbul), circa 532 CE, longitudinal section; drawing Lübke&Semrau *Grundriß der Kunstgeschichte*, 1908**

When this perception met Christianity, which became the dominant and eventually the official religion of the Roman Empire in the middle of the fourth century CE, architecture moved a step further away from classical ideals. A prime example of the architecture that emerged in this cultural environment is Hagia Sophia, the cathedral of the new capital of the Roman Empire, Constantinople. It was built within five years, from 532 to 537 CE, according to the plans of two mathematicians, Isidore of Miletus and Anthemius of Tralles. Two decades later the cupola collapsed because of an earthquake and was rebuilt somewhat differently—though the overall impression to the visitor should not have changed radically. It seems that the aim was to make it as difficult as possible for the visitor to categorize the building into its constituent parts, which were simple geometrical shapes, so that he/she would be left speechless by admiration. The cupola sits on the so-called pendentives, which connect it with the square hall below. Along the building, the lateral thrusts created by the cupola are taken on by lower lying quarter spheres, which in turn transfer them to other smaller quarter spheres below; width-wise the lateral thrusts are taken up by massive external buttresses which are invisible in the interior. The visitors' comprehension of how the dome is supported is constantly refuted, unlike the Pantheon where the hemispherical dome rests prominently on the underlying wall. The multicolored mosaics make the image that one faces when lifting one's gaze even more complicated. The lower surface of the dozens of windows at the cupola's base was con-

**Hagia Sophia, Constantinople (now Istanbul), circa 532 CE,
interior view**

figured to reflect the sun's rays to its decorative gold mosaic. All of these
elements make the cupola seem as if it is hovering in the air, as the sixth-
century CE historian Procopius pointed out.[2]

Justinian, the emperor who ordered the construction of this
church, was probably very clear in his mind about what he wanted to
achieve: to legitimize his authority by constructing the most impressive
edifice ever built, and to amaze anyone who set foot in it, visualizing, one
could say, the kind of truth the new religion professed—the revelation. "We
shape our buildings and afterwards our buildings shape us," Sir Winston
Churchill pointed out in a speech in the British Parliament in 1943.[3] With
the invention of large dimensions interior space, architecture's power to
influence the minds and souls of people skyrocketed. The architects' drama
is that they often cannot tell with certainty, sometimes not even presume
beforehand how the buildings they design will affect us in the long run ...

### Notes

1  Seneca: *Epistulae Morales* LXXXVI.8, Loeb.
2  Procopius: *Buildings* I.1.34.
3  Churchill, Sir Winston: "House of Commons Rebuilding",
28/10/1943, *8th session of the 37th parliament of the United
Kingdom of Great Britain and Northern Ireland, 9th vol. of session
1942-43*. His Majesty's Stationery Office1943, 403.



### Selected Bibliography

Corso, Antonio: "Attitudes to the visual arts of classical
Greece in late antiquity." In: *Eulimene*, 2, 2001, 1 ff.
Hetland, L.M.: "Dating the Pantheon." In: *Journal of
Roman Archaeology*, 20 (1), 2007, 95 ff.
Krautheimer, Richard: *Early Christian and Byzantine
Architecture*. Penguin Books 1965.
Lamprecht, Hans Otto: *Opus caementicium*. Beton-Verlag 1984.
McDonald, William Lloyd: *The Pantheon: Design, Meaning,
and Progeny*. Harvard University Press 1976.
Yegül, Fikret: *Bathing in the Roman World*. Cambridge University Press 2010.

# ISSUES OF SCALE

## Angkor Wat

"The one thing people know about southern barbarians is that they are coarse, ugly, and very black.... When it comes to the women of the palace and women from … the great houses, there are many who are as white as jade, but that is because they do not see the light of the sun.... They wear their hair in a topknot and go barefoot. This is the case even with the wives of the king. The king has five wives, one principal wife and one for each of the four cardinal points. Below them, I have heard, there are four of five thousand concubines and other women of the palace. They also divide themselves up by rank … Any family with a female beauty is bound to have her summoned into the palace.... At the lower level, there are also the … servant women who come and go providing services inside the palace and number at least a thousand or two…"

The quote above was written by Zhou Daguan, a member of the Chinese delegation to the Khmer capital in 1296, in his memoirs of his visit to Cambodia.[1]

In this passage, references to architecture are limited and elliptical. And yet, despite its shadowy presence, architecture is the context in which the words of Zhou Daguan acquire their full meaning. The number of five thousand concubines and women is impressive because they all lived and worked in the same compound. The fact that families from the whole country sent their beautiful daughters to the palace implies that the huge building complex was the seat of a highly centralized authority. That the king chose the number of his wives to establish a spatial correspondence between his authority and the heavens, informs us about the order and the hierarchy of an empire that had invested so much in architecture only to collapse, probably not least because it was carrying out one of the most ambitious building programs in history—the stones required for Angkor's temples were more than those used in the great pyramids of Giza.

I am not certain which parts of the *Record of Cambodia* give us the most essential information on its architecture. Those in which Zhou Daguan provides factual data, such as that the audience hall had golden windows and the houses of the king's relatives had thatched roofs? Or, perhaps, those in which the man-made environment is merely the stage upon which the social life unfolds? Or, perhaps, those in which architecture is a topic of the narrative, but references to it are indirect, such as the part in which he describes the bridges crossing over the moat that surrounds the city; descriptions referring substantially only to the sculptural décor of these bridges, the fifty-four deities carved in stone supporting parapets in guise of serpents with nine heads?

I have the impression that the most successful way to talk about architecture is exactly what Zhou Daguan did—a combination of all these approaches. Abstraction is a mental function that varies considerably even among people who partake in the same cultural environment. Vitruvius noticed that while everyone can judge architecture, only architects are able to conceive what a building will look like before they see it completed.[2] This suggests that only architects are able to distinguish the features that give each building its specific identity. But the juxtaposition of factual data can be perplexing even to them, especially if they come from a different cultural background. When in 1414 Poggio Bracciolini and his assistants located a manuscript in the library of Saint Gallen's monastery, which in turn was the copy of an older one, and contained Vitruvius' treatise on architecture, they realized that all the accompanying drawings had been lost. The successive illustrations attempted by the editors of this work until at least the nineteenth century are too far away from what we know today that the Roman writer wanted to describe. Such misconceptions, of course, not only have disadvantages, because they are often productive and lead to new ideas. The case of the Renaissance is telling: the erroneously understood Vitruvius inspired an outstanding new architecture.

The experience offered by direct contact with many of the most famous edifices in the world, cannot be obtained by everyone, even today when traveling has become part of our everyday life. In Zhou Daguan's times, images of buildings were extremely rare, and rather schematic when available. Human constructs invested with mythical status—for example, the city of Venice or Baghdad—were known to people from random descriptions passed down orally from generation to generation. Since architects generally wrote few accounts, today we may miss peer-compiled descriptions (of dubious usefulness, anyhow), but we have a rather strong indication of what the layperson observer noticed and chose to convey to his/her audience.

Zhou Daguan focused his attention on three aspects of the city: the wall and the moat that surrounds it, its square shape and the position of the palace and the temples, and the semiology of building materials. The Chinese official's main topic, though, is the people; the people

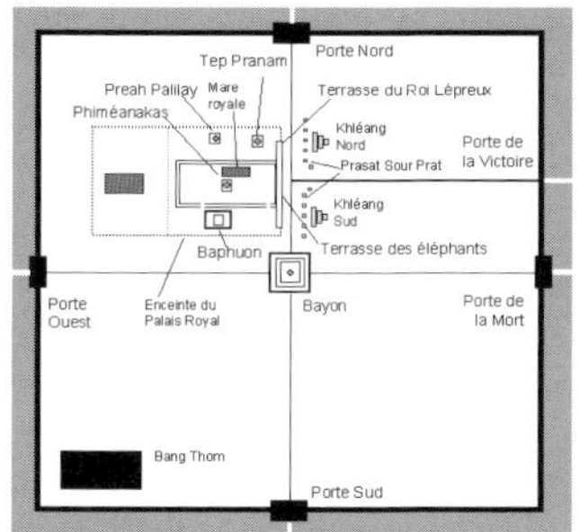

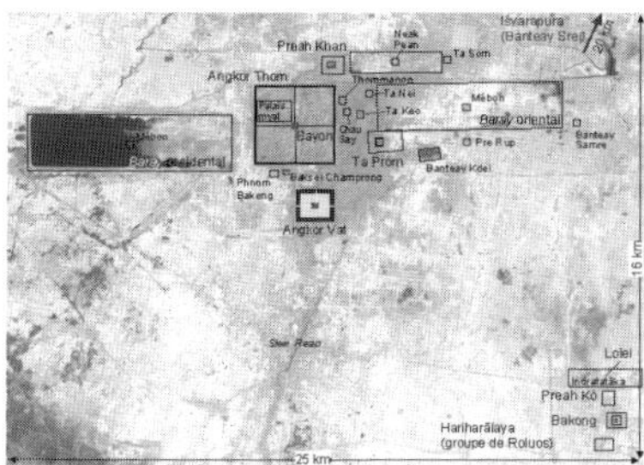

Angkor Thom, circa 1180 CE, plan, and Angkor, twelfth
century CE, map; drawings: Lozère

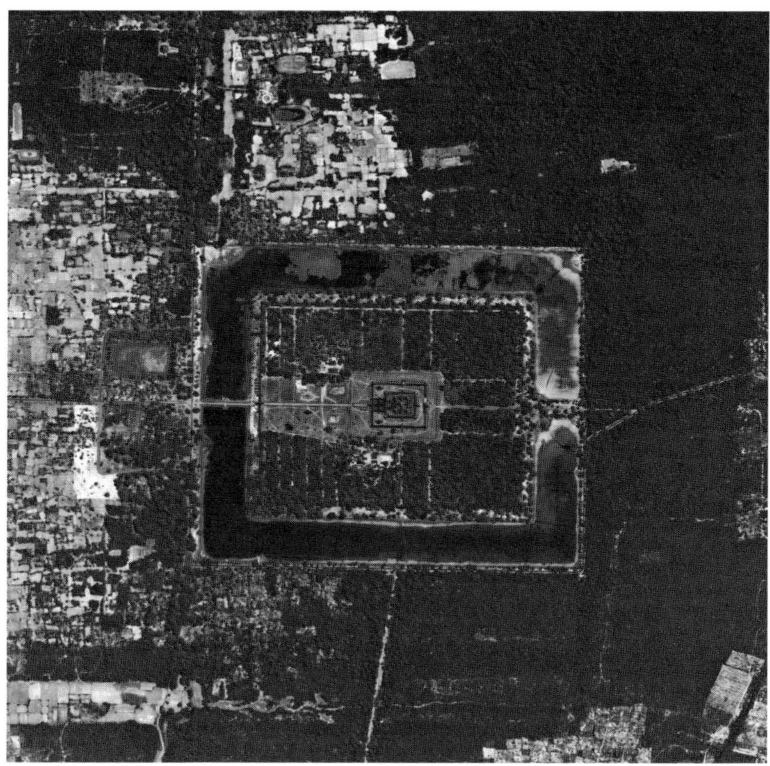

Angkor Wat, early twelfth century CE

whose everyday lives were regulated to a significant degree by customs or laws. What the diverse pieces of his narrative have in common are the ubiquitous allusions to the order permeating the "hardware" and the "software" of the city (its buildings and the conduct of its people); and the resulting symbolism.

As much as the symbolism embodied in the dressing codes, religious rituals, and annual festivals could overcome the city's limits, so too could the symbolism discernible in the layout and form of the edifices, and in their sculptural décor, even if only through narration: at times when word was the dominant vehicle of transmitting information, symbolic architecture reached out to the general public more than any other.

King Jayavarman VII radically transformed the Khmer capital when he set out to rebuild it after its destruction in 1178 by the Cham, a people situated to the east of Cambodia. The mighty king had spent several years of his youth in their land, and most probably had ambitions to unite them with the Khmer under his rule; a controversial policy that left its marks on the stones of one of the city's most prominent buildings, Bayon. Initially, the ruler who more than any of his predecessors embraced Buddhism, without excluding major Hindu gods Siva or Vishnu, turned his attention to public infrastructure projects: hospitals, cisterns, and inns along roads. After completing this network, he built two large temples dedicated to the memory of his parents. And finally, he launched the huge project of converting a complex human artifact—a city—to an image of the universe, an *imago mundi* to use a phrase from another cultural environment. The classical Hindu conceptions recorded in *Śilpa-śāstra* (textbooks of manual arts and crafts including architecture), were still dominant: quite typically, older—in this case Hindu—paradigms in architecture and space management are evidently anchored deep in people's minds although popular beliefs do shift, for instance, toward Buddhism during the rule of Jayavarman VII. The foundation of a city was a religious act of secularization and demystification of space: humans settled where forces and spirits of nature were solely active. They were obliged to conform to *dharma*—a Hindu concept transmitted to Buddhism, designating the universal Law, what is right, and ultimately the truth—reproducing the cosmic order on the building and city scale.

The city, which was named Angkor Thom at some point, is square shaped with its sides measuring about three kilometers. It is walled and surrounded by a wide moat. An inscription informs us about the ruler's intention to connect the city's rebirth with the creation of the universe. The wall and the moat of the city are compared with the mountains and the Ocean of Milk; according to Hindu cosmological conceptions this was the fifth circle of the cosmic system, where Cambodia was situated. In a world where spirits were attributed a place in the lower levels of the supernatural, these structures were named: Jayagiri and Jayasindhu, respectively. Moreover, one of the most important myths of Hinduism—the elixir of immortality surfacing after the stirring of the primordial sea by the *devas* and the *asuras*—is depicted in all the city gates next to figures thought to be Buddha or the king himself, or some combination of the two.

A large temple, the Bayon, is located at the exact center of the city, looking east. Crosswise, four straight roads begin from the temple toward the four cardinal points, leading to four out of the five city gates; monumental temples in the region have somewhat similar layout, which was drawn on the ground with complex rituals. The Bayon is extremely formal in its design, and it lacks an outer wall, probably denoting the openness of Buddhism professed by Jayavarman VII.

From the fifth gate of the wall, another straight road leads directly to the eastern gate of the palace, which is located immediately north of the Bayon; it is surrounded by a three-kilometer-long wall and also faces east. Zhou Daguan seems to have been impressed by the sheer size of its halls, but his remark that walkways are "complicated" and the "soaring structures … rise and fall"[3] indicates that the palace's layout conformed to the specific requirements of the inhabitants and the strictly ordered life it sheltered, rather than to the demonstration of a clearly articulated conceptual scheme.

The social hierarchy entirely determined the city's image. This was by no means a novelty, since in Hindu tradition, villages often housed people of the same profession and—something more or less equivalent—of the same caste. Moreover, the cities were divided into districts, each inhabited by people belonging to the same social class. Not just the size of the buildings, but also the materials with which they were built, were as indicative of each landlord's social status as were the garments he was allowed to wear. In the palace, the "main building" was covered with lead, while the remaining structures with yellow tiles. The semantics of color are omnipresent in architecture: in Çatalhöyük, in Rome, and in imperial China; in the whiteness of the first period of modernism; in the polychromy of postmodernism, in the red and green lining of the seats in the House of Lords and in the House of Commons of the British Parliament, respectively. In Angkor Thom, the king was reputed to sleep in a golden tower; the houses of the officials had thatched roofs, except for the bedrooms and the family temples, which were allowed to be covered with tiles. The size of the officials' houses corresponded to their office. The houses of the common people also had thatched roofs; their size depended on the financial status of their owners, but they weren't allowed to be comparable to or to imitate the houses of the state officials.

In short, in Angkor Thom, visibly perceived order became increasingly apparent as one moved from the small to the large scale—quite the opposite of what is happening in modern cities, where visible order is manifested in the small scale (in individual buildings and building blocks), but the large scale (the city as a whole) completely lacks geometric regularity. The homes of the members of the working classes—all of which have now more or less disappeared—were probably the most irregular and rough structures, which most certainly underwent constant modifications depending on the needs of each family, thus also demonstrating lack of order over time. The houses of the officials and the palace were more orderly and larger; the temples were constructed with resilient materials and were absolutely symmetrical and tidy, like the city itself. This image was reinforced by the dressing etiquette and the overall appearance of the members of different castes in daily life and in official ceremonies. The intended meaning was clear: we pass gradually from the ever changing sordid world of daily life—where people are condemned to the perpetual struggle to overcome mistakes of the past—to an increasingly stable, organized, and clean world, and from there to the world of the divinities; from the world of illusory sensations to the world of universal truth.

Managing the distilled knowledge and traditions of centuries, the monarch constructed what was perceived as a replica of the world. By appearing to tangibly reproduce the structure of the universe, he affirmed in the eyes of the community his status as the intermediary between the divine—or the absolute—and mankind, a *bodhisattva*, as Buddha described himself as being prior to his full enlightenment.

Angkor Wat, early twelfth century CE



Jayavarman VII's city offered the ideal transition from the non-significant—from the small and the chaotic to the large and orderly—leaving to each its particular physiognomy. It accurately visualized the coexistence of the fundamental features that make up the city: the structures serving daily life, which was characterized by chaotic disorder, and those representing the state and cosmic order.

The coexistence of different qualities made feasible through the meditation of symbols is typical for Angkor.

**Angkor Wat, early twelfth century CE**

The construction of what is probably the largest religious building in the world began a few decades before the Khmer capital's reformation. Despite its massive dimensions Angkor Wat—possibly the mortuary temple of king Suryavarman II—was not the only large temple in the area for long: the equally colossal Preah-Khan broke ground in 1191 CE (during the reign of Jayavarman VII) a short distance to its immediate north. Angkor Wat's low outer wall forms a rectangular measuring about 1,000 by 800 meters and it is surrounded by a moat nearly 200 meters wide. The main temple, with a total height of about sixty-five meters, is arranged in three main levels forming a stepped pyramid. This is a common temple layout in the region and is perceived to reproduce the form of Mount Meru, as stated in inscriptions. Meru is the world's axis and unites the different cosmic levels—i.e., our world with the heavenly, where the gods of the Hinduism Pantheon reside. Its five peaks are heavenly worlds—part of the level or the world of desire, *Kama*—inhabited by lesser gods. The world's axis is visualized through a trench, (in theory) as deep as the building's height above the ground; the mountains and the ocean surrounding Meru are visualized through the walls and moats, respectively. The temple is crowned by five towers, one in the center and four at the corners of the upper tier, corresponding to the five peaks of the holy mountain.

Not everyone, of course, can ascend the sacred mountain: as we can see repeatedly in history, controlling the access is, and has always been, a medium of affirming a strict social hierarchy. Ordinary people seemed to have had access only to the lower tier of the temple, in order to pay tribute to the temple's resident, whoever he/she was, by moving around it.

Galleries and porticoes gave a functional and visual complexity to the otherwise very simple geometry of the temple, a set of squares and crosses. The square had a special place in religious architecture: it was the shape of the altar, which in turn was supposed to reproduce the shape of the universe in early Hindu cosmology. The complexity was increased with what we would tend to classify as architectural decoration, but it is actually a composition of small-scale architectural parts. The successive moldings that joint the tiers do not correspond to floors, nor do the small columns that joint the galleries correspond to the halls behind them. Their sole purpose is rather to frame the reliefs and create meaningful sculptural entities, which in turn amplify the temple's visual complexity. This kind of mismatch between the building's structure and form led to the structural failures that are visible today. This mismatch, however, was the result of keeping a tradition developed for centuries in the Indian subcontinent, as showcased at the Shiva Brihadeeswarar temple at Thanjavur in Tamil Nadu. Constructed in 1010 CE, it manifests most clearly that the structural and the functional honesty, as we understand them today, are totally irrelevant. The building should be created from the composition of many individual architectural elements, each with its own, distinct, form and particular symbolic content; forms and symbolic content that varied geographically and in time. What is located behind these architectural elements, the temple's "interior"—the long corridors and the hypostyle halls—cannot be determined by those standing outside the temple.

Despite Angkor Wat's size, the shapes and figures depicted in stone are crafted with great detail and precision (befitting rather a small-scale artifact) by a multitude of workshops with thousands of carvers working simultaneously; we know that in Bayon some galleries were adorned by images installed by individuals or villages probably to commemorate their ancestors. The physical effort needed to decipher this visual pande-

Brihadeeswarar Temple, Thanjavur, circa 1010 CE, detail

monium—the dances of the nymphs, the battles of the asuras and the devas, the exploits of the ruler evolving along hundreds and hundreds of meters—makes visiting the temple particularly demanding for the mind and the eyes. The attention to the perplexing sculptural detail, in as much time as one needed to go around and around the temple in ritual procession, must have transferred the faithful outside space and time, and blurred in their minds the boundaries between the depicted mythological traditions and historical events.

The creators of Angkor Wat were able to manage convincingly one of the most difficult problems of architecture: the relationship between the part and the whole, the character of the small scale in reference to the character of the large scale. The hundreds and hundreds of figures depicted on the temple's stones, each one unique and aesthetically self-sufficient, as well as the dozens of moldings and friezes are ultimately parts of a large composition that unfolds with the appropriate magnificence to convince us that it deserves to assimilate the individual elements that constitute it. The architectural and sculptural details, chaotically complex in the small scale have been integrated in a markedly simple large-scale, grand scheme.

For ages, architects pondered—and still do—whether they should seek to conform the physiognomy of the small scale to the physiognomy of the large; to design the city and the doorknob in the same spirit. As indicated by Angkor, it is not necessary for the part and the whole, for the large and the small to be similar to each other, as far as the carving out of their shapes in concerned; it suffices for them to be permeated by a common principle, whether that is the aspiration to representing cosmic order or the demonstration of positivist approach to their design, as modernist twentieth-century architecture vowed to do. Our answers to the question of the relation of the small scale to the large define architecture even today.

### Notes

1 Zhou Daguan/Harris, Peter: *A Record of Cambodia: The Land and Its People.* Silk Worm Books 2007, 54-55.
2 Vitruvius: *De Architectura* VI.8.10.
3 Zhou Daguan/Harris, Peter: *A Record of Cambodia: The Land and Its People.* Silk Worm Books 2007, 49.

### Selected Bibliography

Cœdès, George: "La destination funéraire des grands monuments Khmèr."
In: *Bulletin de l'Ecole française d'Extrême-Orient*, vol. 40–2, 1940, 315 ff.
Glaize, Maurice: *Les monuments du groupe d'Angkor.* A. Portail 1944.
Eliade, Mircea: *The Myth of the Eternal Return: Cosmos and History.* Princeton University Press 1971 (1954).
Mitchell, George: *The Hindu Temple.* University of Chicago Press 1988.
Rovedo, Vittorio/Clark, Joyce (eds.): *Bayon: New Perspectives.* River Books 2007.
Yung Wai-chuen, Peter: *Angkor: The Khmers in Ancient Chinese Annals.* Oxford University Press 2000.

# REGULARITY AND IRREGULARITY

## Medieval Cities and Gothic Cathedrals

In the context of our neat and predictable world, we may find attractive what defies regularity and appears to be a product of procedures with unpredictable outcomes. Walking in medieval European towns, we appreciate the geomorphic non-rectangular street grid, the warmth of the unpretentious, the constant refutation of the expected, the imperfections, and the many phases of buildings' construction and retrofitting—each of which has left visible traces. These qualities are the very opposite of the classical ideals, namely the principals of symmetry and the more or less immovable in time order. Symmetry in Greco-Roman antiquity meant the balanced, harmonious, synthesis of distinct architectural elements; while order meant the rank in the magnitude, positioning, and succession of the elements or parts that constituted a whole—whether it was a building or the speech of an orator. Perhaps medieval cities' only feature that corresponds fully to the classical ideals is the clarity of their boundaries in contrast to modern dispersed cities. We should keep in mind, though, that Hellenistic and Roman cities didn't have clearly defined boundaries either, since mansions and gymnasia, theaters and odea were often built where there was available land, namely outside the walls.

As seen in Chapter 4, cities in ancient Mesopotamia, as well as several Greco-Roman cities developed without a preconceived plan. Their layout was the result of a rather cumulative build up. It did not follow a blueprint—but was not unreasonable or disorderly—and was the result of action by a multitude of agents and the balance of opposite forces. The inconvenience caused by building a new house or adding a new room had to be minimized by shaping it to avoid friction among neighbors, rather than according to some inflexible ideas translated into a strict comprehensive building code. Respecting the family hearth limited the ability of central authority or the ruler to shape the city according to his/her desires—although the expropriation of property and the demolition of houses were taking place, as we have seen in Chapter 2, at least from the Oval Temple's era. In medieval Europe, the walls defined the boundaries that constricted the expansion of the cities. The pressure to occupy the unbuilt space for housing was counterbalanced by the necessity to ensure free access to everyone and to maintain the functional width of the streets.

Throughout history, "organic growth" was often not left completely unchecked, but was delicately regulated with the enactment of appropriate legislation or through customary law. From what we know from the Roman eastern provinces of the late imperial period, for example, it was forbidden to build a new edifice in way that prevented the lighting and insolation of existing neighboring buildings. Undoubtedly such provisions—which were adopted by the Byzantine empire and helped shape the medieval European legislation—were vague enough, allowing a wide range of interpretations. Frequently, more precise provisions existed: for example, that cantilevered overhangs of newly erected buildings could not be located closer than ten feet to respective overhangs of existing neighboring buildings. In ancient Athens, such overhangs were banned altogether around 500 BCE; in medieval Rome, in 1452 CE.

**"Allegory of Good Government," Ambrogio Lorenzetti, circa 1340 CE, Siena, Palazzo Pubblico**



Such provisions complemented a body of moral practices and customs that were formed over time; they regularly defined the position of a new building in relation with the existing ones and not each building's position regardless of the others in a Cartesian coordinates system. The resulting cityscape is very familiar to us because its structural logic unfolds slowly before our eyes. The buildings' sequence corresponds to our walk and is not governed by principles better understood when looking on the map. In Ambrogio Lorenzetti's frescoes (painted around 1340) in the Palazzo Pubblico (the town hall) of Siena, at a time when it was governed by the democratic oligarchy of the Nine, the ideal city is depicted, as a metaphor for the Good Government; this is very different from the perfect, orderly Renaissance city we see 150 years later in the paintings at the Pallazo Ducale in Urbino, attributed to Piero della Fransesca's circle. In the medieval ideal city, the buildings are crammed one next to another without geometric order and discipline, but without one overshadowing the rest, some still under construction—i.e., with unknown final form yet—which makes the city a work in progress in every sense of the word.

During the centuries of Roman domination, the cities had developed administrative, financial and cultural centers whose survival depended on a sophisticated transportation and disposal network for the products from the countryside. Due to the loss of territory, the dissolution of the central authority, and the disuse of the transportation system, the cities were desolated or lost large portions of their population, who either died or relocated to the countryside in order to survive. Even in cities that retained part of their population, people turned to agriculture: the fields and pastures were now closer or adjacent to their homes, often within the city walls.

The first signs of recovery appeared a few decades before the year 1000, in some cases even earlier. Several medieval European cities inherited the street grid as it was shaped in the Roman period. In some cases, this survived almost intact—in Pavia, for example. In other cases, as in Florence, the densification of the urban fabric gradually but radically reformed it between the fourth and twelfth centuries. The fortification of the compounds of powerful families and the creation of stores and workshops narrowed or completely blocked the once straight roads and created impediments and blind alleys; the initial lack of strong administration allowed cities to be transformed into medleys of small enclaves. In some cities, the traces of their older phases disappeared almost completely. Often the ruins of monumental buildings were recycled and used as foundations for modern constructions—the Piazza Anfiteatro in Lucca is situated exactly where the Roman amphitheater's arena stood and has exactly this shape: it resulted by constructing in its perimeter, on the foundations of the seating sections, new edifices; a similar procedure transformed the Stadium of Domitian in Rome to one of the most beautiful squares of the city, the Piazza Navona.

Many European medieval cities, especially in the north, began from temporary settlements outside a religious installation, as in the case of Speyer, the Roman Nemetum, which was the seat of the local bishop. Wealth, knowledge and considerable political power were gathered there, i.e. the right conditions for business transactions: trade was the activity that contributed arguably more than any other in the creation of the first urban nuclei several hundred years after the collapse of Rome.

Compared to the countryside, the cities were another world. Slowly, from the eleventh century on, their inhabitants were organized, mainly through their closed professional associations, the guilds, into political entities, the communes. Gradually, the emerging urban economy was partially disengaged from rural production, relying also on trade and handicrafts and using money as a medium of exchange; money that could be accumulated and then invested in any enterprise considered advantageous. In this environment, the inhabitants of the cities gradually gained from the nobility and the church what we nowadays call basic human rights: the right to work and do business, the right to own property, and the right to a fair trial. Generally speaking, peasants were still deprived of these rights, since they were mostly serfs—i.e., annexed to the land where they worked. The emergence of cities significantly affected their lives as well. "Stadtluft macht frei" (urban air makes you free) is a German medieval saying, referring to a customary law that decreed that if a serf took refuge in a city and lived there for a year and a day he became free; he could no longer be reclaimed by his master and became bound to the city. This law was partially abolished in 1232 when several cities in Central Europe were fairly strengthened and threatened to bleed the great landowners dry of their available manpower.[1] Further south, however, the situation unfolded quiet differently: in 1256, for example, as the culmination of a tendency to abandon serfdom—which was not as widespread in Italy as it was in other parts of Europe—all the serfs of the territory controlled by the city of Bologna were freed, which resulted in the immediate increase of the city's population by 5,000.

In contrast to the ideal Renaissance city of the circle of Piero della Francesca, Lorenzetti's fourteenth-century ideal city is full of people—people who work, trade, display their wealth and social status. The limited public space of the medieval city, and especially the central square, was rich with activities: most of the trading activities were conducted there; the authorities made announcements and important issues of the city were discussed, something that was originally done in churches; public spectacles were presented and religious processions were organized; justice was administered and the witches were burned.

The complex balance of forces within each city was manifest in its form. From early on, the competition to control its configuration was fierce: where there is high concentration of people this is worthwhile. The church, representing a God who inspired fear and awe, was always a powerful political and cultural player, and regularly claimed the role of community leader; tellingly, the cathedrals were molded as the city's most prominent buildings. Political supremacy was often also claimed by the commune, whose relations with the church ranged from outright competition to cooperation to submission. Political bipolarity was transferred to space, with the cathedral and the city hall featuring the large square in front, regularly being the two pivotal points. The mighty were highlighting their power in various ways. In central Europe, kings and local nobility, monastic orders, and the communities themselves did so by building castles at the highest point of the city; in central and northern Italy, families with great influence and wealth, not least by building towers whose height often exceeded seventy meters, while their surface was limited to one room. Moreover, the aim of the powerful (for practical reasons and for reasons of prestige) to be close to the areas where the social, political, and financial power were concentrated resulted in the construction of the largest and tallest buildings in the city center, and the less impressive and humble structures toward the periphery.

As communities became stronger, they often tried to shape the cities in ways they believed reflected their political identity. Furthermore, in order to accomplish this, they acted drastically. In some cases, they clashed directly with nobility over the city's image, a domain that extended from aesthetics to symbolism. For instance, when the balance of power allowed it in the second half of the thirteenth century, several Italian cities enforced the reduction of the towers' height or their demolition altogether. In Florence, the maximum height for buildings was set at twenty-nine meters. In Bologna, only two of a total of nearly two hundred towers remained. Siena followed an equally harsh policy; moreover, like Florence, it usurped the symbols that the nobles had used up to that point to highlight their power: it built a town hall with a tall slender tower. In San Gimignano, a city only a few kilometers away from Siena, fourteen of the about seventy medieval tall towers have survived and still dominate the skyline of the city.

**Town hall and central square, Siena, early fourteenth century**



The management of the city's image was used by the most vibrant communities as tool for enhancing collectivity. Conceiving of the city in its entirety as a work of art, and not merely focusing its attention on monumental buildings, each commune elaborated a series of measures aimed at harnessing individual initiative to serve the common purpose: the creation of an aesthetically sound and orderly city.

Siena probably attempted this more systematically than any other city. On the one hand, gauging how the care for public spaces was indicative of its priorities, the community assigned the cleaning of the roads to the adjacent owners and introduced fines for offenders. On the other hand,

**The Basilica of St. Denis choir, Abbot Suger, circa 1140**

it embarked on the endeavor to homogenize the form of the city: firstly, by imposing a monopoly on the bricks, i.e., the basic building material, a move primarily designed to generate great revenue; and secondly, by introducing a body of building regulations. These measures were explicitly stated to aim at the city's beauty and the satisfaction of all its inhabitants[2]; their result was that the new buildings that gradually replaced the old—especially in the most central parts of the city—had many more common features between them, than the buildings depicted in Lorenzetti's ideal city. In it, the traces of the past were still vivid, especially in the form of tall slender family towers, which would eventually cease to excite the imagination of the inhabitants of the Italian cities in the fourteenth, and especially in the fifteenth century when a new paradigm for the houses of the powerful emerged in the form of the Renaissance's palazzi.

The width of the streets of Siena was set at approximately six-and-a-half meters for the main arteries and at three meters for the secondary streets. And it was determined that "any edifices that are to be made anew anywhere along the public thoroughfares ... proceed in line with the existent buildings and one building [shall] not stand out beyond another, but they shall be disposed and arranged equally."[3] Particularly strict regulations applied to the rebuilding of mansions in the main square, despite them housing some of the city's most powerful families. These, then, were to be uniform; their windows were to be shaped like those of the city hall and balconies were banned. Located next to each other, their façades formed one large surface embracing the town hall, placed at the lower part of the square, which spread amphitheatrically before it. Paved with red bricks forming nine circle sectors, the square commemorated the community's governance by the Nine.

The town hall, which began around 1300, has three wings: the central wing is somewhat reminiscent of the town hall in Florence, Siena's eternal rival in Tuscany, which in turn seems to have been inspired by the domiciles of the powerful of the era; the two lateral wings are lower and positioned at an angle to the central wing so that the town hall's façade is gently incurving, giving the impression that it is an organic part of the square. The references to the mainstream architecture at the time—the crenellations and the tall slender tower, all useless remnants of the past—abound. The town hall is thus integrated into a whole comprised of both the public and private buildings as *primum inter pares*, the first among equal buildings of the city.

In stark contrast to the town hall stands the cathedral, which dominates the city on a hilltop 200 meters away. Its construction began about eighty years before the construction of the town hall. Over one hundred meters long, richly decorated, and with the colors of the Sienese coat of arms, the cathedral markedly stands out from all the secular buildings of the city: such a great straight line as the cathedral's axis does not exist anywhere else in the city, nor does such an elaborate and consistent decoration.

More than in Italy, Gothic architecture in Central and Northern Europe contributed to making the cathedrals the exceptional structures they are. The early features of the new architecture, which swept across the continent and the British Isles within a few decades, date back at least to the eleven-thirties, when Abbot Suger—a close associate of French kings Louis VI and Louis VII—set out to rebuild the basilica of Saint Denis to ease congestion and to flood it with light.

With immense height, the delicate, graceful Gothic cathedrals absorbed a great part of the local population's wealth and energy for generations. It seems that in erecting them, people saw the opportunity to transcend the rather harsh reality they faced in their everyday lives and to partake in the quasi virtual world of amazing edifices they themselves created, and which they more or less perceived as constructs made possible through divine intervention.[4] They inspired others to follow suit and create similar wonders in their towns.

The extremely impressive appearance of the Gothic cathedrals is due, clearly, to their daring static taking full advantage of the stone's strength, which is stressed to its extreme—even subjected to tension, where applicable. But this is also due to their display of a high degree of regularity combined with extreme visual complexity. The drawings of Villard de Honnecourt—a monk from Picardy who lived in the middle of the thirteenth century—preserved in a folder with thirty-three parchment sheets, clearly demonstrate this characteristic trait of Gothic architecture: people's faces and Gothic buildings' ornamentations, worked in detail, are organized

**Siena, Cathedral, circa 1215**

according to simple geometric principles. The blend of elementary geometry with visual intricacy is present in buildings across the globe: in Chapter 9, we saw that this was the case with Angkor, too. This alone would suffice to make Gothic cathedrals distinctive from the edifices that surrounded them, and were distinguished for the opposite qualities: for the irregularity of their outline, combined with rich variation in texture and the lack of finely worked details.

Walking in Siena today, we appreciate not so much its order and homogeneity—the declared objectives of its leaders, especially during the administration of the Nine—but, again, for the irregularity that we perceive in it. Our judgment is not completely arbitrary; those who regulated and

**Drawing, Villard de Honnecourt, circa 1230**

controlled the building activity in the thirteenth and fourteenth centuries envisioned a regularity that was not in the same league with what was sought after and realized the following centuries (and we are now accustomed to). On the one hand, they had in front of them the strictly regular cathedral of their city; on the other hand, the pandemonium of the small, private buildings with walls that stooped from the passage of time, the openings at irregular intervals, columns, arches, and windows rarely uniform, the repeated additions and extensions. They followed a middle path and attempted to give the city a unified appearance, relating the distinct parts that comprised it to each other. It was an appearance that did not result from detailed planning, but was not shaped without principles. It was based on relative positioning and not on geometric patterns, on gradual evolution and not on predetermined schemes, on balance and not on repetition, on ingenuity and not on a model; a form, which in our eyes balances between regularity and irregularity.

This occurred neither for the first nor for the last time in history. The great Greek temples of Asia Minor of the sixth century BCE are typical of such balance: their columns (all the same height, needless to say) were very different from each other, prepared by different workshops, which had great freedom of choice. Next to each other, the columns formed the colonnades supporting the epistyles and the friezes. No one could argue that in sixth-century BCE Ionia, the sense of individuality was more advanced than in Pericles' Athens when the Parthenon was built, where the columns—also made from different workshops—have the slightest possible differences between them.

With the construction of the huge Gothic cathedrals, and the increasing regulation of the city form, a major shift in people' s perception became apparent of the line that separates diversity from chaos, unimaginative severity from order, and dry repetition from homogeneity; perception that never ceased to shift in time.

### Notes

1 *MGH, Friderici II Constitutiones*, no 171, 5/1232, 211-13.
2 Archivio di Stato di Siena, Consiglio Generale: *Deliberazioni*, 139 ff. 52r.-53v., 6 Dec 1346.
3 *Ibid.*
4 Abbot Suger: *The Other Little Book on the Consecration of the Church of St-Denis*, II.

### Selected Bibliography

Bordone, Renato/Sergi, Giuseppe: *Dieci secoli di medioevo.* Einaudi 2009.
Bowsky, William M.: *A Medieval Italian Commune: Siena under the Nine, 1287–1355.* University of California Press 1981.
Le Goff, Jacques: *La civilisation de l'occident médiéval.* Champs 1964.
Oraiopoulos, Philippos: *Le modèle spatial de l' Orient hellène – le discourse néohellénique sur la ville et l' architectrure.* L'Harmattan 1998.
Toman, Rolf (ed.): *The Art of Gothic: Architecture, Sculpture, Painting.* Könemann 1999.
Waley, Daniel Philip: *Siena and the Sienese in the Thirteenth Century.* Cambridge University Press 2006

# ARCHITECTURE AND MATHEMATICS

## The Alhambra

"As we walk into the Alhambra, I'm immediately struck by the reflective power of the water. It seems as though the palace is built on water. Tiny little streams run from one fountain to another. The architecture of the palace already demonstrates a vertical symmetry: the left side of the façade is perfectly reflected in the right side. Standing at one end of the pool in the Courtyard of the Myrtles, one sees another perfect copy of the building reflected horizontally in the surface of the water. This vast expanse of water stretches to the very feet of the columns of the façade, and the palace and its reflection combine to give the impression of a crystal suspended in the sky. Some girls thrust their hands into the water, trying to touch the fish swimming there, and the symmetry is destroyed. It doesn't take much to disturb the water's calm surface and fragment the palace's mirror image. That is the message in the water: perfect symmetry is hard to obtain. The natural world knows that. The Moorish architects loved the symbolism of the fragility of the symmetry in the water. The tension between the eternal nature of God and the transience of our fragile earth was captured by the dialogue between the solid symmetry of the palace and its elusive reflection in the pool."[1]

This description belongs to Marcus du Sautoy, a distinguished Professor of Mathematics at the University of Oxford. Du Sautoy is an expert in group theory and in number theory, which is increasingly revealed as the narrative of his most recent visit in Alhambra progresses:

"The walls of the palace are covered with tiles of different colors arranged to make patterns. There is a rhythm created by the symmetry which almost makes the walls pulsate, giving the effect of a moving image, hinting at the infinite expanse of the space … This is another reason why the Muslim artists were drawn to symmetry: as an artistic expression of God's infinite wisdom and majesty … Hiding behind each tiling pattern is one of only seventeen different varieties of symmetry that is possible on a

**El Partal, Alhambra, Granada, early fourteenth century and later**

two-dimensional surface. We can look at the array of different shapes that the artists dreamt up and wonder whether they thought there was no end to the catalogue of symmetries…. It would be another five hundred years before mathematicians proved for certain that the medieval Moorish artists would never have been able to squeeze an eighteenth type of symmetry out of the tiles on the walls."

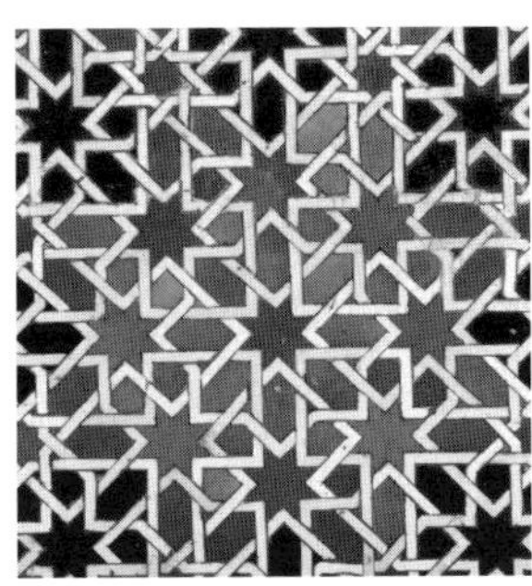

**Wall tiling, Alhambra, Granada, early fourteenth century**

The Alhambra Palace in Granada, Spain is situated on a plateau, on the top of a small hill that rises over the Darro River. Initially, it was a small citadel of the Muslim Moorish rulers of tenth-century Andalusia, which was expanded in several phases. The construction of its most famous sections began around 1330, when the town hall of Siena was nearly completed. It was known as "a pearl set in emeralds" and was praised by poets—not unduly, because it was a real paradise, green and with running water in a dry and warm land. The entire complex is enclosed by a wall from which thirteen towers loom, which contributed to the palace's defense but also provided the opportunity to enjoy the view. The large park stretching on its foot was planted by the Moors with myrtles, orange trees, and roses, and was watered by an aqueduct that drew water from Darro before its descent into the valley.

The twelfth-century philosopher and astronomer Abu-l-Walid Muhammad ibn Rushd, who was known in the West as Averroes, came from Andalusia. He was among the most prolific and influential of Aristotle's medieval commentators, continuing a centuries' old tradition. In his era, a large number of ancient Greek texts on logic, cosmology, astronomy, medicine, and mathematics had already been translated to Arabic. In the following centuries, European students of the Greek classical texts turned for guidance to the commentaries of the Arabs translators; Averroes' commentary on *Physics*, *On the Heavens* and other works by Aristotle were translated into Latin—the European lingua franca of that time—a few years after his death in 1198. Euclid had been translated into Arabic in the late ninth century; in fact, the first translation of this work into Latin was made from Arabic in the twelfth century. The earliest translations into Latin of several works by Aristotle, Galen, Ptolemy and Archimedes were also made from their Arabic versions.

The Arabs, along with their Persian contemporaries, made major developments in ancient Greek science. Among their achievements, they laid the foundations for algebra on the basis of ideas developed by Indian mathematicians, and they also made significant progress in optics. Their advanced knowledge and their love of mathematics and physics contributed greatly to the advancement of Islamic architecture and art—as can especially be seen at the Alhambra and in other masterpieces, from Fez to Esfahan and from Samarkand to Delhi.

Geometry was repeatedly employed to illustrate the cosmic order and to recreate it in our world. The rectangular domed structures, for instance, have probably visualized the creation of the multiplicity (our world) from the One (God), the primordial unity represented by the dome unfolding into the quadrature represented by the isotropic three-dimensional cubic structure beneath it. Moreover, Muslim architects and artists turned to geometry in order to create abstract images with which to decorate their buildings, since Islam is especially skeptical toward representation of living beings.

The Great Mosque, Cordova, 785–987 CE

The application of mathematics in architecture and arts occurs more or less in every region of the world and every cultural context. The ancient Egyptians, as we know, often used the elementary geometrical shape of the pyramid—with very particular size ratios—for some of the most important buildings they constructed: the tombs of several pharaohs and high-ranking officials. Some of the most famous ancient Greek sculptors produced statues with strictly predetermined proportions in the body limbs' sizes and invested their practice with a full-fledged theory. Several centuries later, Vitruvius conveyed to us that the Dorian, Ionian, and Corinthian orders represented the male and female genders and young girls, respectively. Therefore, the buildings that were built in these styles were constructed on the basis of different proportion systems: the Dorian order was more robust with ratio of height to columns' diameter smaller than that of the Ionian order; the Corinthian order had the most delicate proportions, corresponding to the virgins' grace and beauty. On the other side of the world, in the Indian subcontinent, the proportions of the moldings and friezes and tiers on Hindu temples were also strictly prescribed—the list is virtually endless.

The social status of architects has varied greatly during the course of history, and it was not unusual—as was the case in classical Greece— that their trade was considered to some degree vulgar, unlike, for example, music or rhetoric. In this context, mathematics offered architecture more important services than just providing assistance in solving practical design problems: it helped to upgrade it. Mathematics always excited peoples' imagination; the notion that this abstract system, founded only in axioms, could describe in a simple and explicit way, the laws governing the seemingly chaotic complexity of the world, was "fascinating,"[2] and the people who knew their secrets enjoyed respect.

Architects quite often resorted to geometry and to specific numerical ratios to configure and decorate their buildings in order to bestow them with prestige and beauty: prestige, since the affinity of the produce of architecture with the creations of God or Nature would supposedly be manifested; beauty, since something of the World's harmony could be transferred to the buildings. Is this not also the case with music from the time of Pythagoras, who discovered that harmonic sounds were produced from chords whose lengths have simple numerical relations between them?

In the West, architects regularly incorporated simple numerical ratios in their buildings. Prime numbers were imbued by philosophers and occultists with metaphysical qualities in line with a tradition of eastern or Pythagorean origin, until at least the seventeenth century. In many instances, the first integers were considered to correspond to structural units of the universe; some other numbers—such as 6, 10, 256—were regarded for various reasons to express perfection. Rather less frequently, architects in the West used simple geometric shapes, such as circles, quadrangles, or octagons. Geometry itself had a special place in cosmology: Plato believed that "God is always doing geometry"[3] and that the world—spherical in shape, since the circle is the perfect shape—consists of the five regular solids corresponding to earth, water, air, fire, and ether. Aristotle had vigorously opposed this point of view and Averroes had written a lengthy commentary on this topic, which was later translated into Latin. Buildings

**Po-i-Kalyan Mosque, Bukhara, 1172 CE**

incorporating simple numerical ratios and geometrical shapes would reputedly confirm, just by being there, that the Universe is structured according to secret laws expressed with prime numbers and elementary geometry: a self-fulfilled prophecy that would cause the admiration of a public passionately seeking the hidden meaning of things. Rarely, though, would it gain the respect of philosophers or mathematicians who probably saw in such application of mathematics the excessive simplification, if not the trivialization, of elaborate concepts.

In Islam things were a bit different. Architects and artists adopted the Greco-Roman tradition of using proportions in their designs—the Great Mosque of Damascus is typical. However, they mainly used geometry, developing a design philosophy applicable in smaller as well as in larger objects, from carpets to mosques. It can be summarized as using simple geometrical shapes—quadrangles, rhombuses, circles, cubes, hemispheres—inscribed with highly complex smaller units.

According to a widespread view, which was also shared by several philosophers and theologians in the West, the perfection of the geometrical shapes reflected the perfection of the creations of God Himself, even if, according to Averroes, the Supreme Being did not have unlimited free will, and governed the world not with the arbitrariness of an absolute ruler, but through a structure of necessary causes which He had decreed Himself. The way that mathematics—especially geometry—was founded perfectly matched this cosmological perception. Building on a long Sufi tradition, the great master Ibn Arabi, who too came from Andalousia, and was a generation jounger than Averroes (whom he met in his youth), also used geometry extensively to illustrate his cosmology.

The extremely complex symmetries like those we encounter on the walls and floors of the palace of Alhambra corresponded to the world as understood by Averroes, or by the Sufis. They matched even more with the so-called occasionalist approach of many orthodox Muslim theologians and philosophers, who rejected the Aristotelian idea of an eternal world and endorsed Democritus' view that matter is not eternal and immutable, but it consists of particles that meet and bind together. In this process, they argued, God intervenes changing the world according to His will. If, therefore, even today specialists are often unable to discern in Alhambra (as well as in other works of Islamic art) the mathematical structure of complex geometric decorative motifs and architectural members—which however present high regularity—then it is certain that in the eyes of a layperson several hundred years ago, these would have seemed to correspond to works of a power with the ability to mix the ingredients of matter at will producing, nevertheless, perfect results.

The occasionalist worldview was formulated around 1000 CE and was adopted by Caliph Al-Qadir, the leader of the Sunni Muslims based in Baghdad. It coincided with the invention—possibly in Baghdad as well—of maybe the most characteristic feature of Islamic architecture, the *muqarnas*. The muqarnas are small-scale corbelled brackets and niches forming concave three dimensional segments mainly used in zones of transition from flat to curved surfaces and for the decoration of the soffits of arches and vaults. They were possibly devised as an answer to a difficult design problem that architects faced—joining a hemispherical dome with a square hall. The typical solution, the squinch, probably dates back to Iran of the early Sassanid era—the dynasty that ruled the country from 224 until 651 CE—long before the advent of Islam. Squinches are the three-dimensional structures at the corners of the square hall beneath the hemispherical dome. Insofar as the dome symbolizes the sky, these visible supports did not coincide with the explicit assurance of the Qur'an[4] that the sky is not supported anywhere. Muqarnas, on the other hand, made the domes appear as if they were suspended in air. Moreover, neither the clarity of the contour of the classical hemispherical dome, nor its smooth surface matched the complexity of the world according to the occasionalist approach of the orthodox theologians of Islam. But the adornment of the entire dome with muqarnas could visualize it instead. The dome was now deconstructed in small but distinct units arranged in a visually complex manner, which with their protrusions and recessions gave the impression that they were held together by an invisible hand.

The muqarnas were not only used in mosques, but in buildings of every kind—indeed an early example appears in the ninth century in private residencies in what is now Iraq—and not only in domes but in capitals, where again there is the problem of joining the cylindrical shaft with the arch above. This suggests that we are facing a rather typical case where architecture and ideology met halfway for reasons of mutual benefit. A nascent ideology—the occasionalist view of the world—adopted one ele-

**Patio de los Leones, Alhambra, Granada, mid-fourteenth century**

ment, the muqarnas, with which the architects were experimenting at the time. The occasionalists supported its dissemination; appropriating architecture's power ideology would become more attractive and increase its discernment in the public. On the other hand, architecture gained prestige with the allegation that its creations and the world at large were governed by the same set of laws.

In Alhambra, the art of muqarnas reached a peak. Exceptionally designed and crafted, they give buildings a completely airy feel, in absolute harmony with the fragile calmness of the large water surfaces. In combination with the sounds of water running from small fountains and with the breeze cooling the shady covered areas arranged around the successive courtyards creating conditions of comfort for its inhabitants, they make the palace seem as if it were built from the material dreams are made of.

This is perhaps what makes the Alhambra palace a masterpiece: the sense that what the assignors and the architects attempted to convey with the broad use of mathematics is universally perceived even today, and indeed complements rather than destroys other qualities of architecture. One need not be a mathematician or a philosopher to gain the impression, wandering the halls and the courtyards of the palace that the perfection there is based in an almost incomprehensibly complex arrangement. Nor does one need to be king to appreciate the tranquility and beauty that prevails everywhere one turns his/her gaze.

Although the use of mathematics in architecture is, as discussed above, very common, it very rarely achieved what was accomplished in Alhambra. In the course of history, there have been attempts to transfer music harmony to buildings—e.g., by making the relative position of architectural members correspond to musical intervals. This would supposedly suffice to accomplish what German philosopher and poet Johann Wolfgang von Goethe summarized in his famous quote: architecture is congealed music.[5] Goethe's dictum, though, probably should not be taken at face value, but understood as a metaphor. The application of the laws governing musical harmony to architecture may well end up being a mind game, which cannot be perceived by the senses to which it is allegedly addressed. It is not at all self-evident that a rhythmic alternation of architectural members in space will be perceived in a manner similar to a melody, where the notes succeed one another in time. On the contrary, it is quite probable that some other properties of these architectural members—size and weight, the texture of their surfaces, their conservation status—will dominate the image obtained by the observer and will overshadow the fact that they are placed at distances proportional to the musical intervals of a melody.

Today, architecture once again resorts to mathematics in order to create forms. Some architects use advanced software to design in a mathematically consistent manner (which is essential for statics and construction) irregular forms that have emerged from their imagination. Others set only a few parameters, and the computer program creates quite unpredictable forms—the result of this parametric design is bestowed the exceptional prestige of the higher mathematics that produced it.

In both cases, while the architects assign a large part of their role as creators of forms to software—i.e., mathematics—they seem reluctant to relinquish their most fundamental right: to decide themselves which of the thousand alternative forms generated by the computer is worthy of further work, or which of these forms deserves to be built. The architects' judgment in these fundamental issues remains primarily based on the most old-fashioned aesthetic criteria mixed with a sense of what constitutes a welcomed novelty or, instead, a low-profile proposal, appropriate for an environment dominated by posh neighboring buildings.

This behavior of architects is not contradictory. They know that the criteria with which a building is judged now and in the future—by people from one or another cultural background, by the public as whole, as groups, or as individuals, winter or summer, day or night, after a tiring day or in the weekend, in times of prosperity or recession—are too complex to be replaced by whatever clever mathematical functions that the software uses to generate a form.

The architects of Alhambra used mathematics precisely to achieve the perfect result. Let's keep them in mind when we turn on our computers in order to design.

### Notes

1  du Sautoy, Marcus: *Finding Moonshine.* Harper Collins 2009, 62 ff.
2  Einstein, Albert: *Geometry and Experience, an expanded form of an address to the Prussian Academy of Sciences in Berlin on January 27th, 1921,* 1.
3  Plutarch: *Symp.* 8.2.
4  *Qur'an* 35,10.
5  Eckermann, Johannn Peter: *Gespräche mit Goethe,*
Mon. 23 März 1829. Transl. John Oxenford.

### Selected Bibliography

Akkach, Samer: *Cosmology and architecture in premodern Islam: an architectural reading of mystical ideas.* SUNY 2005.
Department of Architecture Sint-Lucas Brussels (ed.): *Symmetry: Art and Science,* Vol. 2 (new series), n. 1–4, 2002.
Grabar, Oleg: "Symbols and Signs in Islamic Architecture." In: Holod, Renata/ Rastorfer, D. (eds): Architecture and Community. Aperture 1983, 25ff.
Jacobs, Michael/Fernández, Francisco: *Alhambra.* Frances Lincoln 2009.
Ruggles, D. Fairchild: *Gardens, Landscape, and Vision in the Palaces of Islamic Spain.* Pennsylvania State University Press 2000.
Tabbaa, Yasser: "The Muqarnas Dome: Its Origin and Meaning." In: *Muqarnas III: An Annual on Islamic Art and Architecture.* E.J. Brill 1985.

# ARCHITECTURE AND UTOPIA

## The Forbidden City

Since Thomas More used the word "utopia" to name the imaginary commonwealth that he devised somewhere in the middle of the sixteenth century, this word has become synonymous with something ideal, which, however, does not have a place in our world. The word utopia is made up from the Greek words for "no" and "place," and it means: a reality that does not exist anywhere, i.e., a reality outside the real world; a reality that we would wish to exist, but we acknowledge that it cannot.

Architects flirted frequently with utopia, carving there a refuge for their proposals, which were doomed in advance not to be built. Utopian architecture might be unbuildable for a whole range of reasons. The technology to support it might not exist, the money to materialize it might not be available, the society to accept it might not be there; or a combination of the above. Nevertheless, utopian architecture has a great advantage: it is not subjected to the limitations of architecture intended to be conveyed into matter; and it is emancipated from the obligation to serve its usual audience directly. So it can often express with great clarity thoughts and intentions; thus it can eventually have a huge impact on future applied architecture.

In the West, utopian architecture became a separate branch of architecture virtually from the time of Romanticism in mid-eighteenth century. At that time, the artists became increasingly independent from the mighty, who used to commission the works, and produced art regardless of whether there was already a predetermined recipient. Needless to say, utopian architecture has existed in some form since antiquity. Vitruvius informs us about the story of Dinocrates, a story whose details may be fabricated, but educational.[1] Dinocrates was an architect who wanted to present his ideas to Alexander the Great, but he could not find a way to approach him. After all his attempts failed and not knowing what else he could do, he dressed himself in a lion's skin, took a club in his hand, and stood among the crowd. Everyone turned toward him—including Alexander, who asked him who he was. Thus Dinocrates found the opportunity to talk about his plan to carve a huge statue of the king in Mount Athos, holding in his arms a new city. Alexander was flattered, but he asked calmly how this city would be supplied. After he found out that there were not enough fields in the region to feed its inhabitants and that its provisioning would depend exclusively on imports, he declined politely Dinocrates' proposal. Nevertheless, Alexander kept Dinocrates by his side and he assigned him, among other things, an equally ambitious project: the design of a city in Egypt bearing his name, Alexandria, which was to become the center of the Western world for the next two centuries. The city in Mount Athos was marginally feasible from a technical perspective; however it was not sustainable, since other cities would have to support its survival.

Sometimes, plans completely feasible from a technical perspective, plans not intended to remain on paper, were labeled utopian by those who were opposed to their implementation. When in 1834 Karl Friedrich Schinkel proposed building the palace for King Otto of Greece on the Acropolis, directly adjacent to the Parthenon, the advisor of the king of Bavaria and father of Otto, Ludwig I, the architect Leo von Klenze, described the plan as "a wonderful Midsummer Night's Dream." At that time, the Romantic movement and the worship of ancient Greece were in full bloom, and preserving the ancient monuments free from any modern admixture, no matter how brilliant, was of outmost importance; only thus could they offer the opportunity for unobstructed and undistracted contemplation. The plans for a palace on the Acropolis turned out to be ideologically non-viable in the early nineteenth century—the emphasis is on the early nineteenth century: Demetrius the Besieger, one of Alexander's successors had turned Parthenon itself in his palace somewhere around 300 BCE.



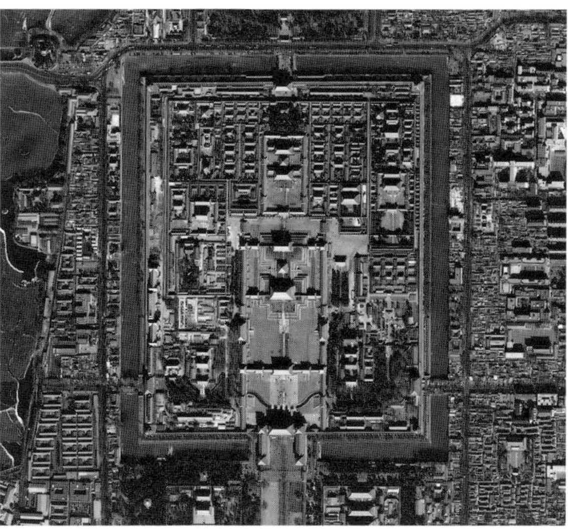

**Forbidden City, Beijing, 1420**

Sometimes the opposite happens: some ideas and suggestions, which could have been rendered utopian when they were initially formulated, proved, in the end, that they could find a place in the real world. One of the most formidable among these is the Forbidden City, the palace of the emperors of China from 1420 until the beginning of the twentieth century. The Forbidden City was built within fifteen years on orders of Zhu Di, the third emperor of the Ming Dynasty, who named the period of his reign "perpetual happiness," Yongle.

Zhu Di was the fourth son of Zhu Yuanzhang, the rebel leader of humble origins who drove out the Mongolian Yuan Dynasty; he proclaimed himself emperor by overthrowing the emperor Zhu Yunwen, son of his firstborn brother. The Yongle Emperor tolerated the various religions of his subjects and was able to achieve peace in the interior, and subsequently the prosperity of his people. Fully aware that knowledge is power, he commissioned his Grand Secretary, Xie Jin, to compile all Chinese writings and books—a project that led to the publication of an encyclopedia 420 years prior to that of Diderot and d'Alembert. Zhu Di also organized successive expeditions led by Admiral Zheng He, who with a fleet of vessels (some of which were rumored to have exceeded the 150 meters) probably reached the coasts of East Africa.

**Forbidden City, Beijing, 1420, south gate, interior view**



The Yongle Emperor moved the seat of government from Nanjing (South Capital) where it was located from 1368, to Beiping (North Peace), which was renamed Beijing (North Capital). This city was the seat of the Mongolian Yuan Dynasty; it was then called Dadu (Great Capital) and had previously been a minor capital for some periods. Yongle loathed Mongolian influence on China and tried to eliminate it. Among other things, he

ordered the city's cleansing from the remains of the Yuan palace, which
his father had burned down in 1368, and founded his own city a bit further to the south, leaving the areas of Dadu found outside its reformed
section to decline.

**Formal hearing of Emperor Qianlong, mid-eighteenth century, For-
bidden City, Beijing, 1420; unknown artist; in the background the Hall
of Supreme Harmony**

In a move to integrate into China and its culture, the Yuan had
adopted as the official state ideology many of Zhu Xi's views, which were
formulated in the second half of the twelfth century and reinvigorated
Confucianism; Confucianism was a kind of applied philosophy principally
aimed at creating a layered society that could ensure the peace and prosperity of all its members. Kublai Khan—the founder of the Mongol Yuan
Dynasty—arranged the layout of Dadu based on guidelines recorded in
*Kao gong Ji*, a manual intended for the training of craftsmen. *Kao gong Ji*
was probably written initially in the fifth century BCE, and included instruc-
tions for designing private residencies as well as planning cities in the
spirit of Confucianism: for instance, the guidelines for private residencies
confirmed the privileged position of men and helped perpetuate the established domestic hierarchy.

Kublai Khan's Dadu, then, was planned as a square with a total area
of about fifty square kilometers, as big as the "intramural" Paris of the mid-
nineteenth century; its walls measured twenty-nine kilometers in length
and had three gates each on their south, east, and west sides and two on
the north. The palace was located in the southern part of the city, in slight
violation of *Kao gong Ji*'s guidelines that wanted it in the city's geometrical
center, for reasons probably related to water supply.

The Yongle Emperor, who did not want to give pretexts for challenging his legitimacy to rule, also adopted the guidelines mentioned
in *Kao gong Ji*. It seems that Nguyen An, a eunuch from what is today
Vietnam, took over the planning of the city as well as the supervision of
its construction. He maintained the city's orientation to the four cardinal

points, each corresponding to one of the natural elements, one of the seasons, and one of the primary colors: west corresponded to spring, wood, and green; south to summer, fire, and red; west to autumn, metal, and white; and north to winter, water, and black. The city center is located where the axes of the city meet; that is where the supposed world axis passes through and corresponds to earth and its color, which is the imperial one, yellow. There, the palace is situated, which would become known as the "Forbidden City," or more precisely, the "Purple

**Forbidden City, Beijing, 1420, minor buildings**

Forbidden City," after the color of the polar star Chinese astrology considered to be the abode of the Celestial Emperor. Actually, the city shape is only roughly a square, with the palace located not exactly at its center, possibly because it was not planned on entirely virgin soil. In its layout, Beijing followed Dadu in reviving a tradition long forgotten and reintroduced by the Yuan. Most notably, Chang'an (modern Xi'an), a very important capital of China had followed a different tradition, at least during its reform in the Tang era at the beginning of the seventh century CE, which wanted the palace situated in the northern end of the city, a location also surrounded by the prestige of a multitude of cosmological symbolisms.

The Yongle Emperor's Forbidden City is approximately 960 meters long and 760 meters wide, and is surrounded by a wall and moat. Its layout is similar to that of Chinese palaces, as it was developed over many hundreds of years; it effectively served both the intended symbolisms and the emperor's daily strictly ritualized routine. Its almost 8,700 rooms—distributed in 980 buildings—housed both the emperor's living quarters with the multitude of his spouses and concubines, and the administrative center of the empire. A subtle line divided the private quarters of the palace from the public ones.

The administrative center of the empire was housed in a complex of buildings around the great central courtyard, known as the Outer Court, which is approximately 180 meters long and 200 meters wide and was the third in a row encountered by the visitor. The north side of the Outer Court is dominated by the Hall of Offering Heaven, which was renamed 250 years later as the Hall of Supreme Harmony. The emperor's most formal throne was in this hall and looked, as imposed by the tradition, toward the south. Behind the Hall of Supreme Harmony there is a smaller hall, the Hall of Central Harmony, where the emperor prepared for his public appearances. Behind it is another great ceremonial hall, the Hall of Preserving Harmony. The three most important halls of the state were thus placed in direct relation to each other. In this layout, one could see the Qien hexagram, which symbolized heaven and corresponded to the leader; and regarding the family, to the father; and regarding the parts of the body, to the head and the lungs.

Behind the Outer Court is the Inner Court, which was the center of the emperor's private quarters. It also has three successive halls, smaller, though, than those of the Outer Court. They are: the Palace of Heavenly Purity, i.e., the emperor's residence, representing the yang and the Heavens; the Palace of Earthly Tranquility, the empress' residence, representing yin and the Earth; and, between them, the hall where the yang and yin met to produce Harmony—the Hall of Union. The rest of the private quarters to the right and left of the Inner Court were organized into groups of six buildings where one could see the Qian hexagram symbolizing the earth and corresponding to the mother, the abdomen, and the reproductive organs. Thus, the Forbidden City appears organized on the basis of the opposites— yin and yang. The meanings conveyed by its layout, the colors of the roofs, and the orientation of the halls were easily perceived and understood by a large number of people who were familiar with this symbolic language.

Although the representative halls of the palace were renovated thoroughly during the 500 years that the Forbidden City was the seat of the Chinese Empire, it seems that their configuration did not change substantially and continued to manifest the fundamental features of classical Chinese architecture. Decoration resulted from the structural elements and was not applied as ornamentation on a finished construct. The roofs—covered with yellow tiles—are concave, double-tiered with upturned eaves, and supported on a highly complex set of beams and interlocking brackets whose succession per height followed strictly prescribed rules. The columns were placed in such a way that the distance between them is greater as we approach the center of the hall, forming bays of different sizes. The interiors of the halls were thus made rather hierarchical than homogenous, with their importance increasing as we approach the centrally placed imperial throne. The column layout and the complex, therefore expensive, construction upon them sustains, if not prompts, the curvature of the roofs

Chon Yang Dian Hall in the Yongle palace, circa 1300; model Chinese
Academy of Cultural Heritage

resulting in their tranquil magnificence; the curved roofs were traditionally considered to repel evil spirits. One could say that the sophisticated
network of columns, beams, and bracket sets supporting the roofs corresponded to the intricacy and multiple layers of the Chinese bureaucracy.

For selecting the senior administrative personnel of the empire,
the Yongle Emperor reinstated an objective examinations system. The
last phase took place in the heart of the Forbidden City, in the Hall of Preserving Harmony, reflecting the significance that the head of the state
attached to choosing the more capable—a pillar of good governance. Neo-
Confucianism was the official state ideology, although the Yongle Emperor
maintained the army's strong position in state affairs and often resorted to
quite un-Confucian extreme violence to impose order—or something that
served the same purpose, to denote imperial authority. He executed numerous relatives and associates of his predecessor Zhu Yunwen when he
overthrew him; he ordered the execution by "slow slicing" of 2,800 wom-
en whom he deemed were actively involved, or by their silence culpable,
in the death of a favorite concubine—not a small number if one considers
that the China of his era numbered fifty to sixty million people. In addition,
he gave the order to hang thirty beautiful women when he died so that
they would be buried with him. This was not unusual, however, since the
rulers of the Sang Dynasty (second millennium BCE) used to take their
harems, domestic servants, even armies with them in the afterlife, quite
often only symbolically.

The Yongle Emperor was a warrior like his father, but with few
exceptions, succeeding emperors preferred to spend their time in the
palace where eunuchs acquired increasing power. Although condemned

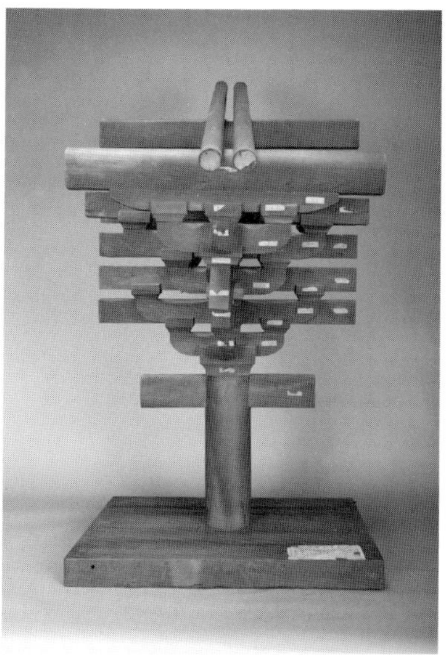

**Typical timber construction, Song Dynasty (960–1279 CE), detail; model Chinese Academy of Cultural Heritage**

by orthodox Confucianism as defective human beings, the vast majority of eunuchs voluntarily chose castration to make a career in Court: those with the least qualifications as servants, and the most intelligent, capable, and educated as officials. During the middle and late Ming period (mid-fifteenth to mid-seventeenth centuries), they were often in favor of a policy advocated by the literati, who studied the classical texts in schools founded with increasing frequency in the safe haven of southern China—approximately eight schools per year between 1520 and 1560. This policy valued Chinese civilization to the point that it aimed to exclude any influences from abroad, and prevent the integration of different peoples and cultural traditions.
As we will see in Chapter 17, the relations with the nomadic tribes of the north soured, the exploratory activity was brought to an end, and the dissemination of information about the voyages of Zheng He was banned. The residency of the emperors and their advisors in the perfect, utopian environment of the Forbidden City may well have contributed to China's introversion. In a rare, for its clarity, estimate about the effect of residence on personality, Goethe wrote on March 23, 1823: "Splendid edifices and apartments are for princes and kingdoms. Those who live in them feel at ease and contented, and desire nothing further. To my own nature this is quite repugnant. In a splendid abode, like that which I had at Carlsbad, I am at once lazy and inactive. On the contrary, a small residence, like this poor apartment in which we now are, and where a sort of disorderly order—a sort of gipsy-fashion—prevails, suits me exactly. It allows my inner nature full liberty to act, and to create from itself alone."[2]

In a sense, the society envisioned by Confucius was a utopian society that never lost its contact with reality—in some way a "feasible" utopian society. The Yongle Emperor conceived of an ideal state of things that he wanted to accomplish, and part of his utopia revolved around architecture: the creation of an man-made environment perfectly balanced in terms of functionality, aesthetics, and symbolism. He was not the first to do so, since the Chinese emperors pursued it systematically. If they were not able to materialize the ideal, they (or their successors) tried to enforce a reading of reality in full correspondence with the ideal. For example, a multitude of city plans, which we find in books of the thirteenth century and later, do not show each city exactly as it was, but as close as possible to what was considered to be theoretically perfect at the time. Most notably, the plan of Chang'an, which was published in the Yuan-era *Henan Zhi* (Record of Henan Province), shows the palace at the city center, as recommended by *Kao gong Ji*, while in reality it was located in the northern end of the city.

With the assistance of his architect, the Yongle Emperor was able to achieve the ideal with great accuracy, and he did so by making do with the means provided by architecture in the narrow sense of the term—with wood and stone. This is not a minor achievement: although quite a few architectural utopias have been implemented, few of them manage to maintain their appeal when they leave the realm of imagination; this is because they usually require a type of human being in short supply, or because they attempt to redesign people, too—which they eventually fail to do. In contrast, the Forbidden City belongs to the materialized utopias that have maintained their prestige and magic until the present day.

**Notes**
1 Vitruvius: *De Architectura* II, pr. 1.
2 Eckermann, Johannn Peter: *Gespräche mit Goethe*,
Mon. 23 März 1829. Transl. John Oxenford.

**Selected Bibliography**
Barmé, Geremie R.: *The Forbidden City*. Harvard University Press 2008.
Gong Qing-yu: "Structural Carpentry in Qing Dynasty—A Framework
for the Hierarchically Modularized Chinese Timber Structural Design."
In: *Transactions of Tianjin University*, Vol. 8, no. 1, March 2002, 17 ff.
Liang Ssu-ch'eng: *Chinese Architecture: A Pictorial History*. Dover 2005.
Little, Stephen/Eichman, Shawn: *Taoism and the Arts
of China*. The Art institute of Chicago 2000.
Nerdinger, Winfried (ed.): *Die Kunst der Holzkonstruktion; Chinesische
Architekturmodelle*. Architekturmuseum der Technischen Universität
München & Chinese Academy of Cultural Heritage, Jovis 2009.
Satzman Steinhardt, Nancy: "Why Were Chang'an and Beijing
so Different." In: *Journal of the Society of Architectural
Historians*, vol. 45, no. 4, Dec. 1986, 339ff.

# ARCHITECTURE AND OBLIVION

## The Great Temple of Tenochtitlan

The majority of the Mayan cities, including those of the Classical period (roughly 250–900 CE) were rather dispersed settlements, adapted to a lowland tropical environment that allowed food production amidst man-made structures; lacking urban character, they loosely developed around religious, political, and ritual centers. In contrast, the Aztec city-state of Tenochtitlan was densely populated. It was founded in 1325 on a small island in Lake Texcoco. One-and-a-half centuries later, its population had grown to over 200,000 people. It was surrounded by a wall with gates at the four cardinal points, and was connected with the coast by causeways. Designed on the basis of astronomical calculations, its religious and political center occupied a 300-meter square and was dominated by the great temple; it was walled with four gates at the cardinal points. The city was divided into four zones, each with its own local center, and each zone was then subdivided into twenty districts. The poorest houses had only one floor; the houses of the rich had two, each of which with a garden and courtyard. All of them were whitewashed, unlike the temples, which were painted red, blue, and ochre.

The Aztecs settled in the highlands of central Mexico sometime in the twelfth century and offered their services as soldiers to the Tepanec of Azcapotzalco, one of the regional powers. Soon, they were able to establish themselves as an independent power and—allying with the city-states Texcoco and Tlacopan—founded an empire controlling an area extending from the Atlantic to the Pacific Ocean. They seem to have had a policy of extracting a rather mild tribute from the conquered peoples, which allowed them to enjoy relative prosperity. They also imposed restrictions in the trade and exchanges between subject cities, making them directly dependent on Tenochtitlan.

Astronomy was significant in Mesoamerican cultures. Being especially skillful in astronomical observations, the elite appeared to be capable

**Temple of the Great Jaguar, Tikal, Guatemala, circa 730 CE**

of reading the supposed "signs" of the sky. Drawing on such readings, extremely complex and imaginative myths were constructed to justify the strict social and political hierarchy, as well as the value systems that supported it. The worldview of the Aztecs was deeply influenced, as was their art and architecture, by that of people who had flourished in the region in earlier periods. They believed that death was essential for the perpetuation of life, and that people had to offer their blood constantly as a payment to the gods in order to maintain the world order. These beliefs may have helped keep population growth at bay, so that the natural environment's capacity was not exceeded; a dubious way to achieve sustainability even at times of limited family planning methods. Neither the nobility nor the priests were excluded from the blood toll, participating regularly in self-wounding and self-mutilating rituals. However, the toll was clearly heavier for ordinary citizens and much heavier for the subjects of enemy cities.

Aztecs conducted highly ritualized warfare. The battles with tribes who shared the Nahuatl language were prearranged. An equal number of warriors from both sides participated. The purpose was not to exterminate the enemy but to capture as many prisoners as possible for sacrifice. This type of warfare may have had a practical advantage for the Aztecs: being more numerous than their opponents, they could eventually wear them out and subjugate them.

Social hierarchy depended heavily on martial virtue. Young warriors from lower social classes went into battle knowing that if they repeatedly failed to capture a prisoner, they would be reduced to porters, which were considered to be the lowest social class. Indeed, the work of the porters must have been especially hard, as Mesoamericans had not invented the wheel, nor did they use draft animals; consequently, the roads of the empire were suitable only for traveling on foot. In contrast, if the young warriors captured an enemy, they enjoyed prominence and honors, and were eventually even allowed to enter the noble class, whose members were trained from an early age in the art of combat, administration, astronomy, history, mythology, and poetry. Their prestige and power grew with the number of the captured enemies—particularly if it included prominent warriors. Their ascent up the social ladder was made clear for anyone to see in their costumes, which became accordingly more and more impressive.

During the festivals, prisoners were led one by one to the shrines at the top of the pyramid-like temple to be sacrificed. The executions were conducted not only in Huey Teocalli, Tenochtitlan's great temple, but also in every district of the city. All residents were involved in some way—either by preparing the ceremony, by taking care of the severed head, or by taking part in the dismemberment and sharing of the corpse.

Executions followed a strict ritual. Four priests restrained the prisoner, while a fifth—or the king himself—made an incision from the abdomen to the diaphragm with a blade and cut out his heart, while it was still beating. He placed the trophy in a basin at the statue of the god, while the body was left to slide down the pyramid's stairs to its bottom, where it was then decapitated.

One in about 400 prisoners suffered a somewhat different, but even more terrifying ordeal. In the period prior the execution, he enjoyed rich hospitality. His captor visited him regularly and looked after him, calling him "my beloved son"—the reply was "my dear father."[1] On the feast day, a priest escort led the prisoner to an elevated platform, where the large execution stone was situated. He was tied with a rope and given his weapons: four throwing clubs and a warrior sword with feathers instead of a sharp flint; iron was unknown in this part of the world.

"The victim," writes Inge Clendinnen,

"elevated above his opponent and released from the inhibition against killing, which prevailed on the battle field, could whirl at him heavy clubs and strike at the head of his antagonists with unfamiliar freedom. The [Aztec] champions were also presented with a temptingly easy target. The victim could be disabled and brought down with one good blow to the knee or ankle, as on the battlefield. But such a blow would simultaneously abort the spectacle and end their glory, so the temptation had to be resisted. Instead, their concern under these most taxing and public circumstances was to give a display of the high art of weapon handling: in an exquisitely prolonged performance to cut the victim delicately, tenderly with those narrow blades, to lace the living skin with blood. Finally the victim … exhausted by exertion and lack of blood, would falter and fall."[2]

John Keegan adds:

"He was finished off by the ritual opening of his chest and the tearing of his still-beating heart from its seat. His captor took no part in this lethal mutilation but watched from below the execution stone. As soon as the body was decapitated, however, so that the skull could be displayed at the temple, he drank the dead man's blood and carried the body back to his home. There he dismembered the limbs, to be distributed as sacrifice required, flayed the body of its skin, and watched while his family ate a small ritual meal of maize stew topped by a fragment of the dead warrior's flesh … Later, however, the captor … changed his garb again. He took to wearing the flayed skin of the dead man and lending it out to those who begged the privilege, until it and its scarps of attached flesh rotted into deliquescence."[3]

A formal architectural analysis of the execution setting should take into account the worldview and value system of the people who built it, in order to avoid the grave mistake of projecting our own onto a building of the past—so goes the theory. Or maybe not?

In addition, we should see if there are timeless virtues in it, since this is what separates the great from the good but otherwise ordinary architecture. We would have to consider whether the stone, on which the ritual battle with the foretold outcome took place, corresponded to the functions that it was expected to serve: whether it provided enough space for the prisoner, without allowing him to escape his attackers; whether it was situated at a height suitable for the gathered crowd to watch the spectacle comfortably; whether its overall configuration corresponded to the importance attached to the blood-shedding and the symbolisms incorporated in it.

Templo Mayor, Tenochtitlan, Mexico, 1487 phase; model in the National Museum of Anthropology in Mexico City



This is also how we should proceed with the critical analysis of the Huey Teocalli. The Templo Mayor—the great temple—of Technotitlan, which impressed Hernán Cortés—the Spanish conquistador who overthrew the Aztec Empire—with its grandeur and art,[4] was modeled after the temples of the Maya, as a stepped pyramid, crowned with twin shrines, not unusual for the Aztecs; one was dedicated to Tlaloc, the god of rain and fertility, and the other to Huitzilopochtli, god of sun and war. It is estimated that there were 62,000 skulls attached to the walls and ramparts of the great temple, which had been removed from the victims of human sacrifice. They had a primarily symbolic function, denoting the human toll needed to be paid for the sun's daily return to our world. Nevertheless, they probably also fulfilled an aesthetic function, by literally providing vivid manifestations of what we call "the human scale"—thus highlighting the temple's size—and by adding variety to the large stone surfaces; similar to Angkor-Wat's sculptures or to the decoration of the Doric architrave with triglyphs and metopes.

The temple was built on the exact spot where the gods supposedly revealed the signs that this was the Aztec Promised Land. It represented Mount Coatepec, the birthplace of Huitzilopochtli. The god killed his sister Coyolxauhqui there because she conspired against their mother; he dismembered and decapitated her body—a tale reenacted repeatedly by real people and with real people. The great temple also symbolized the world axis, where the thirteen levels of heaven and the nine steps to the underworld come together. Additionally, the gap between the two shrines at its top could be understood as the cosmic crack leading to the underworld—which in a way was the source of life. Since the temple was oriented with precision to the four cardinal points, during the vernal and autumnal equinox, the sun appeared to those who were standing in front of it, to rise between the two shrines.

The temple was founded and refounded repeatedly between 1325 and 1521, when the Spaniards demolished it. In the first phase, it was constructed from earth and wood, but around 1400, it was refounded in stone, with relatively small dimensions. After the Aztec victory over Azcapotzalco in 1428, it was extended five more times with additions to the existing bulk, a grotesque repetition of the (obviously independent) pursuit of the ideal form of Djoser's pyramid by Imhotep 4,000 years before. By expanding and rededicating the temple, powerful kings—who at their ascension to the throne were recognized by their subjects as "our lord, our executioner, our enemy"[5]—propitiated the gods and conveyed to their subjects the idea of their unwavering authority. With each new addition, the human sacrifices were made even more spectacular than they already were; the perpetuation of the blood-tainted ritual was made more attractive by means of architecture. Probably exaggerating his feat, king Ahuizotl boasted to have sacrificed 80,400 prisoners within a few days, during the sixth dedication of the temple in 1487.

At its base, the pyramid measured approximately eighty by one hundred meters, and its height possibly reached sixty meters. Two exceptionally steep parallel stairways led to the twin shrines on the top—an architectural virtue if their main purpose was to allow the corpses and the blood of the victims to roll to the temple's base after the removal of the hearts. During the days of mass human sacrifices, as in the dedication of the temple in 1487, the blood of thousands of victims per day seems to have flown unceasingly, proving firmly that the gradient of the stairways was the appropriate one. The pavement of the Great Plaza in front of the temple enhanced the dramatic effect of the blood flowing down the steps since it did not absorb it rapidly, which would have been the case if it was simply set with dirt, as adjacent public spaces were—obviously the right architectural choice.

The house of Eagle Warriors, one of the most prestigious military orders, was located a short distance from the great temple. Constructed around 1469, it was decorated among other things with images of the warriors heading toward a *zacatapayolli*, a grass ball where Aztecs plunged their bloody blades during the self-sacrifice rituals.

**The ballcourt of Monte Albán, south Mexico, circa 800 CE**

In the axis of the great temple stood the ballcourt, a common feature in Mesoamerican cities. Typically, it was an oblong square with transverse flanges at its ends in the shape of an I-beam. The ballcourt was flanked by sloping or stepped walls, so that its floor would symbolize the cosmic crack. The ballcourt was painted in blood as well. The rules of the game are not known, but its outcome was again human sacrifice, although it is not absolutely certain whether the victims were the losers or the winners. In these facilities, women had the dubious privilege of enjoying relative equality with men, in contrast with other aspects of their daily lives. The priests of the temples dedicated to Mixcoatl, the god of hunting, demanded women as well as men for their sacrifices. After hitting them in the head with a stone axe, they cut their throats and decapitated them. After dedicating the head to the god, they dragged the body in order to bathe the ballcourt floor in human blood.

The largest of the seven *tzompantli*, which were erected in Tenochtitlan's religious and political center, was located on a raised platform next to the ballcourt. As we can deduce from a 1524 drawing made by Cortés himself, it consisted of a three-dimensional grid of posts and crossbeams, unlike other tzompantlis, which were usually two-dimensional. It was sixty meters long, thirty meters wide, and thirty meters high (i.e., as tall as an eight-floor building). Attached to the crossbeams were specially processed human skulls—about 136,000 of them. Those worn out by time were replaced by others; rarely, though, was the renewal as profound as on the eve of the ceremonies for the 1487 dedication of the temple, when the order was given to remove tens of thousands of skulls in order to replace them with the severed heads of the new victims.

The great tzompantli was located immediately to the west of the great temple and in the continuation of the ballcourt axis. The equinox sun appeared to rise from the holy mountain Coatepec, from the gap between the two shrines, to descend to the underworld and be reborn from the crack of creation—the ballcourt floor—and to ascend to the heavens and the Galaxy, which was substantiated by the tens of thousands of severed heads of the great tzompantli.

I expect the reader who has reached this section of the chapter to ask: how can we still talk about architecture?

Furthermore, how can millions of tourists admire the Colosseum unobstructed by its history, which they know only too well? What is it about this and every other similar building, which has had the power to inspire Lord Byron and Charles Dickens?[6] It is hard to believe that anybody would feel particularly comfortable smelling the gladiators' sweat and blood, if a magical power transported him/her back in time to basement's maze of corridors during a day of games. Why does the other, less visible, blood associated with architecture have such a small role in its evaluation: the lives of those who died for the erection of the Qin Shi Huang wall, as we shall see in Chapter 17; or the lives of the slaves who died in the silver

**Altar with relief skulls, Building B, Tenochtitlan, Mexico, fifteenth century**

**Steps, Templo Mayor, Tenochtitlan, Mexico, 1487 phase**

mines of Laurium, which financed the large building program of classical Athens, the erection of Parthenon being its most prominent product?

The part of the question concerning human nature in general—what one can feel regarding the pain of others—is the responsibility of other disciplines to answer. However, the other part of the question specifically concerns architecture.

Buildings are all too easily disconnected in our minds from the events associated with them. People not only use buildings in any way they think appropriate—which absolves our peers who did not knowingly design buildings serving morally unacceptable practices of any wrongdoing—but they also project on them whatever they wish. More than merely keeping memories alive, buildings allow for a constant rewriting of history. The Athenians rebuilt the Parthenon although they pondered leaving the remains of the temple burned by the Persians as an eternal reminder of their past; and New Yorkers, despite initial hesitations, had a new World Trade Center built ten years after 9/11. The Athenians and New Yorkers probably knew that the burned-down Parthenon and the absent World Trade Center would lose their power to convey specific messages and would eventually be opened to an infinite variety of interpretations and experiences. But if memory is important, so is oblivion. "It is more important to lose than to acquire. If the seed does not die, it does not produce fruit. We must live drawing from the life reserves created not only by memories, but also from oblivion," Boris Pasternak writes in his autobiography.[7]

The products of architecture are durable in time as physical objects, but vulnerable as cultural ones. Their preservation beyond the human life span creates on its own the conditions of continuous revaluation. And thus, subsequent generations end up regarding buildings in which people were tortured and executed as picturesque. We focus our attention on the timeworn stones or on the small details of a relief or on the size of the building blocks, and we ignore the blood of people we never met—blood, which after all has been washed away by centuries of rain. The "here and now" is the strongest foundation of architectural experience.

### Notes

1 Keegan, John: *A history of warfare*. Hutchinson 1993, 111.
2 Clandinnen, Inge: *Aztecs. An interpretation*.
Cambridge University Press 1991, 87.
3 Keegan, John: *A history of warfare*. Hutchinson 1993, 112.
4 Cortés, Hernan: *Second Epistle to Charles V* (1520).
5 Keegan, John: *A history of warfare*. Hutchinson 1993, 110.
6 Lord Byron: *Childe Harold's Pilgrimage* (1812-18), esp. CXLIII; Dickens, Charles: *Pictures from Italy*, (1848), X: Rome. Reprinted in: *American notes for general circulation and pictures from Italy*. Chapman & Hall 1913, 308 ff.
7 Pasternak, Boris: "An Essay on Autobiography". Reprinted in: *Poems 1955-1959 and an Essay on Autobiography*. Harvill Press 1990, 39.

### Selected Bibliography

Aguilar Moreno, Manuel: "The Mesoamerican Ballgame as a Portal to the Underworld." In: *PARI*, Vol. III, nos. 2 and 3, 2002–2003.
Mendoza, Ruben: "Divine Gourd Tree. Tzompantli Skull Racks, Decapitation Rituals and Human Trophies in Ancient Mesoamerica." In: Chacon, Richard/Dye, David (eds.): *The Taking and Displaying of Human Trophies by Amerindians*. Plenum 2005.
Moctezuma, Matos: *The Great Temple of the Aztecs*. Thames & Hudson 1988.
Serrato-Combe, Antonio: *The Aztec Templo Mayor: A Visualization*. University of Utah Press 2001.
Sharer, Robert J./Traxler, Loa: *The Ancient Maya*. Stanford University Press 2006.
Smith, Michael E.: "City Size in Late Postclassical Mesoamerica." In: *Journal of Urban History*, Vol. 31, 4, May 2005, 403 ff.

# TRADITION AND INNOVATION

## Sant'Andrea in Mantua

According to literature theorist Hans Robert Jauss, some of the most important works are those that are completely outside the horizon of the expectations of the public, but in the long run contribute decisively in changing this horizon.

If this also holds for architecture, then few buildings would seem as important as the Basilica of Sant'Andrea in Mantua. In contrast with the Gothic cathedrals, Sant'Andrea did not aspire to give the impression that it was reaching the sky. Neither did it seem, due to its daring static, to be standing by god's will, nor did its walls evoke lace. It did not have a portal decorated with hundreds of statuettes depicting saints, people, and animals. Sant'Andrea—a huge church one hundred meters in length—was distinguished by its serenity. The overwhelming robustness of its massive piers, the huge barrel-vaults, the Corinthian pilasters, the cornices and coffers—all gave it the majesty of Roman buildings of similar size, many of which were still preserved in rather good condition. A few years later Michelangelo would convert the *frigidarium* of Diocletian's thermae in Rome into a church, the Santa Maria degli Angeli; only the painting and the chanting during the mass would have reminded worshippers that this magnificent space was devoted to religion. Sant'Andrea, erected only fifty meters from the medieval town hall, differed most decisively from the buildings that surrounded it, in that its façade was clearly inspired by Roman triumphal arches. The typical Gothic cathedral front, with its one central and two side entrances had been transformed into a statement of intentions for a new architecture anchored in the past.

Although it was a period for admiring the Ancient World and seeking in it the support for a new beginning—a Renaissance—the very idea that a Christian church could unreservedly adopt Roman buildings forms, was if nothing else, original. Half a millennium earlier, the attempted revival of Roman architecture, the Romanesque, remained a world apart

**Sant'Andrea, Mantua, Leon Battista Alberti, 1470**

from its ideal and soon, in the twelfth century, developed into a clearly distinct direction, leading to Gothic architecture. The decades required for Sant'Andrea's construction—which commenced in 1470—gave the public the time to accept this completely unusual building. As Rem Koolhaas points out, architecture is slow.[1] In Sant'Andrea's case, this might have been a good thing. Architecture is lacking compared with the activities it has to accommodate, not to say it is inconsistent with them in regards of time. When the marble tiers of the theater of Dionysus were constructed in the southern slope of the Acropolis hill at Athens, the major theatrical writers—Aeschylus, Sophocles, Euripides—were already names of the past; their plays were still performed along with the current ones, which were of a much inferior quality by contemporary standards, as well as those of today. If we expect the various arts to be on the same pace, then this marvelous building appeared with a delay of approximately one century.

Leon Batista Alberti was Sant'Andrea's architect. He was born in Florence in 1404 and among other things he wrote a treatise on painting, *De Pictura*, and one on architecture, *De Re Aedificatoria*. Although Alberti's treatise followed Vitruvius' *De Architectura* in its division into ten sections ("books"), one can discern the Renaissance author's sense of superiority toward his predecessor. This probably derived from the fact that Alberti had more extensive knowledge of ancient Greek and Roman literature than Vitruvius, who was an army officer; Alberti resorted to it at every opportunity to substantiate his arguments. Moreover, Vitruvius seemed to miss the point in identifying the essential features of Roman buildings, because he primarily referred to Hellenistic architecture, which he admired; an architecture that was nevertheless absent in fifteenth-century central and northern Italy. In the Renaissance, ancient Greece existed only in the writings of Aristotle and Plato, Aeschylus and Herodotus, Euclid and Galen. At the time, Athens, Delphi, and Olympia were practically inaccessible to

Western architects and scholars. Hence, there was only Rome as far as architecture was concerned.

Alberti offered a full package of theoretical support and practical advice to utilize this great inheritance. The new architecture, though, never stooped to the actual replication of Roman architecture: it was a rather creative, and at times libertine, reproduction of the latter (regularly much more libertine than in the case of Sant'Andrea, whose architect had studied Roman ruins systematically in his youth). The practical spirit of the Middle Ages was still alive, and people built in a way that served them best, ignoring faithful compliance to the original.

On top of that, Alberti himself did not seem to have taken at face value what his predecessor had said. If the symbolism has some significance, his *De Re Aedificatoria* was the first printed treatise on architecture in the Western world. It was completed probably around 1452—i.e., almost three decades after the discovery of Vitruvius' *De Architectura*—and was printed in 1485, a year before Vitruvius' text, which circulated for decades in manuscript copies.

The aesthetic advocated by Alberti can be summarized by the rule that beauty is achieved when nothing can be added or removed from a building without disturbing the harmony of the whole.[2] This classical principle, formulated with much more elegance than Vitruvius', condenses the break with the medieval tradition: the latter was a dynamic architecture, permanently incomplete, an architecture balancing between regularity and irregularity. Apart from some later examples, non-religious edifices were usually the result of additive and conjectural design and construction. Slowly, during the late Middle Ages, it was recognized that regularity adds prestige—cathedrals may have contributed decisively to this shift—and that in order to attain it, sacrifices in functionality or in the defensive qualities of

**Ospedale degli Innocenti, Florence, Filippo Brunelleschi, 1419**

the buildings had to be made: a window in a position somewhat different from what practicality would have required (in order for it to be in the same level and in the same distance from the rest); a door bigger than necessary (in order to fit aesthetically in the floor's height), and so on. Loggia dei Lanzi, for example, built between 1376 and 1385 right next to Florence's town hall to house the assemblies of the citizens and the official ceremonies of the city, was one of the buildings heralding the new era.

With the confidence in regularity established, pioneer architects at the beginning of the fifteenth century were ready to go even farther. Considered as the very first projects of Renaissance architecture, the dome added to the then incomplete Gothic cathedral of Florence and the Ospedale degli Innocenti (i.e., the city's orphanage)—both works by Filippo Brunelleschi (construction begun in 1418 and 1419 respectively)—inaugurated with their simplicity the new visual culture in Europe's built environment.

The wear of the Roman ruins' ornamentation made the purity of their geometry even more clearly visible. In the Ideal City depicted in the paintings of the Palazzo Ducale of Urbino dated in the late fifteenth century and attributed, as we saw in Chapter 10, to the circle of Piero della Francesca, all the buildings are square or circular. But the choice of using elementary geometrical shapes for the outline of the building's layout was also due to the intellectuals' fascination with Platonism and Neo-Platonism. This was despite of the fact that the geometry-based Platonic cosmology was unconvincing and particularly incompatible to the Christian worldview.

The circle was considered to be the most perfect shape and thus churches were often given this form or some variations of it. Moreover, the circle brought emphasis to the congregation and this was fully consistent with the humanist spirit of Renaissance. Similarly the "scientific" perspective invented by fifteenth-century painting brought the viewer to a very privileged position by making him the ultimate reference point of the painting—i.e., by structuring the painting in such a way as to give to the viewer the "right" feeling of depth. The small church (*tempietto*) of Saint Peter built in 1502 on the presumed location of the founder of the Christian Church's martyrdom in Gianicolo, Rome, has a perfectly circular shape. Eighteen hundred meters to the north, Saint Peter, the most important Western church—built on the location of the original basilica erected by Constantine the Great—was also conceived with a centralized plan by Donato Bramante, who envisioned a huge dome rising above the saint's tomb. Although the plan was altered many times by the architects who succeeded Bramante, Michelangelo's final design also made provisions for a centralized church. Eventually, this plan was revised during the Counter-Reformation, in the early seventeenth century, so that the church would obtain an elongated shape. After the Council of Trent, the balance had tilted decisively in favor of the Latin cross as the appropriate shape for Catholic churches: after all, the faithful had to be reminded (somewhat inelegantly) that the road to salvation is not a short one.

**Ideal City, Circle of Piero della Fransesca, circa 1470; Palazzo Ducale, Urbino**

During the European Middle Ages, the world was perceived to be full of signs and symbols, like the night sky is for astrologers. An epidemic was not just an illness, which for some unknown reason was transmitted from person to person, but also a warning from God to a society of sinners. The fall of a meteor was not simply a celestial phenomenon, but an obscure message that had to be deciphered.

Man-made artifacts were similarly perceived primarily as signs. If the Holy Communion bread was the flesh of Christ, the churches represented his body and the crenellations in the town hall of Florence were the symbol of the community's determination. Of course, symbolism in architecture is not a novelty of the European Middle Ages. In fact due to their additive character, most of the buildings of this period were not particularly appropriate for embodying symbolic meanings. Architecture is a communicative art par excellence and communication is carried out through signs and symbols, which have the capacity to function independently from their physical size. Christians and Muslims respect the crucifix or the Qur'an respectively, regardless of whether they are carved in monumental proportions or printed palm-sized. In architecture, the situation is more complicated because our senses do not allow us to ignore certain fundamental physical aspects of its products; these include size, material, texture, and so on. In good architecture, matter effectively supports the symbolism embodied in buildings; in the case of Egypt, for instance, imperishability was convincingly substantiated with granite. But this was not always the case. Often the total submission of sensory experience to prefabricated ideologies was demanded through the authority of symbols. Architecture had its share of responsibility in such attempts, as in the case of church domes three meters in diameter, in which worshippers had to recognize the heavens.

Renaissance architecture built on the mentality of seeking hidden meanings in things. With a far less mystical approach than that of the Middle Ages, it created a completely new system of signs and symbols that could be applied to buildings. It was a comprehensive language understood by scholars and by the members of at least the upper classes, which remained in use for nearly 400 years (until Romanticism and Classicism took hold in the late eighteenth and early nineteenth centuries, and in some cases even later). Language means standardization in the transmission of meanings, and has the great advantage of not leaving much room for mis-interpretations and runaway imagination.

The Greco-Roman columns replaced, among others, the tall, slender medieval towers as symbols of prestige and authority. The hierarchy of the architectural orders was established on the basis of the placement of the columns in the Colosseum of Rome—a building revered through the ages. Its lower band is adorned with Dorian half columns, the band above with Ionian, the next with Corinthian, and the last with composite pilasters. Consequently, during the Renaissance, the Tuscan order was considered inferior compared to the Dorian, and it in turn inferior to the Ionian. The Corinthian was held in higher esteem and the composite one was on the top. The "lesser" orders symbolized nature and wildness and were placed at the building's lower tier or base, which was often constructed by roughly dressed stones—the so-called *ordine rustica*. The "higher" orders symbolized culture and civility and were used on the upper floors in the order mentioned above. Artificial caves with allegorical figures adorned the gardens. An especially detailed iconology—pairing images to meanings—was developed based on mythology, ancient history, and the Bible. In a way, it was an extension of the more advanced one used in painting and sculpture.

**Palazzo Rucellai, Florence, Leon Battista Alberti, 1446; drawing Lübke&Semrau, *Grundriß der Kunstgeschichte*, 1908**

This system of signs and symbols would have been excessively constraining if there was no distinction between those features of the building that gave it appropriate character, and those that gave it variety and grace—*decorum* and *ornamentum*, respectively. The modern observer might be slightly confused because the same architectural elements—columns, pediments, moldings—could either be perceived as parts of decorum or ornamentum.

Decorum's fundamental principle was that buildings should correspond, in terms of layout, size and wealth of decoration, to the purpose of the building and to the social position (and to some extent to the financial background) of its owner. The Tuscan and Dorian orders professed robustness and raw power and were regularly used in rural buildings—and in banks, which later gained their own independent roof. The Corinthian order gave magnificence; it was the Roman order par excellence and thus its use was not "allowed" in auxiliary buildings, such as warehouses and workshops. The first floor of mansions had to have the largest ceiling height and be the most decorated since the owners lived mainly there: it was regarded as the most privileged even in late nineteenth- and early twentieth-century apartment buildings until the popularization of the elevator and privately owned vehicles. It was the *piano nobile*; the servants lived in the attics. The corner stones had to be dressed more smoothly as one climbed from floor to floor, since this was the world order: the triumph of man—the crown jewel of the creation in Christian faith—over wild nature had to be heralded. The products of civilization were considered superior to naturally grown things; *opera di mano* had precedence over *opera di natura*—a belief that remained steadfast in the West until Romanticism. Furthermore, the building as a whole had to be distinguished for its order and balance.

Ornamentum allowed much more freedom, which architects and building proprietors rushed to exploit. The diversity of Renaissance private mansions built in Florence and Rome in a few decades is impressive; they include the Palazzi Pitti, Rucellai, Medici-Riccardi, Strozzi in Florence, and della Canceleria, Farnese, Madama in Rome. Although each of them has a more or less cubic shape with a central arcaded courtyard, the elaboration of their exterior surfaces makes each absolutely unique.

The almost unlimited possibilities of expressing creativity and imagination allowed by ornamentum soon led to experimentations with the norms imposed by decorum. The ruler of Mantua, Federico II Gonzaga, commissioned Giulio Romano in 1524 to design a summer mansion immediately outside the city walls. The Palazzo del Te, as it became known, is a typical *villa suburbana* of the period, aside from some deliberate deviations from the established rules which make it almost sacrilegious. In the courtyard's wall, a triglyph of the Dorian frieze seems to have slipped from its place and slid down; a rusticated stone block is situated between smooth blocks; a window stands where it should not be (directly under the slipped triglyph); a keystone of an arch is disproportionally large in relation to the

**Palazzo dei Conservatori, Rome, Michelangelo, 1536**

pediment gracing the opening, etc. The paintings that adorn the rooms of the villa, a necessary complement of architecture at that time, were equally "transgressive."

The so-called Mannerism, where personal "manner" or personal style played a dominant role in the shaping of the buildings, sought its "official" recognition. In 1536, Michelangelo designed the front of the Palazzo dei Conservatori in the Piazza del Campidoglio in Rome, so that "colossal" Corinthian pilasters (extending from the ground to the top of the building) were placed exactly next to the much smaller Ionian columns adorning the ground floor loggia and the windows of the first floor. This layout created a dynamic whole with great inner tension threatening its balance: the pilasters were 2.5 and 3.3 times larger in height than the columns of the ground floor and the first floor respectively, corresponding to sixteen and thirty-three times larger volume respectively. Without fanfare, Michelangelo was testing the boundaries of the rules—the reign of balanced proportions and symmetry—not in a private villa, but in the most formal building complex of Renaissance Rome.

Yet the architects and painters of Late Renaissance were not the only ones who claimed the right to write and rewrite the rules. Critics wanted to have their share as well, defining the ways audiences perceived art—first and foremost, through the use of the term *rinascita* (Renaissance). It was Giorgo Vasari, painter, architect, and writer of *Lives of the Most Eminent Painters, Sculptors and Architects*—a book published in 1550 and the first treatise of history of art in the West after antiquity—who popularized the term, which had been already used on various occasions. In the margin of his personal copy of the second edition (published in 1568) of *Lives*, El Greco noted in a way revealing simultaneously anger and admiration: "the critics are those who do and undo things and thus from this point of view the various judgments of Vasari are true."[3] Already around 1600, a leading artist acknowledged that the audience had the need for mediation in order to appreciate art, and this mediation was equally an integral part of art, as were the works of art themselves.

An audience trained to accept the unexpected, open to new interpretations and views that were set to constantly overturn its certainties—the creation of this intellectual environment was perhaps the most important contribution of Renaissance to architecture and art. It was an environment that nurtured the radical changes that occurred in the centuries that followed.

**Notes**

1　Koolhaas, Rem: *Content*. Taschen 2004, 118.
2　Alberti, Leon Battista: *De Re Aedificatoria* 6.2.
3　Marias, Fernando: *El Greco y el arte de su tempo; las notas de El Greco a Vasari*. Real Fundación de Toledo 2001, 53.

**Selected Bibliography**

Burckhardt, Jacob: *The Civilization of the Renaissance in Italy*. Penguin 1990 (1860).
Burke, Peter: *A Social History of Knowledge: From Gutenberg to Diderot*. Polity Press 2000.
Hohenberg, Paul/Lees, Lynn: *The Making of Urban Europe, 1000–1994*. Harvard University Press 1995.
King, Ross: *Brunelleschi's Dome*. Penguin 2000.
Panofsky, Erwin: *Meaning in the Visual Arts: Papers in and on Art History*. Doubleday1955.
Wittkower, Rudolf: *Architectural Principles in the Age of Humanism*. Norton 1971 (1949).

# LESS IS MORE

## The Rock Garden of
## Ryōan-ji Temple
## in Kyoto

According to a legend recounted by Livy and Plutarch,[1] Romulus, while founding the city bearing his name, marked in the ground with a plough a trench forming a large square. There the walls of *Roma quadrata* would be built. The trench was interrupted in few places: these were the "gates" that allowed one to enter the city. When his twin brother Remus, in an act of defiance, leaped across the trench, he was slain by his brother. Architects may find this version of Rome's foundation legend interesting in that it touches one of the most difficult issues they face when designing: to assess whether the material means they use to transfer to reality their ideas are appropriate for the occasion. According to the legend, a city founded on logic (its square shape), laws (the common agreement to respect the statutory provisions), and power (its impregnable walls) had its limits substantiated through a simple mark on the earth. Two centuries later, two to three small buildings and seventy-centimeter-tall signs defined the boundaries of the Athenian Agora. After another 500 years, imposing porticoes and temples defined the boundaries of the Imperial Fora of Rome.

Are two steps enough to mark out a distinct area in our living room or does it has to be five? Maybe five are too many? On the other hand, are five steps sufficient to mark out a separate area in the Défense Plaza, which is 400 meters long and 120 meters wide, surrounded by skyscrapers? Maybe the 0.3-millimeter-thick lines used to draft the steps on paper or the intense shading in their photorealistic rendering are misleading? Is an eighty-meter-thick wall necessary, as in the Palazzo Pitti in Florence, to separate one room from another? Or is a modern eight-centimeter-thick soundproof wall sufficient? Or maybe a wall made of rice paper as in six-teenth-century Kyoto?

In modern Japan, rice paper walls are also not uncommon. We may admire this graceful architecture, however, it is the observance of strict cohabitation rules that allows people living in such houses to be happy

Scene in *Murasaki Shikibu Nikki* Emaki, Fujiwara Nobuzane (attributed), thirteenth century; Fujita Art Museum

with them. Foremost, however, it is the commitment of each person to any activity whatsoever, that helps remove the disadvantages of the minimal sound insulation and visual isolation that rice paper offers.

The dissemination of Zen, a branch of Buddhism that emphasizes meditation in the pursuit of enlightenment, enhanced the traditionally strong commitment of Japanese people to their occupation. The strictest Zen school, Rinzai Zen (which was founded by the Chinese monk Linji Yixuan during the Tang Dynasty), was successfully introduced into the country in the thirteenth century; slowly but steadily it was emancipated from Chinese suzerainty. The upper class preferred it to Sōtō Zen, whose mild and almost rustic spirit was considered better suited to rural populations. Although supported by the emperor and the merchants, Rinzai Zen owned its substantial influence to its adoption by the rising samurai military class, since it was fully in line with their attitude toward life; eventually it proved instrumental in further shaping their mentality.

Zen reinforced existing mindsets and coated them with the prestige of an integrated and comprehensive worldview. For members of nobility, the boundaries between daily life and art became vague—something that Western art attempted to achieve after 1960. Every activity became art, and each art was an activity whose ultimate goal was anything other than constructing a useful or aesthetically pleasing object. Proper art was an art without practical purpose, an art that, in theory, did not even aim at what Kant would classify as pure aesthetic enjoyment. Its ultimate aim had to be the contact of the person who exercised it with the alleged ultimate reality. Art, such as flower arrangement and calligraphy, required years of intensive apprenticeship followed by a continuous attempt at personal perfection. Although it was extremely difficult to master technical knowledge, this was not enough. One had to transcend it so that art could become "artless," growing effortlessly from the unconscious. In art such as writing short haiku poems, this spirit could be expressed with the greatest clarity; in art such as archery and swordsmanship, however, the collateral benefits from constant exercise—even if this aimed at overcoming the practical purpose (hitting the target with the arrow or defeating the opponent in swordsmanship)—were not negligible and very few refused them.

Zen was disseminated in a period when arts and crafts were blooming, and it probably contributed to their further sophistication. In the fifteenth century, the country was at the forefront of technology; a particularly impressive feat if one considers that the most basic invention, the cultivation of rice, was introduced only in the third century BCE from neighboring China—a country from which a variety of things, methods, and ideas adopted by the country of the rising sun originated. During the period Europe that experienced its Renaissance, Japan produced and exported a multitude of high quality products. Among them were numerous kinds of paper products made for a variety of purposes—even for disposable tissues, useful items that the Americans reinvented 300 years later. Japan's iron and steel were better than the England's, which were Europe's finest; its copper was cheaper than the Sweden's, even after its transportation from Nagasaki to Amsterdam with sailboats. Japanese swords were high-tech weapons and sought after in East Asia. Their blades were relatively small in comparison to those of European swords. They were, however, of such a good quality that could cut through armor "easily as a sharp knife cuts a tender rump,"[2] according to the testimony of a Jesuit monk during his visit to a Buddhist monastery, which was home to a militant order, similar to those in the West, such as the Knights Templar. The blade of the Japanese sword was about seventy centimeters in length and five centimeters wide, and consisted of approximately four million layers of forged and reforged steel—very hard in the edge and rather soft in the rest of the blade so that it would not be brittle like glass, nor blunt like its European counterparts of the same era. The devil is in the detail, and in the case of Japanese craftsmen, this is absolutely true: the good devil of craftsmanship, no doubt.

One of the most cherished activities of the nobility of Muromachi period (1338–1573) was the tea ceremony, which by then had become a status symbol. New preferences emerged, which were inspired by the reputedly pure past. Similar to Europe at the era of Romanticism, in sixteenth- and seventeenth-century Japan, the rural life's simplicity did not only have bad connotations. Thus, the tea ceremony was performed in simple, plain pavilions of relatively small dimensions. In these, both the host and the guests followed a strictly defined ritual precisely specifying their movements, positions, and the procedure of preparing and serving the tea. Many of these pavilions were designed by the tea masters themselves: it was not unusual for users to design the buildings they used before architects gained legally reserved professional rights.

The tea ceremony itself, as well as the pavilions housing it, represented a new aesthetic: the ideals of *wabi*—honesty and understatement—transferred in architecture. At a time when building at the imposing

Great Wall peaked in China, the *shoin* halls with tatami covered floors, suspended ceilings, and sliding doors became popular with the ruling class in Japan. Apart from metaphysics, the occasionally limited financial capabilities of some members of the nobility possibly encouraged their success, as we can infer from the later princely palace of Katsura. The first buildings of the complex—constructed at the beginning of the seventeenth century during a period when its owner's income was very limited—are more modest (and, arguably, more compatible to the wabi ideals) than the buildings constructed when the income of the heirs of the original owner had increased significantly.

Restraint in the usage of material means to accomplish the desired goal was rooted in Japanese mentality from earlier times and was likely derived from the profound conviction of unity between humanity and nature. Applied to all kinds of activities—from martial arts (where the body was the only weapon) to the samurai swords—it strongly influenced architecture, which utilized matter differently than in the West.

To begin with, the main building material of monumental Japanese architecture was wood; Western monumental architecture used primarily stone. Wood is a naturally renewable material, if logging activity is conducted prudently, and it continues to change even after it becomes a beam, column, or floor. The structural integrity of wooden buildings was often due to relatively thin linear elements intertwined in three dimensions; that of the stone buildings was due to mass. The boundary between inside and outside was not very strict in the former, since the timber frame of buildings allowed the extension of the floor toward the garden or the

**Main building, Ryōan-ji temple, Kyoto, initial form circa 1500**

large protrusion of the roofs over the grass; in the latter, the dividing line between inside and outside was clearly defined and this has contributed to creating the habit of us Westerners seeing—as the saying goes—our houses as our castles.

Generally speaking, Japanese architecture from the mid Hein period—i.e., from about the tenth century on—shows preference to group ensembles in which there is no single dominant element. In palaces, villas, and temples, the individual halls were not incorporated into a large building, nor were they placed—except in some early Buddhist temples—in axial succession. Each of these constituted a more or less distinct unit, a detached building that communicated with the rest with narrow corridors. Characteristically, the various halls comprising Nijo Castle (the shogun's quarters, the audience halls, etc.) did not differ significantly in size, nor did any of them have a particularly prominent position that eclipsed the others. Access to the more formal quarters of the castle was conducted via a series of rooms that were not one behind the other in an obvious hierarchical succession. In contrast, Western architecture preferred a central dominant. Indeed, from Hellenistic times to Modernism, with the probable exception of the early Middle Ages and Byzantium, this was often placed on the central axis of symmetry of the composition that was strictly hierarchical; Augustus' Forum in Rome or the Palace of Versailles are typical examples. Moreover, in Japan even the most formal buildings rarely exceed the surrounding trees in height. In the West, tall vegetation was generally kept far from buildings.

In Japanese architecture, rooms were often not dedicated to one function only; and their identity was not defined—especially in urban environments—by heavy furniture as was common in the West. The pillows on which the house residents sat and the mattresses on which they slept were folded and stored in closets leaving the rooms almost empty, ready for every use. The place where the host and the guests ought to sit and the access from the point defined by tradition determined the form and the layout of rooms and building complexes—not elementary geometry. As a result, buildings did not base their identity on accumulation of matter ordered in ostentatiously invented shapes immobile in time; and they did not underscore emphatically the contrast between man-made and nature. Instead, constructed to accommodate their residents' needs with less, they blended successfully with their environment both in terms of immediate visual perception, as well as on a second level in which the perceived is subjected to further cognitive processing.

The architecture using limited material means—an architecture that has built its identity on the use of limited material means—gained prominence during the Muromachi period, because it complied fully with the requirements of the Japanese nobility for elegance. In the beginning of the seventeenth century—i.e., immediately after the end of the Muromachi period—Japan entered a period of extreme seclusion from the rest of the world, sealing its borders and excluding any influence and any stimulus from abroad. Nijo Castle in Kyoto was built then. It may have been decorated with golden leaves and elaborate woodcarvings, but the clarity of its lines and the lightness of its structural elements were entirely in the spirit of tea pavilions and the elegant shoin halls. Furthermore, apart from its double walls with moats aimed at stopping organized armies (a few years later, in the sixteen-twenties, the fortification wall of the Osaka castle was built with huge interlocking granite boulders), it was also equipped with a safety measure that was invisible to the naked eye, in contrast to measures customary in other cultural environments, such as heavy doors guarded by armed soldiers: the floors were designed to make chirping noises when walked upon. Various techniques were used to achieve the effect—which assured that no one could sneak through the corridors undetected—the most efficient of which probably being nails fastened to the wooden boards rubbing against jackets or clamps.

The mentality of using as little material as possible in order to achieve the given objective was manifested in garden architecture, an art already popular and widespread in Japan at a time when practically the only gardens that existed in Europe were those in monasteries, which were planted with herbs useful in medicine and cuisine, as well as some rose gardens. The *Sakuteiki* manual was written in the eleventh century, and its illustrated version was published in the fifteenth century by the gardener-priest Hōin Shingen. Another manual was written in the twelfth century. Both were mystic texts considering the art of gardening as the quintessence of man's metaphysical relationship to nature. The distillation of long and careful observation of natural landscapes aimed at helping choose materials, shapes, and textures that would capture and recreate the essence of nature with the fewest means possible, thereby creating a buffer zone between the building and its environment.

In Japanese tradition, each place had its spirit, which was symbolized by a rock. As time passed by, more symbolism was added, derived from Buddhism and geomancy. Searching for rocks with suitable shapes to take over this complex symbolic load was a very serious affair. Already since the Sakuteiki period—i.e., 1,000 years ago—placing these rocks was the founding act of gardening, the art par excellence allowing the coupling of humans and their artifacts with nature. Zen's influence and the abstraction that it advocated only increased the importance of rocks in Japanese gardening, in some cases excluding all other materials.

Prominent among rock gardens is the one situated in front of the main hall of the Ryōan-ji temple in Kyoto, constructed just before 1500. The ten-by-thirty-meter garden we see today is the one that master Akisato (Shoseki) Rito rebuilt after the great fire of 1797. It is made up of fifteen rocks arranged in five groups on a carpet of course feldspar gravel; there are no trees at all (as far as we know, no other garden in medieval Japan is fully lacking vegetation, which clearly suggests a dating of today's Ryōan-ji rock garden at around 1800, a period when this would not be a rarity).

Although the garden's general layout is extremely simple, it creates great visual interest—according to testimonies, this was also achieved in the original garden, which was evidently not that different from the current version (except that the original garden had a raised corridor running across it). The carefully selected rocks have a size that allows them neither to dominate over the gravel, nor to be lost in it; and they are positioned in a way that from every view point all but one are visible—the monks liked to say that one can see all of them at once when one reaches enlightenment. The shape of each group is somewhat similar to the shape of each one of the rocks comprising it; the impression emerges of one organizing principle permeating the multiple scales of the composition: the fractal principle. The median axes between the groups of rocks (the lines running at an equal distance from them considered in pairs) join like the branches of a tree whose trunk passes almost from the center of the monastery's main hall; the impression created is that of a strictly structured and balanced, although not symmetrical, entity. The texture of the materials used is especially rich: the gravel contains sand as well as pebbles of varying sizes and raking does not allow the formation of a uniform and isotropic surface without differentiations. The walls are made of clay mixed with oil and straw, while moss and lichens add green and gray shades.

As with classical Japanese painting, all of the elements comprising the garden are visible and comprehensible at first glance. This means that they are presented in a way that our mind identifies them with minimal

**Rock garden, Ryōan-ji temple, Kyoto, initial form circa 1500, current form after 1797**

**Enjō-ji garden, Nara, from the twelfth century**

mental reconstruction of the missing visual details—something that also happens, for instance, when we see a horse from the side or a person en face. In this instantly familiar environment, the gaze is drawn by the harmony of shapes, attracted by the clarity of the visual organization and the variety of the texture of the materials. The eye wanders through this visually balanced composition, which is so complex as not to be boring and so simple as not to seduce our senses. The mind travels: in several texts, some of which are from the time before the great fire, the garden is described as tiger cubs crossing a sea.[3]

On the other hand, however, the Ryōan-ji rock garden, immovable in time, lost something crucial: the appeal resulting from the day by day changes as seasons succeed each other, excellently highlighted in other Japanese gardens. In a cultural environment appreciating meditation and poetry through the ages, the yearly circle of nature was a source of inspiration and admiration. A rock garden without other vegetation, except moss growing beneath the rocks, could not offer this experience. This may be why it was forgotten at times, before coming back to the limelight in the twentieth century (initially in the nineteen-twenties and thirties, and then after the Second World War) with the increasing interest in Zen in the West, and, eventually, in Japan itself.

But the fact is that the Ryōan-ji rock garden utilizes the minimum material—raw rocks of varying sizes and shapes—in an amazing way. With an extremely organized and balanced composition, an environment is created that is simultaneously familiar and challenging to the mind. An environment where visual complexity corresponds, even today, to the perceptual capabilities of the observer, enabling him/her to meditate, neither overburdening him/her with the richness of images, nor causing boredom or frustration. It is probably no exaggeration to say that the

Ryōan-ji garden in the present, but also possibly in its original form, as well as the entire complex in which it is integrated, visualize with the best way possible what Mies van der Rohe summarized later with the phrase "less is more"[4]; an architectural maxim accomplished only few times in history.

**Notes**
1  Titus Livius: *Urb.* I.1.7; Plutarch: *Rom.* 10.
2  Perrin, Noel: *Giving up the gun, Japan's reversion to the sword 1543-1879.* David R. Godine 1979, 11.
3  Kuitert, Wybe: *Themes in the History of Japanese Garden Art.* University of Hawai'i Press 2002, 101.
4  Mies van der Rohe, Ludwig: "On restraint in design." In: *New York Herald Tribune*, 28 June 1959.

**Selected Bibliography**
Coaldrake, William H.: *Architecture and Authority in Japan (Nissan Institute/Routledge Japanese Studies Series).* Routledge 1996.
Locher, Mira: *Traditional Japanese Architecture: An Exploration of Elements and Forms.* Tuttle 2010.
Suzuki, D.T.: foreword to Eugen Herrigel: *Zen in the Art of Archery.* Vintage 1981 (1953).
Takei, Jiro/Keane, Marc P.: *Sakuteiki Visions of the Japanese Garden: A Modern Translation of Japan's Gardening Classic.* Tuttle 2001.
van Tonder, Gert J.: "Less is More or Less More: Visual Minimalism in Japanese Dry Rock Gardens." In: *South African Journal of Art History*, 22 (3), 208 ff.
Yamada Shoji: *Shots in the Dark: Japan, Zen, and the West.* The University of Chicago Press 2009.

# THE BUILDING AND ITS SURROUNDINGS

## The Villa Rotonda

According to Massimo Montanari, an expert on culinary history: "… spices, which for a millennium had distinguished the cuisine of the rich and had been desired perhaps above all other things, slowly began to disappear from culinary use, just at the moment when their abundance would have allowed more widespread use (as in fact for a period it did). The procurement of the spices directly from their sources in order to supply this demand had been among the goals of the globe-circling voyages of exploration and conquest. But the inundation of aromas and flavors that assaulted sixteenth-century Europe quickly brought fatigue. When saffron, cinnamon, and 'fine spices' came within the reach of everyone, the wealthy looked elsewhere for signs of distinction. Preferences even turned to indigenous and (in some respects) "peasant" products: in the seventeenth, century the French elites gave up spices and replaced them with chives, shallots, mushrooms, capers, anchovies and the like, more delicate flavors and certainly better suited to the richer cuisine then coming to fashion. Another element was the satisfaction experienced by those who from the lofty height of their wealth could allow themselves to enjoy even 'poor' foods, a sentiment which today is fortunately widespread."[1]

The world of the rich has always been miles away from that of the poor, in both urban and rural areas. What is interesting though from the history of architecture's point of view is how this social and economic gap between the privileged and the non-privileged has materialized. On many occasions, boundaries have been literally impenetrable: the residence of a ruler within a walled city was often protected by a second wall. In other instances, boundaries were not physical, but symbolic, and yet just as impenetrable—dictated, for instance, by the seating etiquette in a church or a parade. Quite often, the rich chose to distance themselves from commoners by adopting a clearly distinct aesthetic taste. In medieval European societies, the figurative distance between the "haves" and the "have-nots" became a reality; the wealthy few literally contrived a way to keep their distance from the masses and the environment in which they lived. "Our Princes and Signori, in order to separate themselves from the great noise of the crowd, make beautiful Villas [i.e., country houses] in their Villas [i.e., farms] … which are near or far from the Cities, whichever pleases their Excellencies,"[2] wrote Anton Francesco Doni in his book *Le ville del Doni*, published in Bologna in 1566.

Since the spatial segregation between higher and lower classes was hardly achievable in the city, the advantages of moving to the countryside, at least for some months of the year, were not only ideological or aesthetic but also practical. That the popular sport of hunting could not be practiced easily if one lived in a city was only one reason. City air reeked of mold, urine, and animals, and the chances of catching a disease were significantly higher than in the countryside. "The benefits [of living in the countryside] are so rewarding that I stay there joyfully and willingly. And first of all because of the air, the chief sustainer of our existence, which in those places I find purer and much superior and more beneficial to my complexion than that of Ferrara, which is … filled with malignant vapors,"[3] wrote another author around about the same time as Doni. If one was not unremittingly undernourished, as was often the case among the rural population, the living conditions in the countryside were clearly much better than those in the city; the rich of Florence took to their countryside houses, when the outbreak of plague reached their city in 1348, killing two-thirds of its citizens.

Throughout the world, moving away from the cities was of course a practice that dated back much earlier than the period in question, and to escape from the masses was clearly not its only motive.

In Classical Greece, the basic distinction people made in perceiving their surroundings was between cultivated and uncultivated land: fields and vineyards and the homesteads of the people who tended them, on the one hand; forests and untamed nature, on the other. It was hundreds of years later that the perception of the environment shifted toward the distinction between the city and the countryside—a shift that can be largely attributed to the repercussions of living in densely populated cities.

With the establishment of peace under the Roman rule, life in the countryside—at least for a considerable minority—definitely became a source of joy, rather than a constant struggle for survival in a hostile milieu, in a domain of irrational and menacing powers that had to be subdued. In an excerpt from the ninth book of his *De Re Aedificatoria*, which deals with private buildings in the countryside, Alberti cites Martialis: "we receive joy from the simplest everyday activities, such as eating, singing, taking a bath, or reading."[4]

The affinity of Roman elite for life in the countryside is also reflected vividly in Cicero's writings, especially his letters to Atticus. The desire of this prominent scholar to retreat to his villa in Tusculum away from the noise of the city had a strong moral dimension: the city was a place for conventions and compromises, challenges and distractions, whereas the countryside was the domain of purity and clarity, reflection and deliberation. Farming the land was an honest business that connected its owner to the finest traditions of the nation. Both Columella and Cato assigned great importance to the efficient operation of estates in a spirit similar to that described by Max Weber in his studies on Protestantism. Recreation recovered its full meaning: the real rejuvenation of body and soul in peace and tranquility.

Roman villas did actually not blend in with their natural surroundings, unlike those in the Far East of later times. While usually built in areas of exquisite beauty, such as the coasts around Naples, they had relatively few openings on their external walls, since most rooms looked onto the inner courtyards or peristyles. And yet, their function was not to protect their inhabitants; if indeed something demonstrated the power of their tenants, this was not crenellations, but marble statues and well-tended gardens.

Villa Medici, Cafaggiolo, remodeling of a fourteenth-century structure by Michelozzo, 1452



Things changed radically in Europe with the collapse of Roman Empire. When the medieval cities emerged, they became the place of disengagement from coercions associated with life in the countryside. By the thirteenth century, however, they had evolved into extremely densely populated urban centers, and it was only natural that city dwellers eventually discovered the joy of escaping to the countryside. The most famous among them was Petrarch, who on April 26, 1335 climbed Mont Ventoux, a steep mountain in the Alps where fierce winds blow incessantly.[5] Notably, the sole purpose of this climb was the opportunity it offered to admire the view, which the poet described meticulously in his notes. To the people who worked the land, such a lack of a practical productive purpose in a laborious activity was rather unfamiliar; this is what firmly separated Petrarch, the city dweller, from the peasants he met on his way. Back then, being able to enjoy the beauty and splendor of the landscape without being bothered by the daily nuisances of life in the countryside was a privilege reserved mainly for those who had secured their livelihoods—an oddity for rural areas organized into strictly segregated social classes and with low productivity.

But this was an era of transition in central and northern Italy. Early in the Middle Ages, the nobility—i.e., the aristocrats who owned land—were based in towers built on vantage points from where they could control their estates. Nonetheless, cities had gradually grown to the point that the nobility could not afford to ignore them; several powerful families chose to build impressive palazzi. On the other hand, the absolute control feudal lords kept over land loosened. Freed of their obligations, many serfs now owned the fields they farmed. Agriculture is unpredictable, though, and the income it generates is subjected to considerable fluctuations. In addition, the nobility often retained the exclusive right to exploit forests, a major source of food and wealth. As a result, some of these farmers were forced to seek financial help from city dwellers who had accumulated capital. Quite a few of the latter eventually invested in land; in exchange, they were entitled to a part of the harvest, a shield against recurrent food shortages at a time when the demand for agricultural products had multiplied. Then, the wealthiest bourgeois would buy land off of them creating large estates. This gradually changed the landscape around cities. Already early in the first half of the fourteenth century, the hills around Florence were dotted with country houses, similar to Terraferma around Venice a little later.

Initially, these country houses were in the style of the country towers that belonged to the nobility. By the mid-fifteenth century, however, this kind of fortified residence was no longer adequate—neither for the actual security conditions, nor for the political and military structure of the time. Attacks by armed groups had now disappeared and defense against organized military forces possessing artillery was largely unfeasible. But the newcomers as well as the old feudal aristocracy were generally reluctant to adapt their houses to constantly evolving preferences; the older their ancestral homes looked, the more they added to their own prestige. Typical of this mentality is the country house of the Medici family in Cafaggiolo, where the most prominent ruler of Florence, Lorenzo the Magnificent, spent a good part of his youth. The castle turned villa, remodeled in the mid-fifteenth century, had high walls, small windows, crenellations, and heavy doors. Rather cloistered, it was built around a courtyard and allowed limited access to the garden from indoors.

In Roman antiquity, country life was to some extent associated with eudemonism; this aspect had been marginalized in the Western cultural environment of the Middle Ages, not least on account of Christianity's distrust of pleasurable experiences. With Renaissance humanism, eudemonism of country life—which was evident as early as Petrarch's time—reemerged never to subside again; not even in the era of Romanticism toward the end of the eighteenth century, when melancholy replaced happiness as the emotion people ought to feel when finding themselves in nature. Acknowledging the aesthetic quality of nature was probably the most important intellectual step toward discarding the medieval model of a country house.

**Villa Medici, Fiesole, outskirts of Florence, Michelozzo, 1451**

Unambiguous signs that something was changing are traced in the Medici Villa in Fiesole, built by the architect Michelozzo in 1455. Perched on a hillside and offering gracious views, the villa was a simple, square edifice with no hint of fortification or crenellations—a luxurious version of the unpretentious rural house.

The Medici family also owned a villa in Poggio a Caiano, commissioned to architect Giuliano da Sangallo by Lorenzo the Magnificent toward the end of the fifteenth century. This was a striking, symmetrical structure with a colonnaded entrance built on a raised platform. The new era had arrived with pomp. A new architectural type had been born.

The quintessence, though, of the *villa suburbana* is the Villa Rotonda, designed in 1565 to be the home of a church dignitary who had returned to his hometown of Vicenza having retired from the Vatican. Its architect was Andrea Palladio, rightly considered the most successful designer of suburban villas in post-medieval Europe and one of the most influential figures in Western architecture altogether; his villas—he built several in Veneto—later fired the imagination of both architects and their clients, in countries such as Great Britain and the United States in the following centuries. Palladio, a former stonemason, is also well known as the author of the architectural treatise *I Quattro Libri dell' Architettura*. As the title suggests, the book was written not in Latin but in Italian, the vernacular language of his homeland, probably for marketing and advertising reasons; large parts of it are devoted to the presentation of his own designs.

**Villa Medici, Poggio a Caiano, Tuscany, Guilliano da Sangallo, 1485**

Symmetrical along two axes, the Villa Rotonda features four identical façades, each with a portico or projecting porch in the shape of an Ionic temple front. Four stairways—one on each side of the building—lead up to the principal floor, the *piano nobile*, which is raised above the ground. The ground plan of the building is formed by a square with an inscribed circular hall. The hall is covered by a dome inspired by the Pantheon in Rome, and is adorned with frescoes. It is a grand design resulting from the composition of a handful of architectural elements; such a visually and symbolically rich outcome achieved with such restricted means ensured that the Rotonda survived as a model structure in the coming centuries.

The villa stands at the top of a small, gently sloped hill and it almost invites people to visit it: the steps leading up to the piano nobile take up half the width of the façade, which was quite original at the time. Devoid of any signs of defense or introversion, it creates the impression that it stands unreservedly open to its surroundings amidst a friendly nature. Because the villa was near the city, Palladio included its plans in the chapter of his treatise on urban mansions. However, he made a point to describe its natural setting in the most poetic terms: "The site is as pleasant and delightful as can be found, because it is on a small hill of very easy access, and is watered on one side by the Bacchiglione, a navigable river; and on the other it is surrounded by most pleasant risings, which look like a great theater, and are all cultivated with the most excellent fruits and the most exquisite vines; and therefore because it enjoys from every part the most beautiful views, some of which are limited, some more extended, and others that terminate with the horizon, there are loggias made on all four fronts."[6]

The Villa Rotonda is an expressive structure unintimidated by the (more or less tamed) nature around it; one cannot fail to detect the whiff of superiority this man-made structure emanates. This was a quite groundbreaking idea, but at that time Venice was not shy of novelties: for instance, in view of the upcoming battle with the Ottoman fleet, which eventually took place in Lepanto in 1571, the Venetians decided to mount large canons on the sterns of their battleships, vastly increasing their firepower, even if this meant that they had to remove their rams—i.e. their primary offensive weapons until that time—to balance the extra weight.

While open to its natural surroundings, the Villa Rotonda highlighted the distance separating its resident from the people crowding the city and the peasants farming the land. In addition to elevating the house above the ground and giving it grand entrances to establish the owner's prominence, Palladio unreservedly used porticoes with columns, architraves and pediments, domes and frescoes depicting scenes from

**Villa Capra or Rotonda, Vicenza, Andrea Palladio, 1585**

**Vaux-le-Vicomte estate, Maincy, France, Louis le Vau, André le Nôtre, and Charles Le Brun, 1657; engraving by Nicolas de Poilly**

mythology. Thus, he made available architectural features, which were reserved originally in the antiquity for temples and for the most official public buildings, to individual members of the upper classes, rather than the community as a body, as Alberti had done in Sant' Andrea. Gradually, Roman-style love for the productive land subsided, and aesthetics and hedonism fully dominated the field.

The direction that the life of the privileged few was taking in the countryside is visualized most clearly in absolutist seventeenth-century France. Nicolas Fouquet, the Superintendent of Finances for the young Louis XIV, commissioned in 1657 architect Louis le Vau, landscape architect André le Nôtre, and painter Charles Le Brun—the team that later made Versailles into what we see today—to rebuild a small chateau he had recently purchased. In Vaux-le-Vicomte, a palace situated about forty kilometers outside Paris, human sovereignty is not restricted to stone but extends to soil, water, and green. Its gardens stretch over three kilometers in length completely subduing nature. There are no vineyards and fields around the building, but geometric gardens, artificial ponds, promenades, and courtyards where the nobility and their escorts could pleasantly pass their time.

The balance achieved by Palladio between artifact and surrounding nature was lost in the grand baroque complexes. It was meant to resurface in another form in eighteenth-century Britain—most notably in Chiswick House. When William Kent refurbished the estate's gardens in 1733, he applied some ideas that can be readily described as revolutionary in the cultural environment at the time. Geometry was not the dominant principle. The lawn unfolded gently and sloped down to the river; views were organized so that not everything was visible at first glance, leaving room

**The gardens at Chiswick House, London, William Kent, 1733**

for imagination and expectation to grow. The building at the heart of this idealized version of nature was the epitome of Palladianism—the architecture movement that adored Palladio. It was designed by Lord Burlington, who knowingly wanted to revive the Roman tradition of countryside villas and who turned to the Renaissance architect for guidance.

Like the farms around Cicero's villa, the land around the Rotonda, and the flowerbeds of the Vaux-le-Vicomte estate, the lawns of Chiswick House were tended by dozens of workers who lived with their families nearby. Distancing oneself from the masses did not mean denying their services or straying from collective achievements.

### Notes
1 Montanari, Massimo: *The Culture of Food.* Blackwell 1994, 119.
2 Quoted in: Ackerman, James: *The Villa.* Thames & Hudson 1995, 109.
3 Lollio, Alberto: *Lettera nella quale rispondendo ad una di m.
Hercole Perinato, egli celebra la villa, et lauda molto l'agricoltura.*
G. Giolito1544, fol. IX v; transl. James Ackerman.
4 Alberti, Leon Battista: *De Re Aedificatoria* 9.2.
5 Petrarch: *Epistolae familiares* IV.1.
6 Palladio, Andrea: *I Quattro Libri dell'Architettura.* D. de'
Franceschi 1570, II.3. Transl. Isaac Ware (1738).

### Selected Bibliography
Ackerman, James: *The Villa.* Thames & Hudson 1990.
Ayres, Philip: *Classical Culture and the Idea of Rome in Eighteenth-Century England.* Cambridge University Press 1997.
Frossmann, Erik: *Dorisch, Ionisch, Korinthisch.* Almquist & Wiksells 1961.
Lapi Bini, Isabella: *Le ville medicee. Guida Completa.* Giunti 2003.
Puppi, Lionello: *Andrea Palladio.* Electa 2006.
Nauert, Charles G. Jr.: *Humanism and the Culture of
Renaissance Europe.* Cambridge University Press 2006.

# THE USEFULNESS OF EDIFICES

## The Great Wall of China

Utilitarian edifices have always been important architectural objects, although rarely did they have the prestige of monumental buildings such as churches or palaces. We can define as utilitarian those edifices whose function completely overshadows aesthetic considerations; edifices judged mainly on how well they serve the purpose for which they were built, at least at the time of construction. Thus "utilitarian" does not mean buildings that completely lack decoration.

We have the impression that walls are the most decisively utilitarian edifices in the history of human constructs and rightly so. Although they always symbolized power and strength, or marked territorial boundaries and limits to the movement of people and goods, walls first and foremost provided the protection that made the difference between life and death.

Walls defined the physiognomy of cities throughout the world. Imposing de facto high population densities in the enclaves they surrounded, walls were perhaps one of the most important factors in creating city culture, which depends heavily on the habitually formed relationships between people who live next to each other. The type of walls always depended on the kind (real, invented, or imagined) of threat faced, and certainly on the resources of each city. The walls of Jericho—their legend maintained in a familiar Bible passage—are the oldest ones identified. These walls are approximately 10,000 years old—i.e., from the period before agriculture's invention. They were built around a relatively small settlement, where objects from far away were found, including obsidian tools from modern South Turkey. These finds made many scholars wonder whether the first cities were born to facilitate trade, and not to accommodate populations that were tied to their land by developing agriculture.

The development of artillery in the fifteenth century brought a radical revision to the design of fortifications. They became obsolete a few centuries later, when the firepower of the cannons had multiplied, and military tactics, political conditions, and war ethics had changed radically. In the early nineteenth century—or in the mid-nineteenth century, as in the case of Vienna—the walls of several major European cities were demolished. In the second half of nineteenth century, railroads finalized their pronouncement as fossils of an era irrevocably gone.

Another hundred years later, a radically different strategy for protecting the population would better suit the demands of the contemporary military technology. Nuclear war appeared as almost inevitable in the nineteen-fifties and sixties, and according to many, the best solution was population dispersion. In several countries, and especially in the USA, the already strong tendency of mass exodus from city centers was reinforced and the model of life based on one- or two-story houses with a garden and intensive car use was promoted. So in a strange turn of events, motorways also obtained a defensive character in the strategic planning of these countries, since they created the most important practical requirement of suburbanization and the subsequent urban expansion. The motorways became symbols of the freedom of movement—until the permanent traffic congestion led us, only a few decades later, to a more dispassionate evaluation of these controversial projects.

However, even before technological developments rendered fortification walls unnecessary, their construction was not always a one-way road. This meant that the usefulness of these supposedly unquestionably useful buildings was often cast in doubt, even by those who were involved in the decision to build them. Perhaps the Great Wall is the most telling example.

The Great Wall is only the culmination of fortification construction in China that lasted for over two millennia, from the sixth century BCE to the end of the sixteenth century CE. The overall length of the walls probably surpasses Earth's perimeter, and that without counting the city walls,

The wall of Ping Yao city made of pounded earth, circa 1370

which were by no means negligible. Emperor Hongwu's Nanjing had an imposing double wall; the interior one, made of bricks, was about thirty kilometers in length and between fourteen and twenty-one meters in height, while the exterior wall was made of mud and clay and was about twice that long. Moreover, in large cities such as Chang'an, the capital of Tang China and the largest city in the world for many centuries, or later Beijing, walls surrounded the *hutongs*, the small neighborhoods each consisting of a number of residences opening up to narrow lanes; and walls regularly surrounded separate houses.

Not all walls were built for the same reason. Some protected the territorial integrity of the smaller states, which comprised China prior to its unification in the late third century BCE. Others were constructed probably for customs purposes or for the central authority to control trade. Most of them, however, were constructed to stop the raids of the "barbarians," *i*, in the land of the "civilized" *hua*. Some demonstrated their usefulness immediately, and others became obsolete a few years after their construction.

**Wall of a house yard in a typical Beijing hutong**



Qin Shi Huang's walls were not the first built but were destined to survive in folk tradition. In 221 CE, Qin Shi Huang became the first ruler of unified China. The title Huang-ti— translated loosely as emperor—was created for him and after his death, he was guarded by a terracotta army of 7,000 warriors, which were buried with him. He standardized weight and measurement units facilitating commercial transactions, as well as the axle length of wagons easing transportation, and he built roads and canals. Qin Shi Huang made the penal system stricter and followed a zero tolerance policy, even for minor misdemeanors. He was equally decisive in his foreign policy. He ordered General Meng Tian to gather a huge army in order to repel the nomadic tribes to the north and to create a line of defense that became known as the "Wall of 10,000 li"—10,000 *li* equal 5,000 kilometers. This line consisted of walled cities—forty-four of them were founded within ten years and were manned with convicts who assumed garrison duties—and of walls in the usual sense of the term, which incorporated sections of already existing ones, as well as natural barriers such as steep mountains and cliffs.

Most of the walls in China, either city walls or those protecting entire geographical regions, were made of pounded earth. This method seems to have been used on a large scale—but not exclusively—for the construction of Qin Shi Huang's wall. The soil was compressed per layers approximately ten centimeters thick, each between wooden molds, similar to those the Romans used and the ones we use today to cast concrete. The soil came from a depth of at least ten centimeters below the ground surface, so that it would not contain seeds and grass. On many occasions, especially in areas with sandy and gravely soil, it was reinforced with red willow and thin reeds—i.e., vegetable material resilient to great shifts in temperature. The faces of the wall were mostly coated with clay; where abundant timber was available, the molds were made of whole tree trunks, and were not removed after completion, forming part of the wall itself.

This construction method did not require a large specialized workforce. Hundreds of thousands of peasants, convicts, and soldiers worked on construction sites, while others worked to supply them with food and other provisions. Coercion surpassed every precedent, and was enforced on the grounds that the wall was being built for the benefit of those who worked on its erection. Some scholars estimate that about half of the population of China was mobilized. The living and working conditions during the very cold winters and hot summers on the edge of the steppes were harsh, resulting in a tremendous loss of human life. Folk songs dating back to the era of the wall's erection sing of the skeletons protruding from its foundations—probably thrown into the moat in front of the wall, which was formed by the removal of soil for its construction. Without doubt, Qin Shi Huang was a cruel ruler who did not hesitate to use every means at his disposal to unite the various Chinese kingdoms under his rule. He pursued his goals by burning classical books and burying Confucian scholars alive; members of China's intellectual elite, who did not accept that just and pious rule could rely on violence. Maybe his critics were right: the dynasty founded by Qin Shi Huang collapsed after a short time and the hated Wall was left to ruin, since it was vulnerable to weather conditions.

The completion of the Wall of 10,000 li was marked with General Meng Tian's suicide, which was coerced by the emperor who succeeded Qin Shi Huang. Submitting to the Son of Heaven's command, the general seems to have searched for the reasons that made him a persona non grata, and concluded that as head of the construction of the wall he had injured the earth by "cutting her veins" when digging to obtain the soil used for its erection. It was the era when Feng Shui theories had begun to formulate, and it seems that the general felt more comfortable with this mystical approach than with prosaic explanations like those given a century later by a writer echoing classical Confucian perspectives, Chinese historian Sima Qian. He maintained that the general was forced to commit suicide because he had breached the principles of just rule, "conscripting forced labor, and did nothing to alleviate the distress of the common people, support the aged, care for the orphaned, or busy himself with restoring harmony among the masses … What did his crime have to do with the veins of the earth?"[1]

Although many of the ensuing dynasties build walls, the Wall of 10,000 li became—among court bureaucrats and intellectuals—the symbol of bad administration relying on brute force. Another 1,600 years had to pass before the creation of such an extensive defensive line was decided on again—an endeavor that lasted several decades; and the erection of the wall was not the only option pondered in the audience halls of the Ming Dynasty emperors.

The issue at hand was to find a way to stop the raids of the nomadic tribes coming from the steppes north of China proper. The previous dynasty, the Yuan Mongols, had followed a carrot-and-stick policy against these tribes. Moreover, the Yuan envisioned a state that would include China's rural heartland, as well as extensive pastures unsuitable for cultivation (because of the extreme climatic conditions), and the peoples living in these areas. The attitude of the court toward the nomads changed with the expulsion of the Mongol Dynasty and its replacement by the Chinese Ming. Hongwu and Yongle emperors were tough warriors and aspired to keep nomads at bay. Their policy was multifaceted: they settled soldiers as farmers at the borders; they created a network of watch and signal towers; they erected new fortification walls in selected locations, and renovated the existing ones. Their goal was to stabilize the territorial gains resulting from well organized expeditions. However, insufficient crops and the transformation of the officers into something like local feudal lords caused the collapse of one leg of the policy. Strangely enough, the Yongle Emperor left the Ordos Desert—south of the bend of the Yellow River—to the nomads; a decision that proved disastrous in the following centuries. It seems that among the reasons for his decision was the lack of adequate funds: state finances were stretched, not only by military campaigns and exploration expeditions, but also by the expenditures for the construction of the Forbidden City. Investing in architecture and its symbolic power often has an overwhelming cost at the expense of a society's other obligations.

With the passage of time, the conflict regarding the strategy for dealing with the nomads became more and more profound. The pragmatists insisted on developing commercial relations and ceremonial exchanges—a trade and tribute system. The nomads were not self-sufficient and had to rely on sedentary populations for procuring clothing and tools; this is why they repeatedly appealed for establishing markets and trade stations along the borders. These appeals, however, were not always phrased with the subtlety of the Chinese court: during a raid in March 1549, the forces

**Great Wall, circa 1600**

of Altan Khan shot an arrow into the camp of the Chinese general Weng Wan-ta—the main architect of the Great Wall—with a note warning that if commerce were not allowed, they would attack Beijing in autumn (when their horses would have been stronger after summer grazing).

The hardliners insisted that it was not proper for the Chinese state to negotiate and trade with the nomads, and that the only appropriate policy against them was that of their complete subjugation or expulsion. More or less equal trade relations with them would be equivalent to a betrayal of the political and moral principle that China was the center of the civilized world and all other people owed allegiance. In order to support their opinion they resorted to a rather narrow interpretation of the classical texts: China was clearly bounded, culturally cohesive, and historically continuous. "Barbarians" had no place in it because they did not follow the Way of the Heaven, i.e., they did not share the same set of values with the Chinese. In this context, the analogy of the walls as the fence of a house—the house represented China—made perfect sense.

This idealized worldview, which was supported by various groups—including ambitious generals, eunuch officials, or the literati of the south—was not compatible with the military and political situation, but it was often predominant in the Court. The ability to organize campaigns that would have brought the decisive victory proved to be increasingly out of reach as years went by. However, the governors of border provinces who helped or tolerated transactions with nomadic tribes were severely punished.

154

Therefore, the only solution for the impasse was to keep the nomads away. New military camps were established and the system of transmitting messages was completed. Mainly, though, older fortification walls were repaired and reinforced and new large sections were constructed. By the end of the sixteenth century, a cohesive barrier 6,500 kilometers in length, the Great Wall, was created. In areas, this barrier consisted of double or triple walls dozens or even hundreds kilometers from each other, and often had branches connecting the main wall with isolated towers.

The Great Wall is more firm and resilient than the walls that had been built until then. The construction of most of its sections demanded a much larger workforce than those manufactured only from rammed earth; China's population, though, having probably surpassed 150 million by the late sixteenth century, was a dozen times larger than in the era of the Wall of 10,000 li. The standard structure consisted of a core of firmly rammed local loess mixed with coarse sand, gravel, and rubble faced with walls made of stone slabs and—more usually—bricks. These bricks were approximately four times larger than those we use today and were produced by the thousands from numerous kilns along the construction site. Aside from the chemical composition of clay, the key to the bricks' resilience is the baking procedure. The temperatures achieved in these furnaces reached 1150°C and the baking lasted up to seven days: today the best ceramic tiles are baked in these temperatures for only a few hours. Moreover, the mortar used to hold the bricks together not only had abundant lime, but also a "secret ingredient." This was recently proved to be a type of rice flour rendering the mortar especially strong—in some cases the mortar is preserved, while the bricks themselves have long eroded. The

**The Great Wall where it meets the Yellow Sea at Shanhaiguan, circa 1600**

THE USEFULNESS OF EDIFICES

**The Great Wall in the Simatai region, circa 1600**

upper surface of the wall was laid with bricks and allowed the movement of up to five rows of armed soldiers. There were towers in small intervals used for relaying messages and also for soldiers' quarters; some of these towers were elaborately decorated and had floors heated by coal fires so that the soldiers' living conditions were good.

While worldwide, the walls of some cities protected them for centuries—the Theodosian Walls of Constantinople, for example, repelled attackers for 800 years—the Great Wall fell into disuse within half a century of its completion. The Manchurians invaded Beijing in 1644 and established the Qing Dynasty. Qing China was approximately twice the size of Ming China and included populations much different from those inhabiting the rural heartland of the country. The definition of what is Chinese and what constitutes China widened to include the new territories and new peoples. Exclusion was a policy of the past.

The Great Wall began to attract the attention of the Europeans who visited China more and more as time passed, and gradually acquired a reputation equal to that of the Great Pyramids of Giza. Voltaire mentions it in five different works, and the completely absurd myth that the Great Wall is visible to the naked eye from outer space is widespread even today. It did not take long for this excitement to seize China itself, and the Great Wall ended up being the symbol of the country—even for the Communist Party. Obviously not for military services, which it virtually never offered, but because, simply put, it is a work of epic proportions. According to an ancient argument, which for millennia did not lose its prestige in Imperial China, the Heavens had designated the boundaries of China (even though its borders contained different geographical regions depending on the ruling dynasty); the walls built from time to time all but locally complemented the work of the Heavens, and for this reason they took advantage of the geomorphology to the maximum extend. The Great Wall of the Late Ming, though, was even driven through rather inaccessible terrain. In the Simatai region, the wall was constructed in slopes with a 70-degree gradient at an altitude of 2,000 meters—in such places, it was just a half meter thick. It was interrupted only when it met almost vertical mountain slopes or rivers. It seems that it was important to denote, as far as possible, the continuity that would symbolize the borders' impenetrability. And so, alongside its length we pass from pragmatism and meeting real defensive needs, to symbolism and marking the limits of Chinese dominion, home (as was firmly believed) to the most advanced civilization on earth's face. The Great Wall, which created according to some of its contemporaries the need for its existence, corresponded to its function in a wide range of ways—from the most practical to the most symbolic.

This fullness of the Great Wall's response to its purpose was intended to be denoted from its construction in locations where it was virtually unnecessary—i.e., from its demonstration as a complete human work. This demonstration seems to have always been the primary aim of architecture, which is possibly connected with an almost fetishistic admiration that people have shown through the ages to material objects. In his famous triptych, *firmitas, utilitas, venustas* (strength, utility, grace),[2] Vitruvius considers that architecture's first concern is to make works that stand—i.e., to demonstrate man's ability to create things. The services that buildings provide are less important than their existence; in other words, it is more important for a building to be, than to be useful. The Great Wall is irrefutable witness of this rank order.

### Notes

1  Bodde, Derk (trans.): *Statesman, Patriotic, and general in ancient China: Three Shih Chi Biographies of the Ch'in Dynasty (225-206 BC)*. American Oriental Society 1940, 61 ff.
2  Vitruvius: *De Architectura* I.2.2.

### Selected Bibliography

Khazanov, A.M.: *Nomads and the Outside World*. Cambridge University Press 1984.
Lovell, Julia: *The Great Wall: China against the World. 1000 BC–2000 AD*. Atlantic Books 2006.
Luo Zewen et al.: *The Great Wall*. McGraw Hill 1981.
Robinson, David M.: "Politics, Force and Ethnicity in Ming China: Mongols and the Abortive Coup of 1461." In: *Harvard Journal of Asiatic Studies*, Vol. 59, 1, June 1999, 79 ff.
Turnbull, Stephen: *The Great Wall of China 221 BC–AD 1644*. Osprey 2007.
Waldron, Arthur: *The Great Wall of China, From History to Myth*. Cambridge University Press 1990.

# MANAGING THE BOUNDARIES

## The Masjed-e Shah in Isfahan

To discourage deviant behavior, authorities in medieval London used cunning methods. There is a record in the Court Rolls of a ward's aldermen and watchmen "entering the house of William Cok, butcher, in Cockes Lane and tearing away eleven doors and five windows with hammers and chisels."[1] This measure allowed neighbors to pry into the private lives of those who lived in the house, and in particular the head of household. It abolished the family hearth's privacy, in order to reassure the community that the commonly accepted rules of behavior were respected and that no morally criminal acts were committed.

Meanwhile, a little farther to the south, in Islamic North Africa, such methods would have been unthinkable: the community members' behavior in the market and the mosque extrapolated their compliance to the accepted mores and religious commandments, and violent behavior at home could be reported to the judge. Hadiths 5366 to 5371 in the Sahih Muslim collection, dating back to the ninth century, stated that one is perfectly justified and would not be punished if he gouged the eye of a neighbor who was caught peeping into his house.[2] Hadiths are sayings or stories reputedly with Prophet Muhammad's approval; as such, they are viewed as jurisprudence and a source of law. Sahih Muslim is one of the most respected Hadith collections among the Sunni Muslims. Other Hadiths specified in detail how guests should announce themselves upon arrival, giving the women of the house the opportunity to cover themselves. This absolute protection of privacy in the home reflected the role distribution within the family: the man was the leader and was solely responsible for overseeing compliance to the rules. The bride's immediate relatives observed his behavior toward her, but without violating the established family hierarchy.

Introverted and with limited openings to the street, houses allowed their residents complete isolation. In this respect, their configuration corre-

**Old town, Tunis, 1899**

sponded to their key role as guarantors of the boundaries between private and public life. As ever, this configuration contributed to the reproduction of the status quo and the stereotypes in the relationships between the two genders and between the generations; not that these same houses could not be used in a different way and to accommodate different relationships between men and women or adults and children; distinguished for its plasticity, architecture allows enormous diversity in the use of its products.

Islam is more than just a religion in the strict sense; it is a form of social organization based on a coherent and integrated set of values. In consequence, cities had to be built in a manner favoring the respect of their inhabitants for these values. Generally speaking, up to the nineteenth century, throughout almost all regions where Islam is the dominant religion, building provisions were based more or less directly on the Qur'an and Sharia, often through the mediation of Hadiths. Their aim was to safeguard the community's morals as a whole and to promote friendly rapport among neighbors, rather than to define the form of the city—which was the case in Siena at the time of the government of the Nine.

The regulation of building activity on the basis of general principles of law and ethics, on the basis of guidelines for behavior toward each other and with respect to religious institutions outline the main features of what we may legitimately call "Islamic cities." Nevertheless, other factors often played a decisive role. In sub-Saharan Africa, the pre-Islamic layout of cities and settlements survived into the new religion with only minor adjustments. On the plains of Iran, houses were often built along water conduits, consequently, the road network—with its main roads, junctions, and dead ends—reproduced the preexistent irrigation network.

Even when cities developed over an existing geometrical background, as the density of the urban fabric increased gradually, it often produced neighborhoods with a maze-like street network and many cul-de-sacs. Just as often, only the location and layout of the Friday mosque, the palace, and the market were determined by the authorities; nonetheless, there have been cases of comprehensive town planning, Baghdad being a typical example. The central market was usually placed next to the mosque. Shops occupied both sides of the streets of a small area defined as suitable for developing such activities. Permanent structures like domes or semipermanent canopies protected the customers and goods. Entry points often had gates, which closed at night. Merchants could not live next to or over their shops, and the passers-by were forced to bypass the market using another route since its roads were part of the settlement's road network. In many cases, there were gates at the entrances to neighborhoods as well—yet another measure favoring the concentration of various ethnic groups in separate areas of the city. To accommodate burgeoning commercial activity typical of Islamic towns, secondary (and less controlled) markets often emerged in other key areas of the city, mainly close to the wall gates.

In the central market, jewelry and perfume stores were set up next to the mosque, whereas food stores with unpleasant odors were kept further away. All other shops in between were grouped per merchandise. Because competition to attract customers was usually fierce, merchandise was displayed to impress. During the daytime, sacks of legumes, piles of oranges, rolls of fabric, and bottles of perfume created a riot of shapes, colors and odors. This is a typical case of space laid out according to an architectural design, but owing its identity to features outside architecture's domain. Rugs and carpets assumed a similar role in homes—as pieces of furniture in the Western cultural environment do today—but they did so with great flexibility, denoting the occasional function of rooms in different parts of the day.

After the advent of Islam, it took roughly three centuries for its value system to be transcribed into written laws. Prominent jurists undertook this formidable task. Their legacy was five schools of law, each in its own geographical area of influence (four in Sunni and one in Shiite Islam), which survived the centuries that followed. Each school assessed, in slightly different ways, the repercussions building projects would have in community life—i.e., whether they would effectively encourage behavior in accordance with the dictates of the religious canon. As a result, slightly different building provisions and, more importantly, case rulings that established judicial precedents, emerged in each area. The Maliki School, for instance, predominant throughout Maghreb before the Ottomans introduced the Hanafi School in Tunisia and Libya, allowed everyone to extend their houses by constructing a second floor—without too much consideration of the impact on their neighbors' sunlight or air—provided the extension would not compromise their privacy and its purpose was not an excessive display of wealth and power. It also allowed anyone to build an annex to their house over a street, as long as there was enough room, both in width and in height, for a camel carrying goods to pass. If the annex were to be partly borne by the wall across the street, obviously that owner would have to give his consent. On the other hand, building a door or window on a wall shared by two properties was expressly forbidden, except when a room could not receive enough light or ventilation in any other way. In that case, however, a whole grid of provisions ensured the privacy of the neighbors, and subsequently their quality of life.

In cities, private and public space are in contact with each other, as is the private space belonging to two different individuals. The management of the interface between them was a major issue in architecture across the Muslim world. The position and shape of doors and windows were obviously important, but not the sole concern in architectural design. Cul-de-sacs created semi-private spaces, which were more like modern-day communal areas in apartment buildings, rather than public space per se. According to the Maliki School, the door of the last house at the far end could be moved forward to occupy what until then was a road, provided it did not block any windows or doors of the neighboring houses. In these semi-private cul-de-sacs, women were often allowed to walk around in their home clothes, which meant that dwellers of that particular neighbor-hood had exclusive rights to these areas and that people from different parts of the city had to respect them.

**Masjed-e Sheikh Lotf-ollāh, Isfahan, circa 1618, interior**

The boundary between private and public space and between two adjacent private spaces often coincides with the boundary between "inside" and "outside." The relationship between inside and outside, and between indoors and outdoors has always been fundamental in architec-ture, especially across a geographical zone enjoying mild to high tempera-

Masjed-e Shah, Isfahan, 1611, courtyard; unknown artist

tures and long periods of sunlight for most of the year (the southern coasts of the Mediterranean, the Middle East and southern Asia), or warm and humid weather conditions (Southeast Asia). Bear in mind, for example, that introvert houses, arranged around an inner atrium, were customary in ancient Mesopotamia. When Islam extended to these regions, it was imperative to regulate at a single stroke both the relation of indoors to outdoors (so that occupants of buildings and dwellers in settlements and towns could live in a comfortable temperature, protected from the sun and the rain), and the relation of private to public space (with the aim to ensure privacy). This was obviously not an easy task. Regional legal provisions, local customs and features of traditional architecture thought to be incompatible with Islam were abolished, whereas those thought to be compatible were kept and enhanced.

Over time, this led to an architecture that was extremely efficient, both in creating spaces of different qualities in direct contact with one another—sheltered and open-air, sunlit and shaded, private and public—and in managing their interface. Its application to monumental buildings, which are heavily symbolic in their own right and have sophisticated functional requirements, produced some exquisitely fine results; among them are the mosques built under the Safavid Dynasty, which ruled Iran from 1501 to 1722.

In 1598, Shah Abbas decided to move his capital to Isfahan, built on a fertile valley irrigated by the Zayandeh River, roughly at the center of his empire. Architect, mathematician, astronomer, and philosopher Shaykh Bahai, a true *homo universalis*, was assigned the task of remodeling the city. His design provided for a representative avenue from north to south, and a grand royal square, 500 meters in length and 160 meters in width, surrounded by markets and mosques. The square proved to be suitable for all types of activities, ranging from an open-air market with stalls and acrobatic shows to polo games, which the Shah and his entourage could watch from the sixth-floor terrace of his palace on the western side of the square. At the south end of the square, Shaykh Bahai designed a large mosque, the Masjed-e Shah, which was meant for the public, in contrast to mosque opposite the palace, the Masjed-e Sheikh Lotf-oll h, which was reserved for royalty. Building the *mihrab* to face Mecca was non-negotiable, so the new square in front of Masjed-e Shah would normally have its main axis oriented to the southwest. Shaykh Bahai designed an ensemble in which the square and the mosque are placed at a forty-five degree angle to each other. This allows the ornate dome to be visible from anywhere on the square, which would have been impossible if it had been built behind the mosque's grand gateway, the *pishtaq*. Saint Peter's Basilica in Rome could not avoid that disadvantage: the church's tall façade blocks the view to Michelangelo's dome from Bernini's oval square, after its central nave was extended by Carlo Maderno in 1607, about the same time that the Masjed-e Shah was being built.

In Isfahan, monumental axiality was sacrificed in favor of a layout that not least maximized visual sensation; architecture emerged as art for display, a notion that took gradually hold in Europe at the time, as well.

The Masjed-e Shah is a mosque with four *iwans*—vaulted open halls with a rectangular, arched façade—one on each side of the courtyard in front of it, a particularly popular layout in Iran. Dating back to 540 CE, the impressive arched vault in the palace of Khosrau I in Ctesiphon—about thirty-seven meters in height, twenty-six in width, and fifty meters in length—served probably as the ultimate model for iwan architecture. Sassanid fire temples (224–651 CE) seem to have frequently had the form of vaulted halls with arched openings on their four sides. As Islam prevailed, many of these temples were converted to mosques: their arch on the wall oriented closer to Mecca was closed off. This made the iwan an acceptable feature that could be integrated in the new religious architecture.

Built with a dome, Masjed-e Shah's central prayer hall has one hypostyle hall on each side, left and right, providing enough covered space for the faithful to join in prayer. Large hypostyle halls are typical of earlier mosques, the one in Damascus being among the oldest and most famous. Beyond each hypostyle hall, there is a religious school, or *madrasa*, with study rooms arranged around a courtyard. Each hypostyle hall is longer than the central prayer hall, so that the wall they share extends along and flanks the arched façade. Each madrasa is, in turn, longer than the hypostyle hall, so that the wall they share extends along and flanks the large courtyard in front of the central prayer hall and the hypostyle halls. This simple layout creates an extremely complex edifice with alternating covered halls and open areas. While not hidden behind closed doors, the halls can afford opportunities for isolation. The different level of lighting creates zones of relative privacy. There is no clear, tangible boundary to set one hall apart from the other; the sense that each hall is quite distinct from the

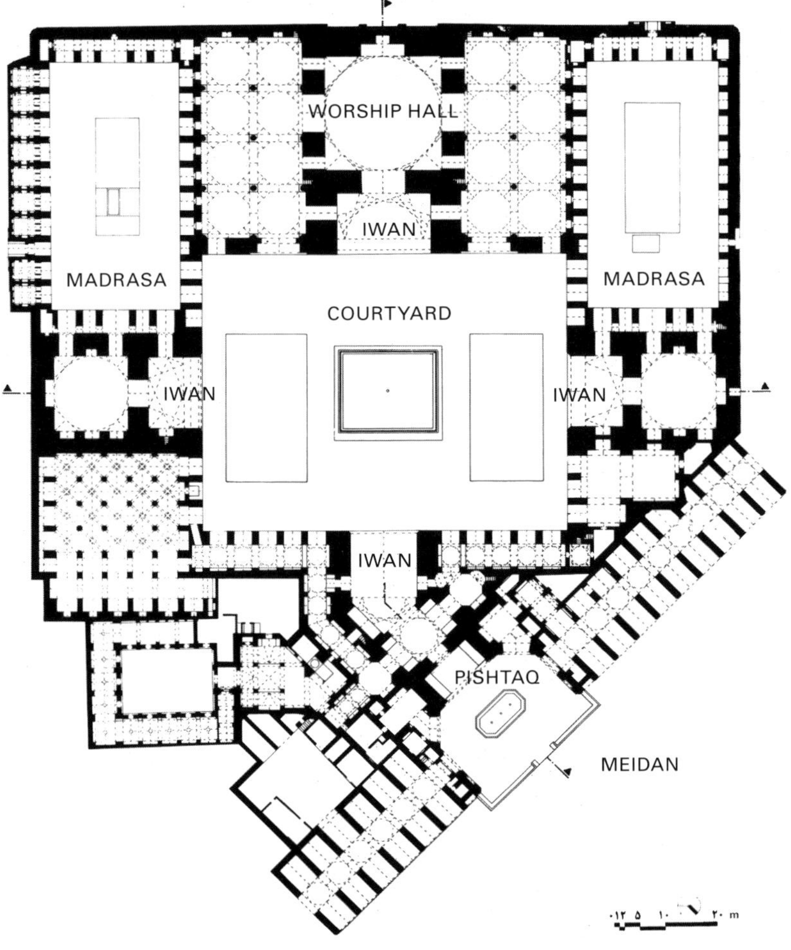


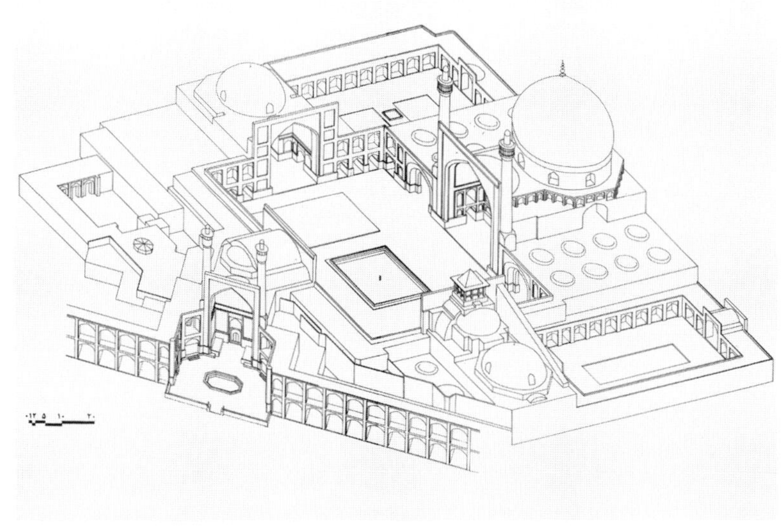

**Masjed-e Shah, Isfahan, 1611, ground plan and bird's eye view; from
*Ganjnameh* II**

**Taj Mahal, Agra, Uttar Pradesh, 1632**

adjacent one is only achieved by their different ceilings, and the different size of their openings. There is certain fluidity to this space, which enables visitors to go on unimpeded (and almost without even realizing it) from one area to the next, which has an entirely different character. The greatest feat of Masjed-e Shah's architecture is that this is achieved without compromising the geometric clarity of either the halls considered separately or the mosque as a whole.

The iwan itself is the epitome of sensitivity to boundaries between spaces of different character. Its grand vaulted niche, with its deep recess, provides a covered area open to the courtyard. The rear wall of the iwan leading to the domed hall is perforated. The balance between the rigid walls and openings, between height and depth, between light and shade edges to perfection.

The same principles in dealing with boundaries are applied to a multitude of other mosques and public buildings. The greatest merit of the Badshahi Mosque in Lahore, modern Pakistan, lies in the simplicity of its design. Its construction started in 1671 on the order of the Mughal emperor Aurangzeb. Badshahi's rival was the other large mosque of the Indian Mughal Dynasty, the Jama Masjid in Delhi, which was built on the initiative of Shah Jahan, Aurangzeb's father and predecessor, before Aurangzeb overthrew him. It has a large courtyard, 170 meters by 170 meters, with study rooms around it, which under British Rule in the nineteenth century were joined together to form arcades. On one side of the courtyard is the main mosque, which has one central and two side halls; all three halls are domed and measure a total of seventy meters in length and twenty-five meters in depth. This simple layout alludes directly—and perhaps more than any other great mosque—to the mosque that Muhammad himself built in Mecca, outside his house: an enclosed courtyard with a simple shed where, protected from the sun, the faithful would gather to pray.

Shah Jahan also ordered in 1632 the construction of the Taj Mahal, a mausoleum built in memory of his beloved wife, Mumtaz Mahal, who had died prematurely. The Taj Mahal is built against a backdrop of geometrical gardens that bring out the majesty of its structure. Its robust yet ethereal character lies not so much in its amazing decor, as in the fact that it is neither a building in the usual sense, nor a sculpture: it has no enclosed halls, since its "interior" is set apart only by means of perforated screens. Yet it is not solid—a piece of finely sculpted marble. The floor area on the level where the sarcophagus of Mumtaz Mahal is placed takes up a surface approximately equal in size to the imprint of the massive pillars, which calls into question speculation on to whether it is the mass or the void that prevails. Higher up, the columns meet forming recesses below them—mass turns into void and vice-versa. Its chamfered corners reveal the building's intention to forgo a feature creating the visual impression of stability. Typically at the time, the dome veers from the strict geometric shape of a hemisphere, ending in a top that tapers into the sky.

The dreamy nature of the Taj Mahal is largely due to the coexistence in the same building of pairs of potentially opposing qualities. One cannot fail to observe, however, that contrary to what the fluidity of space in this magnificent monument suggests, death—visualized in the sarcophagus of Mumtaz Mahal at the geometrical center of the layout—is a state categorically different and utterly distinct from life; a fact that Shah Jahan did not seem to have easily accepted.

**Notes**

1  Ackroyd, Peter: *London: The biography*. Vintage 2000, 64.
2  *Sahih Muslim. The Book on General Behaviour (Kitab Al-Adab)*. Transl. Abd-al-Hamid Siddiqui.



**Selected Bibliography**

Ardalan, Nader/Bakhtiar, Laleh: *The Sense of Unity: The Sufi Tradition in Persian Architecture*. ABC International Group 2000.
Blake, Stephen P.: *Half the World: The Social Architecture of Safavid Isfahan, 1590–1722*. Mazda Publishers 1999.
Blow, David: *Shah Abbas: The Ruthless King Who Became an Iranian Legend*. I.B. Tauris 2009.
Bonine, Michael: "From Uruk to Casablanca: Perspectives on the Urban Experience of the Middle East." In: *Journal of Urban History*, February 1977, 3, 141 ff.
Hakim, Besim: *Arabic-Islamic Cities: Building and Planning Principles*. Kegan Paul 1986.
Tabbaa, Yasser: *The Transformation of Islamic Art during the Sunni Revival*. University of Washington Press 2001.

# ARCHITECTURE AND SPECTACLE

## From Pont Neuf to Vierzehnheiligen

The layout and character of European cities, in which buildings as radical as Sant'Andrea were built, was defined by the medieval perception of unity and the medieval practice of high density. Let us remember, for example, that the urban mansions in Siena's central square were packed next to each other, opposite the town hall with their façades creating the curved vertical surface that borders the plaza; and the houses, even those belonging to very powerful families, opened up in the narrow city streets, fully integrated in the continuous urban fabric of the city. Gradually, however, something started to change. Freestanding buildings—buildings that were not part of the compact medley comprising the medieval cities—were constructed as early as the early sixteenth century. The Renaissance ideal depicted in the Piero della Francesca's circle paintings in Urbino's Palazzo Ducale started to become a reality: a city consisting of rectangular or circular buildings each clearly distinct from the neighboring building.

Palazzo Farnese, one of the most prominent urban mansions of Rome, was built in this spirit. Alessandro Farnese, who was made cardinal in 1493 at the age of twenty-five, bought an older palace in 1495, which he set out to renovate and enlarge; he also bought adjacent houses and demolished them. Farnese opened a road that connected the palazzo with Campo de' Fiori, by then a major commercial hub. When he became Pope in 1534, he embarked on an even more ambitious undertaking. He commissioned the best architects of his era to redesign his palazzo. The building realized has the shape of an oblate cube surrounded by roads—it is a building block on its own—with clearly visible cornerstones and projecting cornice, highlighting its outline. The structure is thirty meters in height, with a ground floor in *ordine rustica*—rusticated stone blocks forming a solid foundation—and windows decorated alternately with triangular and curved pediments. The Farnese insignia and the papal tiara dominate the symmetrical façade, adorning its central window designed by Michelangelo. The building's grandeur could be better perceived from some distance, ideally when approached axially. Therefore, a plaza in front of it was necessary. Alessandro Farnese bought the land to create it and cleared it of all structures. Eventually, the façades of the buildings on the roads leading to the palazzo were rebuilt. Not only was the Farnese mansion designed in detail, but also the terms of its perception.

Ensuring open space in front of important buildings is, of course, a practice as old as monumental architecture. Its post-medieval European version made its most prominent appearance in the sphere of utopia—the ideal city of Piero della Francesca's circle. But we had to wait until the sixteenth and the seventeenth centuries for the new approach to seal the image of the large European cities.

Henry IV, King of France, decided in 1599 to continue constructing the Pont Neuf, the new Parisian bridge that would connect the right with the left bank of the Seine at the height of the western end of Île de la Cité. His predecessor had begun the works in 1577, but two decades later and after successive changes to its initial design, the new bridge was still incomplete.

**Map of Paris (detail), Matthaeus Merian, 1615; at the lower part of the picture the Pont Neuf and the new wing of the Louvre palace along the Seine**

In its new version, the bridge would be an elegant piece of work with semicircular arches—bridge-building was not yet free of Roman templates—and would stand out for one radical innovation: it would not have buildings on it. The wooden bridges common in the early Middle Ages or constructed in small settlements were also free of buildings, since wooden structures could not carry the burden of heavy superstructure. In 1599

Europe, though, stone bridges within the city limits regularly had shops and houses on both sides of the deck—as we can still see today in Ponte Vecchio in Florence. Bridges were of crucial importance for financial and social life; they placed the cities on the map of the regional transportation network and they were an extremely important source of state revenue, because it was feasible to control commerce and the distribution of commodities there. They were a meeting point with unceasing traffic and constant crowds of people, on and around them. Therefore, the bridges were ideal for establishing commercial activities—preferably in permanent structures—and with them came the homes of businessmen who wanted to live above their shops or just be close to the action. What was more natural, then, than to have buildings on the stone bridges, which were increasingly common in late medieval times?

Even so, the king of France had other priorities. He wanted to keep the horizon as open as possible, so that the view from the bridge toward the Louvre palace and its new wing under construction—which would connect it alongside the right bank of Seine with Palais des Tuileries—would not be obstructed, and he was indifferent to the cost. Absolute monarchy was fully imposed, national unification was almost complete and he was its personification. His official residence, seat of the government and heart of the state, ought to dominate the city as much as possible. In order to achieve this, it had to be as visible as possible.

However, a monarch is not only represented by his palace, but also by the entire city and the entire country. The self-promotion ambitions of the kings of France had been concentrated in Paris from the time that Frances I settled there permanently (around 1530); in previous decades, the French kings preferred living in the Chateaux of the Loire valley. The image of the city as a whole, which was the concern and mirror of the community in self-governed cities such as Siena, became the concern and mirror of autocracy; and later of democracy, if we consider Francois Mitterrand's Grands Projets in the nineteen-eighties.

It was Henry IV who realized, more clearly than all his predecessors, that ensuring open space in a densely populated city would be the supreme luxury he could offer his subjects and would give prestige to the crown. In Madrid, the idea of creating Plaza Mayor in a busy quarter of the city center dates back to the fifteen-seventies, but construction started several decades later. In Henry IV's Paris, impressive waterfronts accessible to everyone (specifically to those who dared to take their strolls within sight of the palace) began to take shape on both banks of the Seine. Where the banks were formed by the river's natural flow, embankments and promenades were built, and where were buildings, these were demolished. This was a particularly ambitious undertaking since sharp increase in overseas commerce required the construction of more and more docks and warehouses along the river and as close as possible to the city center. In a 1615 engraving by Matthaeus Merian, one could see this great urban renewal project in progress. It was completed two hundred years later with the conversion of the entire length of the riverbanks into prime public space. By contrast, the banks of Thames in London remain until today devoted to commercial activities, visualizing a priority characteristic of the society that gave birth to capitalism; and in New York almost the entire coastal zone of Manhattan was occupied by docks until the nineteen-sixties.

Before the completion of Pont Neuf in 1606, the remodeling of the western part of Île de la Cité was decided. The banks of the small island were shaped into promenades following the two arms of the Seine and converged with each other in approximately the middle of the new bridge. In this pointed ending of the small island, Place Dauphine was built, named in honor of the successor to the throne and later King Louis XIII—this alone betrayed how much the royal house invested in this project. It was shaped like a triangle and was surrounded by residential buildings with shops on the ground floors. The houses had views of both the plaza and the river, and their façades were identical to one another, creating an ensemble distinguished for its order and regularity.

Almost simultaneously, the construction of another royal plaza, Place des Vosges had begun in the eastern end of Paris. The façades of the houses were also here identical to each other, made of red brick and stone quoins and vaulted arcades supported on squared columns. The pavilions of the king and queen in the south and north sides of the plaza respectively were made taller in order to stand out. The steep roofs may have recalled the old era, the experience, though, offered to the residents of the houses around the square was unique. In the front, they had outdoor space measuring 140 by 140 meters—something unheard of in the city during a period when Notre Dame was still squeezed between crumbling houses, and the area between the Louvre and the Palais des Tuileries, which were connected with the new wing along the Seine to form an imposing whole, was still densely populated.

Neither of the royal plazas was fully integrated into the urban fabric; access to them was not completely straightforward, and entry points were not situated at the end of some important thoroughfares. Moreover, in Place des Vosges, the central area was fenced off and reserved for residents of the adjacent properties—like London's Bedford Square in front of the AA School of Architecture and Gramercy Park in New York still today.

The new type of urban space provided the upper class the urban version of isolation from the crowd offered by the suburban villas. In the medieval cities, the plazas and the few bridges were open to all the inhabitants of the city, since every type of public activity took place there. In contrast, the new royal plazas and the promenades along the Seine were almost exclusively reserved for the flamboyant enjoyment of the privileges of those for whom they were intended: those who could afford the luxury of having time to kill, to wear fine and expensive clothes, to behave in a ritualistically refined and polite manner. In other words, the new type

**Place Vendôme, Paris, Jules Hardouin-Mansart, 1699**

of urban space was devoted to the spectacle staged by the upper class of a society, which now produced surpluses so large that it could support this never-ending theatrical performance.

Thus, it was at the beginning of the seventeenth century, that European cities began to disintegrate into zones reserved explicitly or implicitly for different strata of the population. Aesthetics became increasingly—more or less deliberately—a means of class segregation. The poor were a problem in the areas of this early gentrification. The boundaries between the zones addressing different strata of the population were, of course, fluid. Pont Neuf was under constant pressure to assume the traditional role of the bridges, and seems to have changed character from time to time. In stark contrast to the intentions of its builder Henry IV, people flocked there en masse in the mid-eighteenth century, street artists preformed and permanent pavilions were erected on it. Nevertheless, it took more than 250 years for the benefits of the urban renewal that began in 1600 to be fully capitalized and distributed to the entire population. Then, in the nineteenth century, the private squares and parks were opened to the general population who acquired new habits: taking strolls and going for picnics.

Initially, however, the rather introverted configuration of the royal plazas contributed to the fact that the *hoi polloi* did not dare access them. Here, perhaps, lies their great difference from the squares and avenues created by Pope Sixtus V's orders in Rome in the late sixteenth century—less than two decades before Henry IV's urban renewal project began. The main goal of this great undertaking to transform the "eternal city" was to directly connect the city's seven most important churches visited by the pilgrims. Therefore, Sixtus V's plan addressed a broader audience—an audience for whom showing off was not a priority. Only with the great square in front of Saint Peter's Basilica, designed by Gian Lorenzo Bernini a century later in the mid-seventeenth century, did the theatricality of the faithful's congregation to the cathedral rise to prominence. In this respect, Saint Peter's Square constitutes the "democratic" version of Paris' royal squares; before God's representative on earth, the differences between the social classes ought to lose their sharpness.

Place Vendôme was Paris' most impressive royal square. After the settlement of several ownership issues and some changes in its design, it acquired in early eighteenth century the form it has today: a rectangle with chamfered corners. Initially, just the lavish stone façades, adorned with half-columns and pediments, were constructed. Whoever wanted and had the king's approval and the money, could buy as many bays as he wanted and build his mansion. As in the other royal squares, the property owners waived the right to partake in defining the city's image, by giving to their house the form they considered appropriate. They did so in exchange for the great prestige of owning property in an ensemble representative of the king himself; prestige that was enhanced by the uniformity of its luxurious buildings and the festive character of their architecture: a well ordered urban cohort. Ortega y Gasset, an early twentieth-century Spanish thinker, held the opinion that "more than anything else, the city is the square, agora, discussion, eloquence. In fact, the city does not need to have houses: facades suffice."[1] The Place Vendôme might not have been an agora or a medieval town hall square with a multitude of activities taking place in it, but the façades of the houses surrounding it were enough to create an urban environment that accomplished the function demanded by the times: to highlight the insignia denoting high position in the social hierarchy, and to give those who carried them the opportunity to meet and converse with each other.

This was the baroque era. The forms of buildings, although based on classical principles, tended to subvert all rules. The three-part organization (base, shaft, and cap) was still visible, though the confidence of the horizontal and vertical lines of "beam on post" classical architecture was shaken by the curved ceilings that were conceived as continuation of the walls. The calmness of the straight lines has given its place to vibrating surfaces. The simplicity of the distinct architectural members constituting the buildings—the column, the epistyle, the pediment, the cornices, the walls (which was to resurface in the early nineteenth century as we will see in the next chapter)—was lost behind an runaway decoration unifying all the individual elements of each building to an intoxicant whole.

Baroque was the era of grand compositions. The building complexes unfolded in hundreds of meters in length, constituting the setting of a stylized behavior in public space. The show of presenting one noble to others started in the *cour d'honneur*, the yard in front of the entrance to a mansion or a palace, where the carriage arrived—a sculpture mounted on wheels. The entrance of the guests into the building was an event on its own, as one can imagine seeing the ceremonial staircase leading from the entrance at the ground floor to the piano nobile in the palace of the prince bishop of Würzburg. The construction of the palace—designed by Balthasar Neumann—began in 1720. Its ceremonial staircase occupies 540 square meters and is covered by a domed ceiling measuring eighteen by thirty meters, reaching twenty-three meters in height and is painted by Giovanni Battista Tiepolo.

This was the environment corresponding to the visual appetites of a class that had few moral inhibitions (in the narrow sense of the term), and had placed aesthetic enjoyment on a very high pedestal. The various objects, even the most utilitarian ones, were not the only ones being primarily evaluated on how satisfying they were to the eye. The various activities—from the most routine ones (such as a walk), to the most formal (such as an audience at the palace or attending a concert)—were executed by the elite in a way highlighting their aesthetic quality. Knowledge itself was associated, to an extent unprecedented until then, with visual perception. The Wunderkammer, collections of rare natural objects from corals to

The central staircase of the Residenz, Würzburg, Balthasar Neumann, 1720/1737

strange mammals, were organized in a manner to astonish visitors rather than allow the careful study of the exhibits. In one of the older surviving depictions of these collections, in an engraving to Ferrante Imperato's book, *Dell'Historia Naturale*, published in Naples in 1599—the year that Henry IV of France decided to continue the construction of Pont Neuf—a crocodile is mounted on the roof, a location that does not allow scientific examination, at least not in the way that is customary today.

**The stage of Teatro Scientifico, Mantua, Antonio Bibiena, 1767**

Perceiving reality through the lenses of aesthetics was crystallized in the most characteristic way in Teatro Scientifico at Mantova. Designed by Antonio Bibiena, its construction began seventeen years after the publication in 1750 of Alexander Gottlieb Baumgarten's *Aesthetica*, which introduced this term to philosophy giving to it the meaning it has today. Teatro Scientifico is a theater constructed where once stood the mansion of a member of the ruling family of Mantova. The audience sits in comfortable armchairs covered with luxury fabric. The stage is surrounded—in the rear and on the sides—by a structure resembling the façade of a three-story building, with open arcades featuring semicircular arches and double columns in the elevated "ground floor" and "first floor," and windows in the "second" floor. The audience had access to these in order to see the action on the stage. At the same time, they could exchange glances with those sitting in the auditorium armchairs, or in the boxes, to meet more or less accidentally with spectators of the opposite sex and temporally hide behind the columns. Below, on the stage, all kinds of shows were performed: music concerts, scientific discussions, physics experiments, and anatomy demonstrations. We are already in the age of Enlightenment and the movement of spreading and popularizing knowledge, spearheaded by the *philosophes*, was in full bloom. The wider audience's contact with science (and especially those able to fund this activity) also occurred through highlighting those aspects of the natural world that were of great visual interest. Buildings such as Teatro Scientifico were called upon to serve discovering the natural world as spectacle.

Baroque architecture was not a low-profile architecture creating colorless settings in order to highlight the visual magic offered by other activities. Baroque architecture was a high-profile architecture serving the culture of spectacle, at a time when there were no rock concerts or 3D cinema. Creating rich sceneries, in terms of visual stimuli, baroque architecture did not operate competitively, but complementary to other forms of entertainment. Architecture often assumed similar role from the time that priests climbed the stairs of the first ziggurat, and continues to do so. For example, the emotional stress resulting from watching an exciting football match, increases if the spectator is prepared psychologically by entering an impressive stadium, where tens of thousands of singing and chanting spectators are gathered.

**Vierzehnheiligen church, Bavaria, Balthasar Neumann, 1743**

Baroque architecture helped transform not only the physical, but also the spiritual world into spectacle—something to which Calvinism reacted violently. The Catholic churches built during the Counter-Reformation, but also later during the eighteenth century, used all available means to amaze the faithful. Vierzehnheiligen, for example, another work by Balthasar Neumann of 1743, is one of the dozens, if not hundreds, impressive churches built in Bavaria's rural environment. It was as if the Catholic Church doubted whether the promises of happy eternal life for those following its dictates and the threats of eternal punishment for those who violated them were sufficient to convince the indecisive, and invited architecture to make its message more attractive. Judging by the number of churches built during that period and the money spent on their construction, it seems that the heads of the church felt that the architecture of their time responded successfully to their great expectations. This is an acknowledgment that architecture does not always receive.

### Notes

1  Ortega y Gasset, José, quoted in: Rubert de Ventós, Xavier: "Urbanisation against urbanity?" In: *Ciutat real, ciutat ideal.* Centre of Contemporary Culture of Barcelona 1998.

### Selected Bibliography


Cleary, Richard L.: *The Place Royale and Urban Design in the Ancien Régime.* Cambridge University Press 2011.
Cowan, Alexander Francis/Steward, Jill: *The City And the Senses: Urban Culture Since 1500.* Ashgate 2007.
Kaufmann, Emil: *Architecture in the Age of Reason: Baroque and Post-Baroque in England, Italy, and France.* Harvard University Press 1955.
Lavin, Irving: *Bernini and the Unity of the Visual Arts.* Oxford University Press 1980.
Sennett, Richard: *The Conscience of the Eye: The Design and Social Life of Cities.* Faber & Faber 1991.
Spezzaferro, Luigi: "Place Farnèse: urbanisme et politique." In: *Le Palais Farnèse.* École française de Rome 1981, 85ff.

# THE POSITIVISTIC APPROACH

## 1800: The Grid

In *An Inquiry into the Nature and Causes of the Wealth of Nations* Adam Smith wrote:

"A magnificent high-road cannot be made … merely because it happens to lead to the country villa of the intendant of the province, or to that of some great lord, to whom the intendant finds it convenient to make his court. A great bridge cannot be thrown over a river at a place where nobody passes, or merely to embellish the view from the windows of a neighboring palace; things which sometimes happen in countries, where works of this kind are carried on by any other revenue than that which they themselves are capable of affording…. The expense of making and maintaining the public roads of any country must evidently increase … with the quantity and weight of the goods which it becomes necessary to fetch and carry upon those roads. The strength of a bridge must be suited to the number and weight of the carriages which are likely to pass over it. The depth and the supply of water for a navigable canal must be proportioned to the number and tonnage of the lighters which are likely to carry goods upon it; the extent of a harbor, to the number of the shipping which are likely to take shelter in it. When high-roads, bridges, canals, etc. are in this manner made and supported by the commerce which is carried on by means of them, they can be made only where that commerce requires them, and, consequently, where it is proper to make them. Their expense, too, their grandeur and magnificence, must be suited to what that commerce can afford to pay. They must be made, consequently, as it is proper to make them."[1]

This precise and detached writing dates back to 1776, during a period when the nobility dressed in their fancy clothes, dined in luxurious mansions, such as the bishop's palace in Würzburg—the decoration of its large staircase was completed in 1772—or enjoyed themselves in theaters, such as the Teatro Scientifico in Mantova, which had also just been completed.

Smith's book was one of many indications of what is worthy of naming "the society of the spectacle," two hundred years before Internationale Situationiste had begun to falter. Enlightenment criticized aristocracy's parasitic lifestyle. Goethe has young Werther—in his 1774 novel bearing the same name—expelled from a banquet because the participants did not want anyone not belonging to their class to attend it.[2] The aesthetic serving this society was eventually called into question. The intellectuals began to see baroque architecture as increasingly bombastic and fake. In the cultural environment, which was gradually taking shape in Europe at that time, architecture based on intoxicating seduction—if not deception—of the senses was considered, apart from being wasteful, morally wrong. Its abandonment was just a matter of time.

**Cathedral, Étienne-Louis Boullée, 1778**

Just two years after the publication of *The Wealth of Nations* and independently from it, the French architect Étienne-Louis Boullée unveiled his vision for a new architecture. The buildings depicted were based on elementary geometric shapes and lacked decoration, in stark contrast to what was common at the time; what really distinguished them, however, were their colossal proportions. In the vistas, which emanated a sense of grandeur, the building roofs seemed to touch the sky and the colonnades were lost in the horizon. According to Boullée, architecture should aim at creating feelings in the user, consistent with the purpose of each building—the library ought to inspire respect, the cathedral awe and devoutness, and the opera a celebratory mood.

One of Boullée's most typical designs is Isaac Newton's Cenotaph. An empty sphere approximately 150 meters in diameter sits on a cylindrical base planted with cypress trees. At its lower pole is placed the great physicist's empty sarcophagus. The sphere is perforated, allowing the daylight to create the impression of starry sky, while during the night an armillary sphere hanging in the center represents the Sun emanating light, with the Earth orbiting around it. The achieved "reversal" of time (the sense of night when it is day outside and the sense of day, when it is night outside) contributes to its otherworldly charm. The cenotaph's layout is not groundbreaking, though, since it is a mixture of the Pantheon and the mausoleum of Emperor Augustus in Rome. What makes it different is its size. It is approximately fifty times larger in volume than the majestic Pantheon; that alone shows that it is meant as a utopian design. By declaring the impossibility of its realization, Newton's Cenotaph allows us to focus our attention on the core of the architectural idea: that each building should have a specific character corresponding to its purpose; it does not suffice to be designed according to the general principles of architecture—order, symmetry, etc. In this case, the purpose of the building is to denote society's appreciation toward science, and this had to be eternally plain for everyone to see and to feel, not only to those initiated in the architectural iconography of the time.

Boullée's cathedral is even larger; approximately 600 meters in length and 200 meters in height, it would have dwarfed the admittedly huge Saint Peter in Rome; and the design for his library, with colonnades towering toward the sky and a huge barrel vault, drove monumentality to its extremes.

Boullée's designs maintain their magic even today, although our visual experiences are incomparably richer than those of people at the dawn of the Industrial Revolution. Their author—a professor at a school of engineering, École Nationale des Ponts et Chausses—did not seem to have minded that in some cases the number of columns in the ground plan did not coincide with that in the 3D depiction of the same building. His goal was to move the viewer. Unfettered by the problems associated with their eventual implementation, his designs succeed in exciting us by managing to bypass our consciousness and touch what lies beyond the control of logic. They accomplish this with the simplicity of their structure and the clarity of their configuration—that is to say, by means that allow them to appeal to the widest audience, from the most educated and refined to the plainest of people.

Boullée had responded to the program of the Enlightenment: unity between instinctive emotion and rational mind. True art no longer lay in elaborate decoration but in constraint—understood in relation to what preceded it. The "primitive hut" was recognized as the archetype for architecture. Ancient Greek monuments—inaccessible for centuries due to political circumstances—were studied systematically, revealing another world compared to that of ancient Rome: much more modest, much stricter in its principles, and much more reserved in the use of imaginative forms. In ruins, they touched the romantic soul as much as they charmed rationalists who knew that they were creations of a civilization all European nations wanted to appropriate. Classicism—the return to the architecture of the Parthenon era—triumphed. A few decades later, buildings such as the Altes Museum of Karl Friedrich Schinkel in Berlin—designed in 1823—brought to

**Altes Museum, Berlin, Karl Friedrich Schinkel, 1823**

its peak this architecture of geometric simplicity and functionality, realized with architectural members of ancient Greek appearance.

Boullée's designs expressed in a way the heroic spirit of French Revolution and its great visions. The reality of the late eighteenth and early nineteenth centuries proved to be somewhat different. Effectiveness was the predominant value in the ideology supporting the Industrial Revolution, and this is the thread that runs through Adam Smith's work. One of Boullée's students—an architect working for him—attempted to implement it to architecture.

J. N. L. Durand became a professor of the École Polytechnique in 1796. The institution, which received this name in 1795, was founded a year before by the National Assembly, the legislative body of the French Revolution. Its purpose was to train engineers who would conserve, improve, and expand the aging infrastructure network inherited by Louis XIV for the benefit of the people and the glory of the nation.

Durand developed a strictly rational system of design based on a simple idea, impressive in its power of abstraction. Buildings are comprised of a limited number of architectural components: walls, columns, pillars, doors, stairs, and roofs or domes—a full-fledged modular system. Their successful combination has created buildings for every use and of every character. It is obvious that people have very different requirements of a private house than a church. But in both cases, the columns and the walls were placed at equal spacing from one another in a grid—the use of grid is featured in Egyptian and later in Hellenistic architecture, but it was never the morphogenic principle Durand envisioned it to be.

Durand's buildings were distinguished by their symmetry and the repetition of their constituent parts, and they were predominantly square or circular. The ratio of enclosed area to perimeter was therefore optimal: the outer walls were expensive to build. This layout contributed to the buildings' structural integrity without the use of bulky walls and columns;

on top of that, it supposedly rendered them beautiful, since order as well as good and effective organization of their components responded to our deepest expectations as rational beings.

Durand arrayed a number of designs to demonstrate the superiority of his theory. The most characteristic ones are those featuring in the opening pages in the 1819 edition of his book, *Précis des leçons d'architecture données à l'École royale polytechnique*. In the first one, the mid-eighteenth-century French Pantheon, Ste. Genevieve—a highly ambitious and well-know building by J. G. Soufflot in the shape of a Greek cross—is juxtaposed with his own proposal for a circular building of the same surface recalling the Pantheon of Rome and Villa Rotonda. The illustration is inscribed as an "example of the benefits that would bring in the society the knowledge and application of the true principles of Architecture." Below Soufflot's Pantheon the caption reads: "… this building which is fairly narrow has cost eighteen million"; while below his building: "… it would cost only nine and it would be huge and magnificent."[3]

The second design reveals confidence approaching arrogance—a character quality that often seems to be an asset for architects in their professional lives. In several arts, what we call progress is often motivated by the rather unjustified disdain of what is handed down. Quatremère de Quincy, secretary of the Académie des Beaux-Arts from 1816 to 1839, argued that, "the word Modernism does not seem to mean anything else than opposition to what exists."[4] In this second design, Durand juxtaposed Saint Peter's of Rome with a church of his own with the same surface; his church is a five-aisled basilica with a rectangular plaza in front of it, corresponding to Bernini's oval square in front of Saint Peter's. The illustration is inscribed as an "example of the fatal consequences resulting from ignorance or non-application of the true principles of Architecture." Below Saint Peter's the caption reads, "this building has cost more than 350 million at the time"; while below his church, "design, which if had been applied it would have saved three quarters of Europe from centuries of calamities." It is clear that here Durand referred to the appeal of Luther's preaching to a Central European public frustrated by the constant financial bleeding caused by the funding of the construction of Saint Peter's miles away. The religious wars that followed caused huge calamities in three quarters of Europe.

Durand declared economy as the philosopher's stone of architecture. He thus approached an industry, which in the previous centuries obeyed the demands of the spectacle, from a positivist perspective. But Durand's economy was restricted to the optimization of responses to given programs. Which building would be appropriate for each occasion was not an issue. Durand did not question the need to construct a huge French Pantheon or a colossal Saint Peter; he opted to criticize vehemently the configuration of these edifices as they were being built.

Should architecture be limited to only these duties? Must the architect act in the capacity of a consultant and raise questions regarding the purpose, and the social and financial repercussions of the requisitioned project or should he/she be confined to his/her core assignment to realize a given program and to design in the strict sense of the term? It seems that these questions have not been clearly answered in any cultural environment, in any period. Vitruvius assigned architects alternating roles. On the one hand, he wanted the architect to give the most appropriate form to predetermined programs, especially when it came to temples—i.e., the most formal public buildings whose type, size, and symbolism concerned the whole city and was decided by its authorities. On the other hand, he gave the architect greater freedom of action on rather utilitarian public buildings, such as basilicas or fora. Lastly, he assigned to the architect the leading role in private projects: he repeatedly urged him (we do not know of female architects of that time) to design the houses in correspondence to the social status and finances of its owners and to ignore their impulsive desires.[5]

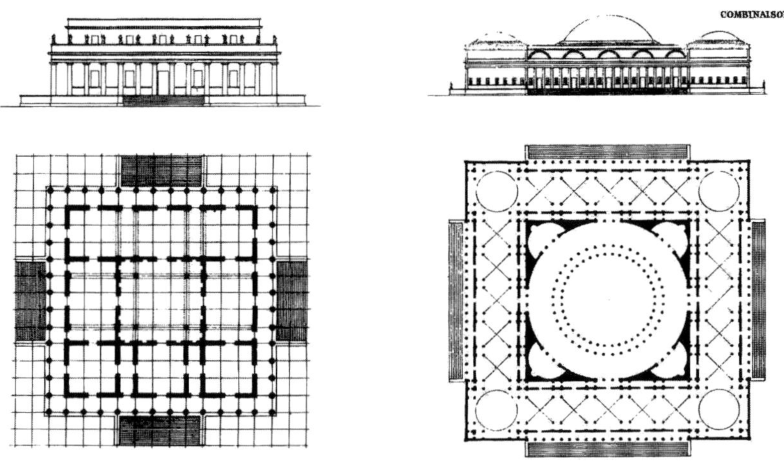


**Architectural compositions, J.N.L. Durand, 1809; private urban mansion (left) and unidentified public building (right)**

The buildings presented in *Précis* were very large, with the exception of some private houses in the city and the countryside, and some provincial town halls or courts. This made them unrealistic, thus practically none of them materialized. Nevertheless, Durand's designs were pivotal in associating classicism with reason: classicism in architecture was already in fashion—inspired by a romantic contemplation of the past—and in dire need of being seen by the public as appropriate for furnishing reasoned answers to contemporary challenges.

Durand's designs were also a source of inspiration for the architecture of the following decades. As we will see in the next chapter, in the course of the nineteenth century, buildings would become much more complex than they had been for hundreds of years, because they had to address increasingly complex needs in increasingly complex urban environments. The systematic way of organizing architectural components (be it columns and walls or halls and corridors) suggested by Durand created a very powerful paradigm, which helped making architectural "composition" synonymous with architectural design. Even the heavily decorated late nineteenth-century Beaux-Arts buildings owe something to the austere plans appearing in the pages of *Précis*; in their layout, they more or less follow Durand's clear principles, so that they can reign over their bursting formal and functional intricacy.

During the time that Durand was teaching in Paris, on the other side of the Atlantic the city of New York resorted to a positivist approach for expanding its urban fabric. With a population placing it "in the category of second-rate cities," its prospects were to increase it in the next fifty years to 400,000. In 1807, three prominent citizens were assigned to draft what would be known as "the Commissioners' Plan." The plan submitted in 1811 provided the blueprint for the street grid that we see today—with a few modifications—in Manhattan. It consisted of parallel avenues approximately 200 to 250 meters apart, and vertical to these, streets approximately sixty meters from each other. In the report accompanying the plan, its authors pointed out that they refrained from "those supposed improvements, by circles, ovals, and stars, which certainly embellish a plan, [author's note: such as in the plan of Washington of 1791], whatever may be their effects as to convenience and utility."[6] Because, they explained, "a city is to be composed principally of the habitations of men, and that straight-sided and right-angled houses are the cheapest to build and the most convenient to live in…"

Pragmatism permeates the Commissioners' Plan, and distinguishes it from earlier urban environments with comparable street layout: the settlements of the workers on the pyramids of Egypt, the planned Roman, Chinese, Indian, or Renaissance European cities. The lack of a park (Central Park was not included in the original plan) was justified with the argument that in contrast to Paris and London, New York is located between large strips of water; considering the very high land prices, it seemed "proper to admit the principles of economy to greater influence than might, un-

**183**

**Magnus Map of New York City and Brooklyn (excerpt), 1855**

der circumstances of a different kind, have consisted with the dictates of prudence and the sense of duty." The street grid is not inscribed in some elementary geometrical shape, but runs up to the rather irregular coastline. The avenues are pointing to a "northerly direction" and not oriented precisely to the north, as would have been the case if symbolism was the main concern. They are adapted to the island's oblong shape with its two roughly parallel coasts running along for about six miles in the east and ten miles in the west; and to a major road (now Fifth Avenue), established in 1785, on both sides of which the city had auctioned off large rectangular plots. And last, but not least, the avenues and streets stretch over hills and valleys regardless of the particularities of the terrain (a deliberate choice since a full survey had made detailed topographical data available). The future proved that the commissioners were particularly insightful. Manhattan's grid came to symbolize and enhance New York's character of a city offering an even field and unlimited opportunities, ready to accept the newcomer and make him/her feel at home. Austere positivism helped create a wonderful city, both familiar and mysterious, orderly and rich in surprises and changes.

The Commissioners' Plan was ultimately highly effective, while Durand's positivism led him to an inapplicable architecture that never materialized, but one that proved to be highly influential in the long run. These two cases from the early nineteenth century make us wonder about the many levels in which the architectural virtues of effectiveness and efficiency are judged. A building may appear to be wastefully configured, but it can create a steady flow of admirers that make it economically sustainable. An architecture can be efficient in using the available materials or the available land, but create buildings that nobody wants to use and thus to prove inefficient. Until someone comes forth, who will appreciate and love them …

**Notes**

1  Smith, Adam: *An Inquiry into the Nature and Causes of the Wealth of Nations* 5.3.1.
2  von Goethe, J. W.: *Die Leiden des jungen Werther*, 15 März.
3  Durand, J.N.L.: *Leçons d'architecture. Partie graphique des cours d'Architecture.* Chez l'auteur 1809, I part, pl. 1 & pl. 2.
4  de Quincy, Quatremère: *De l'invention et de l'innovation dans les ouvrages des Beaux-Arts.* F. Didot 1828, 1.
5  Vitruvius: *De Architectura* I.2.9; III.3.1-9; IV.1.3-10; V.1.2.
6  *Remarks of the Commissioners for laying out streets and roads in the city of New York, under the Act of April 3, 1807.*

**Selected Bibliography**

Buci-Glucksmann, Christine: *Baroque Reason: The Aesthetics of Modernity.* SAGE 1994.
Gratta-Guiness, Ivor: "The École Polytechnique, 1794–1850: Differences over Educational Purpose and Teaching Practices." In: *The American Mathematical Monthly.* March 2005, 233 ff.
Kostof, Spiro: *The City Shaped.* Thames & Hudson 1991.
Perez-Gomez, Alberto: *Architecture and the Crisis of Modern Science.* MIT Press 1983.
Schiller, Friedrich: *Über die ästhetische Erziehung des Menschen.* Suhrkamp 2009 (1795).
Trempler, Jörg: *Karl Friedrich Schinkel. Baumeister Preußens.* C.H. Beck 2012.

# ARCHITECTURE AND TECHNOLOGY

## Tall Buildings

In 1586, a project was finally realized after one hundred years. Domenico Fontana, following Pope Sixtus V's orders, directing 900 workers, and using 140 horses and 40 winches, moved the obelisk lying in the ancient hippodrome of the Vatican and erected it 250 meters away, in front of Saint Peter's. It is a granite monolith—25.5 meters in height and weighing 331 tons—carried to Rome from Alexandria in 37 CE by a specially constructed ship, quite unusual for its time and probably unsuitable for other uses.

The Romans not only placed orders for obelisks in Egypt, they also wrenched others from their location in order to erect them in their city. In each case, they used them as freestanding objects, unlike the Egyptians who normally placed them directly in front of pylons in the entrance of temples. One-and-a-half millennia later, Pope Sixtus V adopted the Roman practice. In order to highlight focal points of his major urban interventions, he used four out of a total of thirteen obelisks bequeathed to Renaissance Rome from antiquity—including that of the Vatican. This large obelisk (forty-one meters in height including his base) cannot compete with Saint Peter's and its 138 meters in height. With its pronounced verticality, however, it could apparently serve as a landmark in a completely different way than the church itself.

The obelisks are not buildings, if this word means artifacts accessible by humans, in the literal sense of the term. The ziggurats were. However, the materials required to build a ziggurat twice the height of Ur, for example, would be eight times as much. Many years had to pass for a radically new idea to emerge. The spiral minaret of the mosque of Samarra in modern Iraq was perhaps the most typical of the early (largely independent of each other) attempts to construct tall slender buildings. From the Kaifeng Pagoda to the tower of the Siena town hall, and from the minarets of the Blue Mosque in Constantinople to the Eiffel Tower in Paris, history is rich in examples of man's pursuit to go high—to the point that this is possible with architecture: the artifacts that liberate us from the shackles of gravity are airships and airplanes and not buildings. And yet, the struggle for conquering the skies with vehicles not very suitable for this purpose continues unabated even today: oddity seems to be inherent in much of what is done in architecture.

A big step toward our disengagement from the ground—practically rather than symbolically—was taken with the construction of livable spaces dozens, even hundreds of meters above earth's surface. This was achieved for the first time in the late nineteenth and early twentieth centuries in the so-called New World.

In 1820, Chicago had approximately 250 inhabitants; by the middle of the century its roads were still largely unpaved. But, located between the developed and densely populated eastern coast of the USA and the then sparsely populated West, it soon became the center of a revolution, the industrialization of agricultural production. In the vast plains of the Midwest, the farms were large and laborers sparse. Slavery was abolished in 1787 and the new settlers overwhelmingly preferred to cultivate the less fertile land themselves, than to work in farms owned by others. The rapid increase in productivity measured per labor unit brought by the agricultural revolution made the difference.

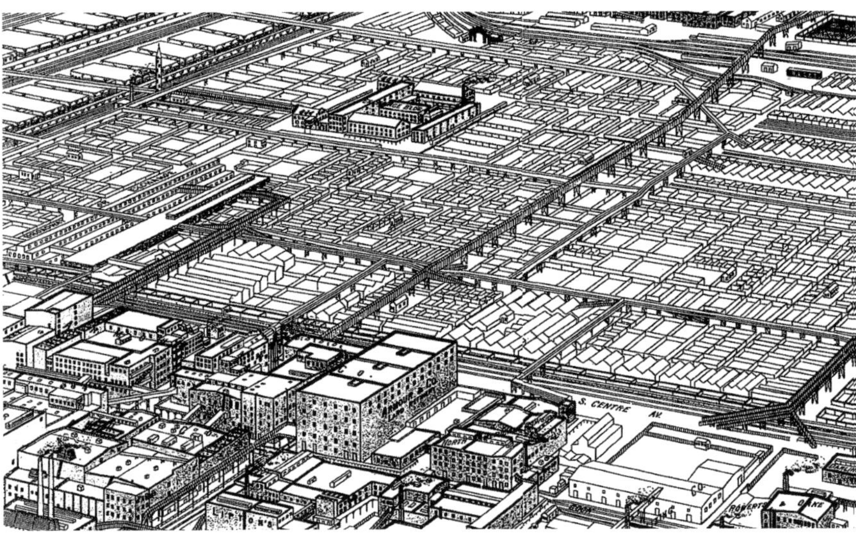



The Union Stock Yard, Chicago, in 1901; drawing Sanborn-Perris Map Co. Ltd



The new way of working the land and harvesting its produces had two pillars: knowledge and machines. The schools of agriculture established in universities furnished the first. The latter was provided by various inventions and patents: harvesters, automatic wire binders, threshing machines, manure spreaders, potato planters, hay driers. The list is endless, and the numbers dazzling: the agricultural machinery factory, founded by Cyrus McCormick in 1847, produced 250,000 harvesters annually by 1860.

Navigable rivers and an extended railroad network allowed raw materials to reach Chicago to be processed and manufactured into goods for a nationwide market. Animals were sadly among the "raw materials"—huge herds of cattle that grazed the Great Plains—and their "processing" was their slaughter, skinning, butchering, and packaging. The stockyard created to the west of the city next to McCormick's factory was from the onset very large; it would evolve in the coming years into a gigantic complex that must have evoked the atmosphere described by Franz Kafka in *Amerika*. In 1900, it was served by a railroad system 200 kilometers in length, and produced 82 percent of the meat consumed in the US. The meat packing companies established nearby had set up proper production lines such as those used in the car factories decades later. The carcasses hung with hooks from suspended rails, and each worker performed a specialized, repetitive job that he could learn quickly.

The second industrial revolution had an aspect far less heroic than steel, electricity, and telephony. The roars of up to 25,000 cattle and pigs manually slaughtered each day by specialized personnel must have haunted the lives of the poor German, Irish, and Polish immigrants who worked twelve-hour shifts in the Union Stock Yard. In this environment, trade unionism flourished. The city in the heart of the industrialization of agriculture became the center of the global eight-hour workday movement. And it was there where the events of May 1886 took place, which led to the establishment of May Day as International Workers' Day.

In order to support the industry, accounting, law, insurance, and transport firms began to settle in Chicago. Demand for commercial spaces became so pressing that entire floors in new buildings were rented to companies even before they were built. Construction peaked after the fire of 1871, which provided the opportunity to replan the city. Six- and seven-story buildings—like those on the large avenues that were cut through Paris in the eighteen-sixties in a thrust to remove its medieval features and modernize it (this venture was directed by the Prefect of the Seine Department, Baron Haussmann)—were apparently inadequate to accommodate Chicago's aspirations. Since the Great Lakes city was neither a nation's capital nor a local ruler's seat, it was free from the obligation to symbolize central authority. Architecture was called to serve the new service economy. And this was accomplished first and foremost by creating a new building type, the high-rise office building.

One of the most innovative edifices of this type was the Home Insurance Building. It was designed by the architect and engineer, William Le Baron Jenney and built in 1884–85. William Le Baron Jenney studied in the USA and then in Paris, in one of the grandes écoles, the École Centrale des Arts et Manufactures; he graduated one year after Gustave Eiffel, creator of the famous tower.

**Home Insurance Building, Chicago, William Le Baron Jenney, 1884**

The hum of the new age sounded in these new buildings; typewriters were invented in 1867. Architecture was no longer willing to sacrifice functionality, good lighting, and ventilation of spaces in controversial aesthetics or outdated symbolisms. The primary objective was to ensure appropriate living and working conditions. The various styles and architectural signs that once monopolized architectural discussion were losing their vital importance. Louis Sullivan, an architect who built on William Le Baron Jenney's ideas—and in whose office he worked briefly—captured the new priorities of architecture in a phrase that would eventually become the motto of modernism: "form ever follows function."[1] Sullivan pointed to animals and plants, apparently not knowing what is common knowledge today: that 99 percent of the species that lived on Earth are now extinct; their configuration did not respond well enough to their "function" to ensure their survival in the long run.

Despite the references to the past—such as the classical tripartite division, and its discreet but rich decoration (which would be abandoned in the next generation of skyscrapers)—Prudential Building in Buffalo, New York, built in 1894, was among the high-rises that opened a new chapter in the process of the buildings' emancipation from style. Its volume eclipsed the cornices and corbels; the seemingly limitless repetition of floors placed one upon the other removed the symbolic power from the rusticated base and the capitals of its pilasters, erased their function as decorum, and reduced them to simple ornamentation: to disposable parts of the façade of a building that owed its identity to its response to present-day practical requirements.

During the same period in Europe, styles were also gradually losing their pivotal role in architecture. For over four centuries, columns and pediments, arches and cornerstones had the power to determine the building's form and character in the eyes of an audience who had learned to recognize and respect them. By the late nineteenth century, this had changed: the buildings constructed in order to accommodate the triumphant bourgeoisie and its culture, which claimed institutions formerly controlled by the monarch or the aristocracy, had multiplied. Since the late eighteenth century, opera performances, art collections, and books ceased to be housed in halls of palaces or monasteries. Buildings devoted exclusively to them were created: theaters, museums, and libraries. As time passed, they started to compete in size and magnificence with churches and palaces, the most powerful symbols of the old regime. Their volume and layout made the treatment of their surfaces look increasingly irrelevant, even if the academic discourse, particularly in the period of Historicism from the second quarter of the nineteenth century onwards, revolved to great extent around it. The Opera houses—with their foyers, amphitheaters, and towering stages—resembled each other, as did the railway stations with their large departure halls, or the huge department stores with their festive disposal of goods, regardless whether these buildings were wrapped in neo-Baroque or neo-Gothic or any other attire. What the audience saw in them were edifices (wearing a nice dress of whatever style) where the episodes of a new type of life—life in the metropolis—would transpire.

It may be that in USA and Europe, the treatment of façades largely lost its ability to define the identity of buildings; but despite this common

**Auditorium Building, Chicago, Dankmar Adler & Louis Sullivan, 1887**

step, in the course of the nineteenth century, cities in these two regions of the world had taken a different course, mainly because of the different management of urban space.

In Europe, the authorities typically designed cities in detail. The various activities were encouraged to be housed in separate buildings, arranged in positions corresponding to the importance attributed to them: when, for example, the walls of Vienna were demolished in 1857, a zone 450 meters wide and five kilometers long was created, in which theaters, museums, the university, the new palace, the parliament, luxury homes, and office buildings were settled.

In the USA, however, space management was to a great extent a market affair; therefore, extremely dynamic and unpredictable. Instead of designing the city, the authorities guided its development by establishing rather non-hierarchical street grids—such as New York's Commissioners' Plan—and by creating incentives and imposing restrictions. The roads, that succeeded one another in a stereotype repetition, could accommodate almost any type of edifice—housing complexes, churches, theaters, warehouses, and office buildings. Private investors erected buildings to respond to emerging market demand for venues to house various activities, on the land they owned. So spots of intense city life formed randomly in the urban fabric, sparked by the construction of edifices such as the Auditorium Building in Chicago, designed by Dankmar Adler and his then partner Luis Sullivan in 1887. It housed a 4,200-seat theater, a hotel, and offices. Unlike the Paris Opera of Charles Garnier or that of Vienna, which were both constructed in early eighteen-sixties, the large theater of the Auditorium Building—like Radio City Music Hall in Rockefeller Center, built four decades later—were fully integrated into their namesake building, which more or less looked like any other large building on the block.

Moreover, already from the transition from the nineteenth to the twentieth century, a large part of the surface of the office buildings constructed did not have internal partitions, so that each tenant could arrange the space according to his needs; this forerunner to "open plan" was a rather direct application of the spirit of laissez-faire in architecture, and constituted a notable break from the tradition that wanted the form of each building precisely outlined before the construction began.

Hence, buildings of a new generation refused to be devoted to only one program, to one predetermined single function or use. Configured externally as generic, multistory, urban buildings, their outline denoted their flexibility in harmony with the freedom of capital movement that investors in building industry demanded. The anonymity of the big city combined perfectly with this architecture.

This did not mean that the building had to go unnoticed; on the contrary, it had to be as visible as possible, so long as its form posed as few restrictions on its potential use as possible. How else could the Empire State Building—this iconic building struggling for decades to find

Empire State Building, New York, Shreve, Lamb & Harmon, 1930; in the back the just completed Chrysler Building

tenants—survive financially? Built in the period of the Great Depression—its construction started on January 22, 1930 and ended 410 days later—the Empire State Building today houses about 1,000 companies employing 21,000 employees. In a tradition whose prime example is Place Vendôme, Paris, the tenants were asked to waive the right to appear individually in the city and settle for collective representation via an aesthetic in which they had no say.

In the Downtown Athletic Club, a building completed in 1930, the anonymity verged on concealment. The narrow plot, approximately twenty-three meters wide, did not discourage its architect from placing in vertical succession the most disparate activities: squash courts on the fourth floor, a golf course with small hills and a creek on the seventh, lockers and an oyster bar on the ninth, a pool illuminated underwater at night on the twelfth floor, a restaurant on the fifteenth, and suites on the floors above it. The steel frame is quite unique in its irregularity, since its columns do not continue through all the floors as usual, but are interrupted adapting to the specific spatial requirements of the individual activities accommodated on the various floors.

Multistory buildings would not even be conceivable if the appropriate technology were not available—the Tower of Babel myth was refuted when steel replaced stones and bricks. In paintings like Peter Bruegel's of 1563, the deadlock of constructing tall buildings with conventional means is visible. The walls had to be so thick that the lower floors were no longer usable.

The incentive, though, for using structural steel in buildings was not initially to save space and materials. In 1796, Charles Bage constructed the Ditherington Flax Mill facilities in Shrewsbury, England. Because of its iron columns, and floors of successive low arches made of shallow brick arches supported on joists and coated with sand and ceramic tiles, this building was less vulnerable to fire than the wooden structures that were common then. Consequently, this construction found many imitators—though not in America where the mills were still built with thick timber, equally resistant to fire. A few years earlier (1779), cast iron was first used in the construction industry. The bridge over the Severn River became an instant landmark and prompted the creation of the Ironbridge village. Does Bilbao not owe its modern rebirth to some extent to Frank Gehry's Guggenheim Museum?

**Empire State Building, New York, Shreve, Lamb & Harmon, 1930**

In the course of the nineteenth century, numerous innovations helped improve the quality of steel and drop its price considerably. Thus, steel gradually replaced cast iron, although for some years mixed construction—steel and cast or wrought iron—was the norm. The volume of the steel frames was a small fraction of the walls made of bricks and stones of comparable strength. Lower floors of tall buildings were usable. The path to conquering the skies was now open.

As usual, the solution to an array of problems is required for developing a new technology—in our case, the construction of tall buildings. One of these was protecting steel from fire; soon many reliable solutions were suggested. Another was the safe and fast vertical transportation of people and goods: tall buildings are inconceivable without elevators. In 1854, Elisha Otis presented his invention at New York's World Fair. He entered the cabin of the elevator he had built and cut the wire rope holding it in check. Its brakes activated instantly and the cabin immobilized instead of

**Downtown Athletic Club, New York, Starrett & van Vleck, 1927**

falling to the void. The sigh of relief breathed was a strong indication that the public would soon overcome its reluctance and trust these machines. The first steam-powered lifts were installed in multistory buildings around 1860, and electric elevators were invented two decades later. Within a few years their speed was increased to the point that they could serve real skyscrapers: electrical motors offer much higher accelerations than the steam or combustion engines. The Empire State Building had sixty-four of them.

The available technology—or what was developed to solve a specific problem—has always defined largely the form of the buildings. The roofs of the ancient Greek temples, for example, initially had very high gradients to drive rainwater away, approximately 1/1. The Corinthians in the first half of the seventh century BCE developed a highly advanced technology allowing them to construct completely flat, large tiles with complex interlocks that made them fit together watertight. This allowed for the creation of roofs (and, consequently, pediments) with gentle gradients as seen in the Parthenon; much later, Roman temples held to the Etruscan tradition of high-gradient roofs and pediments, also adopted by Palladio two millennia later. The change that had occurred with the Corinthian invention was not radical, but it was enough to mark the aesthetics of classical Greece. On the other hand, the Romans who remained attached to the traditional roof and pediment layout developed the *opus caementicium*, the revolutionary material that allowed them to build edifices like the Pantheon, which could do without pitched roofs altogether. Moreover, a few hundred years later, the dome of the Florence cathedral may have been very different if the Pisano shipbuilders—commissioned by Filippo Brunelleschi—had not developed the expertise enabling them to construct ropes hundreds of meters long and strong enough to meet the requirements of this major project.

And we all know that architecture would be completely different today if it were not for computers and advanced software, which allow us to design complex geometric forms with the ease we once drew a straight line with a pencil ...

**Notes**
1  Sullivan, Louis: "The tall office building artistically considered". In: *Lippincott's Magazine*, 57 (March 1896).

**Selected Bibliography**
Condit, Carl W.: *The Chicago School of Architecture: A History of Commercial and Public Building in the Chicago Area, 1875–1925*. Chicago University Press 1964.
Giedion, Sigfried: *Space, Time, and Architecture*. Harvard University Press 1962 (1941).
Hobsbawm, Eric: *The Age of Capital, 1848–1875*. Vintage 1996 (1975).
Hounshell, David: *From the American System to Mass Production 1800–1932: The Development of Manufacturing Technology in the United States*. The Johns Hopkins University Press 1984.
Koolhaas, Rem: *Delirious New York: A Retroactive Manifesto for Manhattan*. Monacelli Press 1994 (1978).
Pinol, Jean-Luc: *Le monde des villes au XIXe siècle*. Hachette 1991.

# AN ARCHITECTURE FOR ORDINARY PEOPLE?

## Modernism

Richard Rogers mentioned in a lecture in 1979 that the Centre Georges Pompidou in Paris—the Beaubourg, which had just been completed—is erroneously considered to have been designed by Renzo Piano and himself; it would more appropriate to say that it is "a work of Piano, Rogers and the Fire Brigade."[1] With this typical British humor, Rogers pointed out that the Fire Department's requirements decisively influenced the shaping of the building. The most significant change requested was to reduce its height in order to allow rapid evacuation of the upper floors in case of fire. The architects devised an ingenious solution. They submerged the building's entrance below grade and placed the emergency staircases at its ends so that they exit in the street level. They gave a slightly downward gradient to the large square in front of the building, similar to that of the square in front of Siena's town hall. The visitors descend toward the building's entrance effortlessly. The hi-tech façade, with the red escalator, is revealed in all its glory. When the visitors exit, they face people swarming in the square, whose theatricality is pronounced because of its gradient toward the building. Fortunately, cases like this one—when a restriction becomes the cause for good architecture— are not rare.

Beaubourg's design was adapted to the requirements of ensuring adequate escape routes for visitors, just in case they are needed (hopefully never). Today, safety regulations in almost the entire world prescribe in detail many features of buildings—from the number of classroom exits to the shaping of the handrails on a staircase. Ensuring adequate movement space alone often determines the layout and the configuration of buildings. Let us consider, for example, that Shinjuku Station in Tokyo serves two million passengers on a daily basis—not a novelty of today, though, as architects faced similar problems in the Colosseum or Saint Peter's Square.

Modern architecture made its goal to serve the general public, not only in the sense of crowd management. It upgraded ordinary people from mere spectators and appraisers of buildings denoting the grandeur of kings or gods, to key players in the formulation of its programs, and its choices in layout and aesthetics.

The conditions for architecture focusing its attention on ordinary people were already formed in the second half of the nineteenth and the first decades of the twentieth centuries. These were firstly political and cultural: the radical labor movement and the demand for more democracy; the metropolis and the anonymity associated with it; the increase of the prestige and power of industry, which by its nature was addressing the needs of the unknown consumer. However, some conditions had to do with architecture proper. As pointed out in Chapter 21, distinct buildings were created to house those activities of urban life that cities considered fundamental for their identity: theaters, museums, libraries. Architecture's symbolic function was downgraded in favor of its usefulness, even if those buildings connoted by themselves the triumph of the new order over the old regime. Already from the time of their construction, the Gare de l'Est or the Grand Palais brought, mutatis mutandis, a symbolic load much smaller than that carried by Notre-Dame seven centuries earlier. Upgrading usefulness meant that buildings had as primary reference point their users, and secondarily ideology or aesthetics.

Next, building activity focused to an unprecedented extent on the non-privileged. With the end of World War I and the Soviet Revolution, it had become apparent—especially in Europe—that social peace would depend to a significant degree on the improvement of the poor living conditions of the working class. "Even if it cost 100,000,000 [pounds], what was that compared with the stability of the State?" David Lloyd George, the British Prime Minister, wondered in 1919.[2] Affordable housing programs, launched in the eighteen-eighties, increased dramatically.

Architecture was requested to assist this gigantic effort, namely to dramatically broaden its target group. For thousands of years, most people took care of their housing on their own, not resorting to architects. Organized workers settlements, though, designed by experts are recorded from antiquity—among them the settlement built for those working on Sesotris II's pyramid at Kahun in Egypt. From the mid-nineteenth century, however, designs for simple, practical, and cheap houses for the lower-income strata became increasingly popular. Modern houses for the emerging middle class and the industrial products servicing them were presented at international expositions all over the Western world. Despite being often technologically advanced, these proposals conformed to the then prevailing concept of how a house ought to be: family structure and role distribution within it were considered, as one would expect, as granted; nor were the prevailing habits put into question. The semantic codes associated with the traditional configuration of private houses were not called into question either. Therefore, the form given to the houses of the unprivileged ranged between military barracks of neoclassical aesthetics with some features from *Little House on the Prairie* and a simplified

**Karl-Marx-Hof, Vienna, Karl Ehn, 1927**

version of the Renaissance urban mansion—until, practically, the early nineteen-twenties.

In the aftermath of the Great War of 1914–1918 the scale began to tip in favor of the then nascent modernism; modernism challenged conservative architecture in the design of public housing, and made its presence increasingly felt in the periphery of the large European cities,

**Carl Legien Wohnstadt, Berlin, Bruno Taut, 1928**

**Bauhaus compound, Dessau, Germany, Walter Gropius, 1923**

until it faced the hostility of the fascist regimes that swept the continent, Italy being a notable exception. Under its influence, excellent buildings were created even in cases where the presence of Classicism remained vividly distinct. The Karl-Marx-Hof, a complex of monumental dimensions with 1,382 apartments and 1,000 meters long—built between 1927 and 1940 in "red" Vienna based on designs by Karl Ehn—is one of the most famous of this category.

Modernism faced the challenges of the times sometimes with an artistic and technocratic perspective, and sometimes at the basis of a leftist political approach on the role of art and architecture in society.

These two approaches were especially noticeable in the case of Bauhaus—the School founded by Walter Gropius in Weimar, Germany in 1919 to succeed the arts and crafts school of the city and which has contributed more than any other in the reform of artistic and architectural education worldwide. Hannes Meyer, its second director who took over in 1928, upgraded the architecture workshop, founded the previous year, and gave the School a strong leftist orientation. The direction that Bauhaus was taking was opposed by the local authorities in Dessau, where it was relocated in 1925; because they funded it, these authorities had a say on the school's direction. Ludwig Mies van der Rohe, who replaced Meyer in 1930, reoriented the School to a technocratic approach despite the students' protests. This was not enough, however, for a Germany that was heading to fascism and turning to a sterilized Classicism for its monumental buildings, and to a neotraditional architecture for residential buildings. Bauhaus was forced to close down permanently in 1933, after a short stay in Berlin.

Functionalism was one of the core doctrines that all modernist architects more or less followed. The buildings had to meet concrete and clearly formulated needs in the simplest way and with optimum means.

This was the mission of architecture. To determine the needs it had to fulfill, modernism devised a median human being. It attributed to it certain characteristics—a specific physique and a specific way of thinking—which it attempted to serve in a "Fordist" spirit. Statistics acquired a central role in large-scale design: our familiar methods of presentation with pie charts, tables, graphs and diagrams of the data, now systematically collected, were devised and standards were established. Ernst Neufert's manual was first published in 1936. In any case, all building projects, even the family hearth, the ark of dreams of ordinary people, could and had to be evaluated in a rational and detached way. The house became "a machine for living in. Baths, sun, hot water, cold water, warmth at will, conservation of food, hygiene…"[3] For many rigid functionalists, especially of the postwar period, nothing more, nothing less. For them, the desires and fears of people who would reside in these buildings should not be taken into account. After all, architecture would change the world and would accomplish this by changing their minds with the new type of houses it professed.

Tiled roofs were considered outdated symbols of an old society and products of the construction technology of the past. Logic imposed flat roofs that could be planted. The dark basements and the thick walls were chains that kept people tied like serfs on their land. Light constructions with thin walls, independent from the load-bearing frame of the building, would set them free.

These ideas found worthy defenders. Walter Benjamin identified dwelling with living in a case, in a secluded and secured area; to him, modern architecture's destruction of intimacy warranted by the well-protected interior was revolutionary. Transparency and the interaction of exterior and interior spaces would bring traditional dwelling to an end, thus leaving modern man with no choice, but to face the realities of industrial era.

Houses were made eventually transparent; light and air penetrated the secluded areas. However, it is doubtful whether modernism created

**The German pavilion at the 1929 Barcelona International Exposition, Ludwig Mies van der Rohe (here a precise reconstruction of 1986)**

a completely different habitation culture and led people to a new way of facing the world. Many of its users opposed its missionary obsession to impose on them a specific way of life through the configuration of their houses and took the matter into their own hands. They made changes whenever possible. This is what they did in Pessac, a settlement next to Bordeaux, designed by Le Corbusier in mid-nineteen-twenties for the workers of Henri Frugès' industries (in 1990 these houses were listed as cultural heritage and were restored to their original form); or manifested antisocial behavior and vandalized private and public properties. Designing houses in an ostensibly positivist spirit does not seem to have had as direct consequence the rationalization of people's way of thinking. The god of modern architecture, the average person, became its nemesis.

The modernists were anything but a single body and their views varied on some extremely important issues. The architects of the "other modernism" wanted to exploit the expressive power of their art and considered as architecture's duty the creation of an evocative man-made environment rich in meanings; Alvar Aalto and Hans Scharoun were the most prominent among them; Bruno Taut was the most combative. He was the head of Berlin's municipal housing service, before being forced to abandon his position and settle in Tokyo and then in Istanbul. Since the late nineteen-thirties, he had distanced himself from mainstream modernism and advocated an earthly positivism: humanistic architecture in the service of its users, who were real people of flesh and blood, children of their time, and not imaginary beings, ideal tenants of ideal residences. His ideas were closer to those later formulated by Theodor Adorno in 1944, in a fierce attack on blatant positivism.[4] Both of them, the former from an architect's perspective and the latter from that of a socially active philosopher, attacked the notion of the house as a machine.

**Villa Savoye, Poissy, outskirts of Paris, Le Corbusier, 1929**

However, as was realized in the following decades, the large windows, the white walls and the functional kitchens were not to blame for people's alienation from their homes, but instead the destruction of public space outside them. The traditional street of familiar dimensions, which was the vessel of a rich social life, was the victim of the noble cause to let the sun enter every house—something that was not so crucial in the mid-twentieth century, as it had been in the mid-nineteenth century. But, as already pointed out, architecture is slow.

**Building of the Berlin Philharmonic, Hans Scharoun, 1960, interior**

In any case, modernism in its prosaic version never really represented the ideas of its founding fathers. The latter were convinced that modern times rendered imperative the radical renewal of forms—the form of cars and books and kitchen utensils and buildings and every other object around us—i.e., the renewal of what we call today visual culture. The basic principle of Bauhaus was that objects had to be designed so that their form makes their function obvious at first glance, and that materials had to be used as effectively as possible and according to their natural attributes. These design principles produced objects of exquisite quality, which withstood the test of time and became classic. This was especially the case for objects in which humans were not involved directly—i.e., those in which the intermediary, largely annoying, link between the creator and his material was largely absent. Tableware and furniture designed by the Bauhaus masters were far less controversial and their forms much more resilient in time than social housing—a vindication for supporters of a more artistic and technocratic approach, and an irony for those wanting a more politically activist role. Technocratic-minded Mies van der Rohe designed the German pavilion for the International Exposition of Barcelona in 1929 as a model residence—perhaps the most important building of modernism. He did this without having to apologize to any tenant for the lack of privacy that he/she probably felt behind the large sliding glass doors, or for the expensive marble walls that made it practically impossible to even hang a painting of one's choice.

Le Corbusier played two angles at the same time: the certainty of strict positivism on the one hand, and the thrill that art can offer on the other. His aggressive functionalism—the belief that form should result from function—was counterbalanced by his position that architecture lies beyond successful response to the given tasks in the engineer's spirit of rationality and effectiveness. "Architecture is the learned game, correct and magnificent, of forms assembled in the light," he stated poetically.[5] Perhaps he had a third angle; having carefully studied advertisement, he used image juxtaposition as a powerful argument that impresses even today's readers of his immensely influential *Vers une Architecture*, first published in 1923.

Generally speaking, authorities worldwide were not extremely impressed by modernism. The architecture of the future, as it eventually turned out to be, was an architecture for the marginalized and

**202**

**UN Headquarters, New York, Le Corbusier et al., 1949**

Barbican Center Housing, London, Chamberlin, Powell & Bon, 1965
and later

under-privileged. Modernist public buildings were rather rare, and many
of them were erected in the colonies, which became test fields for innovations. From early on, though, modernism offered its services to the
members of the upper classes who wanted to be distinguished among
their peers for their taste—indeed many iconic buildings of modern
architecture are expensive villas. Things changed radically after World
War II. Many governments, in an attempt to disengage from images
reminiscent of the past, began to adopt modernism; the building of the
newly established UN in New York, designed in 1947 by an international
committee, with Le Corbusier as its most influential member, marked
the beginning of a new era. Large companies also saw the opportunity
to break free from the tight grip of the forms of the past—cornices,
cornerstones, and Corinthian pilasters. The new visual culture, being
recent, was open to appropriation.

Modernism was soon well established. It is difficult to overesti-
mate its impact. If anything, what characterizes the man-made environment today is that the daily life of ordinary people is considered worthy
of being imprinted on space more strongly than abstract ideas. Because
what else do the vast tracts of commercial and industrial land surrounding the nuclei of our cities denote? They are home to mega-stores and the
parked cars in front of them—and to warehouses and industries producing
soft drinks, refrigerators, televisions, and software for our PCs. Being substantiated in space the trivial was monumentalized.

From the nineteen-twenties, modernism was dedicated into shaping this new reality. It called for architects not to hide facilities such as supermarkets and gas stations behind columns, epistyles, gabled roofs, and regular geometric solids—i.e., symbolically loaded forms. Moreover, it invented an aesthetics that gave these humble activities the right to appear as what they were. Adoption of Luis Sullivan's motto "form follows function" helped modernism to justify the forms of buildings it created; first and foremost, though, it helped architecture redefine its very purpose, in order to be allowed to serve ordinary people, to expand its scope, and to exonerate its occupation with ordinary things not expected to last for eternity.

It seems that the most typical recording of this turn of architecture toward the daily life of the common people is the quote of Le Corbusier: "architecture can be found in the telephone and in the Parthenon."[6] The mere comparison of an ordinary, dispensable, object to a building inhabited by the gods of an exceptional society is almost blasphemous. However, it was characteristic of the new evaluation of things, which was fated to shape the man-made environment and its image for at least one century— perhaps for much longer, time will tell. Furthermore, it gave those practicing this art the impression that they could be considered close associates of Phidias, even if they were designing just one more nice, but trivial, building destined for a limited life span, to be built somewhere in the vast suburban sprawl.

**Notes**

1  Author's personal notes.
2  *Minutes of a War Cabinet Meeting, March 3, 1919.*
PRO CAB 23/9/539, National Archives, 5.
3  Le Corbusier: *Vers une Architecture.* Crès et Cie 1923, 89.
4  Adorno, Theodor: "Asyl für Obdachlose". In: *Minima Moralia: Reflexionen aus dem beschädigten Leben.* Surhkamp 1951, 38.
5  Le Corbusier: *Vers une architecture.* Crès et Cie 1923, 16.
6  Le Corbusier: *Vers une architecture.* Crès et Cie 1923, 7.

**Selected Bibliography**

Colomina, Beatriz: *Privacy and Publicity: Modern Architecture as Mass Media.* MIT Press 1996.
Conrads, Ulrich: *Programmes and Manifestoes on 20th-Century Architecture.* Lund Humphries 1970.
Droste, Magdalena: *Bauhaus.* Taschen 2002.
Heynen, Hilde: *Architecture and Modernity.* MIT Press 1999.
Pooley, Colin (ed.): *Low-cost Housing Strategies: A Comparative Approach in Europe.* Leicester University Press 1992.
Zevi, Bruno: *Architecture As Space: How to Look at Architecture.* Horizon Press 1957.

# ARCHITECTURE WITHOUT ARCHITECTS

## The Age of Motorization

A building cannot be "wrong," as a theory in physics or a medical diagnosis may prove to be, since it is judged by a public that is far from homogeneous, and one whose priorities change with time and circumstances. Hence, architecture can boast that it offers almost anyone who practices it the certainty of recompense: there will always be someone who will say something good about an architect's work.

Is it possible for architecture to make the public see a building with a different view without changing a single brick? Art has been posing a similar question for nearly a century. From Marcel Duchamp's time at the latest, we know that changing the context of an object can reveal aspects that remained hidden to us, or make us feel emotions that we did not suspect the object could stimulate. In this sense, deliberate changes of the conditions and the context in which the public perceives an object can be art, provided that the changes are accomplished with means that the senses can perceive—rearranging the matter surrounding the object, for example, or with images or sounds—although even this is open for debate. Changing our mind through a text belongs marginally to the realm of art. If it is written or presented in the way common for artists—what exactly this means is a topic of another discussion—then it can probably be considered art. If it is written in the style of an art critic, then probably not. And we all generally agree that the use of hallucinogens, which change our view of the things around us, is also not art. The same questions are equally legitimate in architecture.

Often, the image we have for some buildings changes, even if the buildings themselves do not. This typically occurs with the construction of other buildings that make us revisit the existing ones. Did Seneca not recount in the passage quoted in Chapter 8 how dismissive the Romans were of the old baths when the new ones with large windows and high ceilings were built? Is it not obvious that Sant'Andrea made the Mantovese reappraise their Late Medieval town hall?

Quite often we realize that we find a building indifferent or even bad, which had impressed us a few years ago, just because many similar buildings have now been built. The rise and fall of postmodernism is telling. For two decades, surprise, subversion of the rules, and allusion to the architecture of the past were reliable design principles. But rather suddenly somewhere in the early 2000s they ceased to be: this occurred when the buildings that incorporated them exceeded a "critical number" (this is a reminder of how seriously we must take into account quantitative data when we study the history of architecture), and when many of these were with us for such a long time that they became tiring.

The ability to discern when an idea has reached its limits and when a proven architectural feature has been used so much that the public considers it outdated or, instead, continues to seek it as something reassuringly familiar, is often what distinguishes a good from a bad architect. Architecture is to a significant degree a matter of marketing.

**Hong Kong at night**



Two technological inventions at the turn of twentieth century fundamentally changed the conditions under which the public perceives the built environment, and ultimately changed the built environment itself: electricity and motorization. Electricity revolutionized the illumination of buildings and roads, doubling their time in the people's visual field and highlighting their nature as familiar objects in the menacing darkness of the night. Motorization not only allowed the spread of cities, but also created new conditions for visually perceiving our surroundings: one sees other things in a building when one walks in front of it than when one rushes past it behind a car's steering wheel traveling at thirty or sixty miles per hour.

For centuries, artificial lighting was rather rudimentary, especially outdoors. In Medieval Europe, some central roads were illuminated during the winter when it became dark early: in thirteenth- or again in fifteenth-century London, it was decreed that the owners of roadside buildings had to hang lamps outside their properties; in early 1500s Paris, some short of light had to be lit in the windows with a view to the road, while in Rome of the same period, the newly opened Via Giulia was occasionally illuminated by torches. This was roughly the case in other cities of the world, too. The situation inside the buildings was somewhat better, since the most formal spaces—from banquet halls in the houses of the upper class to theaters—were lit with a wide range of live fire devices, from oil lamps to candles affixed to candlesticks and chandeliers.

Gas brought about significant improvements to artificial lighting at the beginning of the nineteenth century. London was probably the first city in the world that started illuminating its streets with gas lamps in the eighteen-tens, though Paris also contests this title. Within two decades, a number of large and smaller cities all over the world followed suit. The representative avenues that lost their luster and splendor when darkness fell acquired a new glory.

Not surprisingly, theaters immediately adopted the new technology. Artificial lighting creates its own captivating atmosphere, and worked well to complement the spirit of the spectacle offered by these institutions. Initially, there were some problems because the gas burning consumed part of the poorly ventilated theaters' oxygen and released toxic by-products. Nevertheless, the successive improvements in the quality of the gas, as well as that of the lighting devices allowed for the widespread use of gas lighting. The most famous of the buildings to adopt gas lighting was probably the Paris Opera House, an iconic public building from the second half of the nineteenth century. To ensure its prominence in the urban fabric, a large part of the city was redesigned, even before the competition for its design was announced, which was eventually won by Charles Garnier in 1861. Today, we might focus our attention on its neobaroque decoration or its large staircase, but what guaranteed the festive mood in its foyers and the impressive spectacle on stage were the forty kilometers of pipes and the 960 gas nozzles for its lighting.

The glory of gas did not last long. By the end of the nineteenth century, the efforts to produce light with electricity had borne marketable fruits. The advantages of electric lighting over gas lighting became immediately obvious: zero exhaust, less heat, easier control and operation. Its use in interior space was soon standardized. In a span of thirty years, it eclipsed any other form of artificial lighting both indoors and outdoors; the municipal employees lighting the city's street lights one by one became a thing of the past, like the servants lighting the candles in the mansions of the aristocracy a century before.

At first, by turning night into day, electric light extended the privileged position conventional buildings had in the city's image, around the

Public transportation in New York, 1917

clock. Soon, though, it began to create a magical world rather competitive with that of buildings made of stones and bricks; a world that appeared and disappeared with the touch of a button. Illuminated signs and advertisements began to differentiate the entertainment and commercial areas of the cities' center from their residential and monumental areas, where architecture in the narrow sense of the term was still predominant.

Large hand-painted signs and advertisements were commonplace in major cities by the eighteen-eighties; entire sidewalls of four- and five-story buildings were often transformed into gigantic billboards. With electricity, this practice reached a new level. As early as the late nineteen-twenties, illuminated signs fixed on rooftops were larger than the façades of the buildings themselves—for instance, buildings on Broadway in New

Public transportation in Tokyo, 2007

York—and whole building fronts were completely covered by signage. The evanescent images and signs created by thousands of incandescence bulbs (later neon tubes)—letters, messages, pictures of merchandise and goods—that appeared and disappeared visualized the very essence of the modern metropolis: the fleeting presence of everyone and everything in it. The zoning regulations applied to Times Square from the end of the nineteen-eighties recognize this phase of our urban visual culture: it is obligatory that the illuminated signs cover the best part of the buildings' façades.[1]

The radical change in the conditions under which the built environment is perceived, though, came with the motorization of transport. In the eighteen-thirties and forties, railways captured the imagination of the public to the point that it attracted huge private investment, although the return was modest by standards at the time. The development of the network was remarkable. The face of Europe changed within a few decades.

Motorized transport within the cities themselves was not yet necessary. Even the largest of them extended to an area that one could cross in a reasonable time; the price was very high population density, a public health hazard in itself. Industrialization had significantly worsened sanitary conditions, even in service cities such as London; they would start gradually to improve in the second half of the nineteenth century after the enactment of Public Health legislation. Anyone who wanted to reach his/her destination quickly and in comfort used a horse-drawn carriage, either his/her own—if he/she was rich enough for the maintenance—or one offered for short lease.

The idea of combining train and carriage into a hybrid vehicle led to the invention of the horse-driven trams. In New York, this first urban public transportation service began operating in 1832, and thirty years later was used by 100,000 passengers per day. The rails were laid in public land—streets—and this raised legal and political issues, which were overcome by cities competing with each other in adopting innovations.

One issue, however, could not be solved: lack of space. In the traditionally compact city, roads were narrow and people and animals crowded in them. How else could the situation be in London, which had its streets laid out after the great fire of 1666 when it had a fraction of its mid-nineteenth-century population of 2.5 million? Eventually, what normally would have been seen as a genuine absurdity, appeared as a promising innovative idea and is still regarded a great one: moving under the earth's surface. The railroad, unable to pass through the permanently busy streets, went literally underground. In 1860, work began on a line linking three of London's main-line stations with the City. This first section of Metropolitan Line, between Paddington and Farrington opened in 1863. Sections of the District and Circle lines followed; the full loop was completed in 1884. Steam locomotives (fuelled by coke instead of coal to reduce the smoke) pulled the carriages; effective ventilation made the traveling conditions bearable. Electrification, introduced in 1890 and fully adopted by the early twentieth century, allowed for the construction of lines running at deeper levels: no smoke was generated, which had to be driven away, and the tunnels were dug underground, causing significantly less congestion on the surface during construction than the "cut and cover" method.

The construction of the Paris underground began in 1898. The subway lines beginning and ending at the gates of the mid-nineteenth-century walls—on the traces of which the Boulevard Périphérique runs today—soon formed a very dense network with stations serving the *intra muros* city.

The construction of the subway in New York began in 1900; the city already had a large network of overhead railways—the Els. As in London, it was partly designed to make remote areas accessible: the companies acquired large tracts of undeveloped land, which they later sold at significantly higher prices to finance the expensive metro lines—a policy that Hong Kong has applied consistently until today.

The temporary abandonment of the city and the submersion into a different, obviously much poorer world in terms of visual stimuli, in order for one to achieve quick movement from one point to another is a triumph of positivist thinking that worships efficiency—although the mystical nature of this underground world can touch some metaphysical chords of the public.

But the consequences were tremendous. In the long term, the popularization of the underground fragmented people's perception of the urban environment, confirming their inability to grasp the vast metropolises they built in their entirety. The city ceased to be a continuum (as perceived when walked through) and became a sum of isolated points (as perceived when one submerges in one metro station and emerges at another): therefore it completed the work of modernism from the "first-person" perspective, which destroyed the continuity of the traditional urban fabric in favor of large areas of grass and cement dotted with individual buildings in unprecedented scale.

The car, the other important innovation of the twentieth century, also changed the city and the experience it offers. The West Coast of the USA was the birthplace of the new urban culture. In 1920, Los Angeles already had a ratio of 1 car per 3.6 inhabitants; this ratio rose to 1/1.4 in 1940. After World War II, private car use became an indispensable part of everyday life for the general population in all the countries of the so-called Western World. Car use is connected with suburbanization—the settlement of city residents in the suburbs, which were in the beginning functionally dependent on the center. Over the years, suburbanization created its own dynamics. Nowadays, suburbs have evolved into real cities, but they are more extensive and dispersed than the traditional ones. Cars are indispensable, although efforts are made worldwide to concentrate populations close to centers served by public transportation.

The car also contributed to undermining the continuity of the city. Ensuring the access of its passengers to their destination in conditions of isolation from their environment during the ride—hearing nothing else but the music of their choice, protected from cold and rain—it ruined the experience of slow transition from one point of the city to

# SPACE - SCALE - SPEED - SYMBOL

**The size relationship between objects (symbols), buildings (architecture), and signs (words) according to R. Venturi, D. Scott Brown, S. Izenour**

another, of the laborious but thought-provoking transit through the traditionally dense urban fabric.

On the other hand, the car ensured the city's continuity; a new type of continuity, in a new type of city. It is a city with a large part of its surface devoted to asphalt; a city dotted with neighborhoods and buildings distant from one another; a city where traditional stone and brick architecture is overshadowed by huge signs designed to be visible when moving at high speeds; a city laid out to serve private car mobility, and adapted to the perception abilities of humans moving at dozens of miles per hour. According to some older calculations by L. Wright, the façade of an eclectic building of 1910 incorporates information 300 times greater than a typical modernist building.[2] However, in order to travel a distance of one hundred meters, one needs approximately seventy seconds by foot compared to only seven seconds by car; the bytes of information we get per second when walking in nineteenth-century urban environment and when we drive through our contemporary cities' main thoroughfares, are comparable. The problem arises when we step out of our cars …

Moving at high speeds has ultimately impoverished the experience that real architecture offers at the building's scale; architecture was

**Billboards in an urban fabric laid out before the advent of the car: New York, 1948**

forced to adjust to the requirements of the visual complexity of quickly moving people. At the zenith of individual, motorized mobility in the nineteen-fifties, sixties, and seventies, frugal but bold seemed like the obvious architectural choice for every building, partly because it met the reduced visual requirements of the car's passengers. The poverty of the largely indifferent buildings' stimuli was compensated for by the feeling that passengers came in contact with a large part of the city without spend-

**Billboards in an urban environment designed after the advent of the car: Las Vegas, 2006**

ing their time in microenvironments devoid of special interest—such as supermarket parking lots, gas stations and junctions of six-lane highways. During these decades, our cities became mazy complexes of extremely easy to read buildings.

Electric lighting and motorized movement, in particular, are probably the clearest cases in the history of architecture of changes in the terms of perceiving built environment, which proved much more profound than changes in the built environment itself, in that they deeply changed our experiences, and eventually the way we build. The changes in architecture follow, in part, changes in our mind—and the changes in our mind, in our way of thinking, in our ideas and in our sensibilities may be due to any kind of stimuli, any innovation, often outside the realm of architecture.

### Notes

1   The City of New York: *Zoning Resolution, Special Purpose Districts, Chapter 1: Special Midtown District*, Section 81-732, Special Times Square signage requirements (02.02.2011).
2   Wright, L.: "How many bits". In: *Architectural Review*, April 1973, 251 ff.

### Selected Bibliography

Augé, Marc: *Non-places, Introduction to an Anthropology of Supermodernity*. Verso 1995.
Bauman Zygmunt: *Liquid Love: On the Frailty of Human Bonds*. Polity 2003.
Jacobs, Jane: *Death and Life of Great American Cities*. Random House 1961.
Lynch, Kevin: *The Image of the City*. MIT Press 1960.
Pinol, Jan Luc: *Le monde des villes au XIX siècle*. Hachette1991.
Venturi, Robert/Scott-Brown, Denise/Izenour, Steven: *Learning from Las Vegas*. MIT Press 1972.

# HUMANS AND ENVIRONMENT

## From Vitruvius to Green Architecture

The ancient Greek writer Plutarch records an incident from the Spartan king Leotychidas' visit to Corinth. The king was led to a room for dining and entertainment. He was impressed by the coffered ceiling and he asked, apparently with some irony, if square trees grew in the area.[1] Although a king, he considered squared logs to be a blatant display of wealth and luxury.

Often in history, societies have modified their environment in an ostentatious way to demonstrate their might and particularly the power of central authority—or have resorted to the display of modifications to the environment motivated by responses to rather practical needs. The huge and perfectly joined granite boulders forming the fortification wall of Osaka Castle, built in the sixteen-twenties, visualized the power of the Tokugawa Dynasty through the display of their builders' ability to handle with absolute accuracy weights 1,000 times heavier than that of their own body. And during Nikita Khrushchev's visit to the USA, as related in Chapter 7, President Eisenhower showed his guest the motorways leading to the suburbs of Washington, the utilitarian and popular equivalent of the geometric gardens and walkways of Versailles built by Luis XIV three centuries earlier.

When does a human construct stop being primarily a liberation tool from the constraints of nature and become first and foremost a symbol of strength? Are the huge infrastructure projects that dot the earth's surface today outrageous demonstrations of power or, on the contrary, simply necessary?

The fact that without them, the survival of large groups of people and life in cities would be impossible does not offer sufficient legitimation to any technical project, either today or in the past. Alexander the Great rejected Dinocrates' proposal, mentioned in Chapter 12, to construct a city in the bosom of a huge statue resembling him because the city would not be sustainable. Long before climatic change and global warming caused

by human activity, the voices calling people to live in harmony with nature
were many. We find one of these in the oldest surviving treatise on architecture. Vitruvius echoing the Stoic philosophers' views—later summarized
by Seneca—regarded construction activity an integral part of humanity, and
placed it in historical perspective:

"It was the discovery of fire that originally gave rise to the coming
together of men, to the deliberative assembly, and to social intercourse.
And so, as they kept coming together in greater numbers into one place,
finding themselves naturally gifted beyond the other animals in not being
obliged to walk with faces to the ground, but upright and gazing upon the
splendor of the starry firmament, and also in being able to do with ease
whatever they chose with their hands and fingers, they began in that first
assembly to construct shelters. Some made them of green boughs, others dug caves on mountainsides, and some, in imitation of the nests of
swallows and the way they built, made places of refuge out of mud and
twigs. Next, by observing the shelters of others and adding new details to
their own inceptions, they constructed better and better kinds of huts as
time went on.

And since they were of an imitative and teachable nature, they
would daily point out to each other the results of their building, boasting
of the novelties in it; and thus, with their natural gifts sharpened by emula-
tion, their standards improved daily. At first they set up forked stakes connected by twigs and covered these walls with mud. Others made walls of
lumps of dried mud, covering them with reeds and leaves to keep out the
rain and the heat. Finding that such roofs could not stand the rain during
the storms of winter, they built them with peaks daubed with mud, the
roofs sloping and projecting so as to carry off the rainwater.

That houses originated as I have written above, we can see for
ourselves from the buildings that are to these days constructed of like materials by foreign tribes....

Furthermore, as men made progress by becoming more expert
in building, and as their ingenuity was increased by their dexterity so that
from habit they attained considerable skill, their intelligence was enlarged
by their industry until the more proficient adopted the trade of carpen-
ters. From these early beginnings, and from the fact that nature had not
only endowed the human race with senses like the rest of the animals,
but had also equipped their minds with the powers of thought and un-
derstanding, thus putting all other animals under their sway, they next
gradually advanced from the construction of buildings to the other arts
and sciences, and so passed from a rude and barbarous mode of life to
civilization and refinement.

Then, taking courage and looking forward from the standpoint of
higher ideas born of the multiplication of the arts, they gave up huts and
began to build houses with foundations, having brick or stone walls, and
roofs of timber and tiles; next, observation and application led them from
fluctuating and indefinite conceptions to definite rules of symmetry. Per-

ceiving that nature had been lavish in the bestowal of timber and bountiful
in stores of building material, they treated this like careful nurses, and thus
developing the refinements of life, embellished them with luxuries."[2]

**Cave dwelling, Gomeda Vadisi, Cappadocia**

Construction activity helped humans in their first steps not only because its products offered them security and protection from unfavorable
weather conditions, but also because its practice sharpened their mind and
improved their abilities.

Well conceived and disciplined building, which is worthy of the la-
bel "architecture," in the long run became associated with some of the finest aspects of civilization, and has been regularly regarded as one of these;
but it should not be practiced unrestrainedly—especially today. Vitruvius
already introduced the concept of economy to architecture, considering it
to be one of its fundamental principles[3]; the term he used is *distributio*.
Economy is achieved when all of the means at our disposal are used carefully—i.e., the building materials (preferably local, so that there is no need
to transport them from afar) and the available land. It is achieved when we
take into account the geomorphology of each site and the climate of the
region. Moreover, economy is achieved when the buildings are constructed
to meet the needs that are worth being met, and when they are appropriate for the people for whom they are intended—social criteria are of crucial
importance.

As Vitruvius has pointed out, responsible environmental management has two pillars: moderation in our demands and know-how in our practice.

Moderation is a quite vague concept indeed. On the one hand, there might be consensus in regarding as wasteful some of the over-ambitious building projects realized in Spain since the nineteen-nineties and two-thousands, today dubbed "white elephants"; or that it is rather unacceptable to close down hospitals because they are environmentally unsustainable or to argue in favor of reintroducing slavery as more environmentally friendly than washing machines and vacuum cleaners. On the other hand, our reluctance to endure some cold in winter or some heat during summer in our homes and workplaces, as long as we can change the temperature by switching on the central heating or the air conditioners is quite controversial. It seems, though, that in all cases our response is similar: we would rather try to make hospitals as effective as possible in terms of energy consumption, and central heating and air conditioners as environmentally friendly as possible.

We rely heavily on technological advances (whose impact is quantifiable and therefore can be precisely assessed) in our effort to reduce our ecological footprint, probably partly because they are much easier to achieve than changing our attitudes. We are increasingly able to see wind turbines and photovoltaic power plants around us. Our edifices are becoming smarter, and building materials are increasingly helping in conserving energy. Architecture starts to contribute actively to the effort for ecological sustainability by seeking and incorporating new technologies; and by offering new, more environmental friendly, solutions to the tasks ahead. But a fully elaborated, really green, architecture, which produces its own, distinct building forms, has yet to emerge.

At the dawn of the age of environmental responsibility, architecture is struggling to demonstrate its active role in our pursuit of sustainability—a nonetheless rather contradictory task for an activity that traditionally modifies nature for our species' short-term benefit.

Admittedly, already much of what is built today displays—to which degree deliberately, is open to debate—the new priorities we have to adopt. Since the late twentieth century, the dominant trend in architecture lauds the capabilities of the contemporary building industry without highlighting the visible and often flamboyant differentiation of human artifacts from the creations of nature. Curved lines and twisted surfaces and the swarm aesthetics increasingly substitute for the straight lines and the strictly horizontal and vertical surfaces of our ordinary multistory buildings with rectangular openings, which have ended up connoting the distance between *opera di mano* and *opera di natura*, rather than rationality and efficiency as they once did.

This trend has its origins in the nineteen-eighties. It was established on the theoretical foundation of deconstruction, the philosophical movement that wanted to demonstrate and subvert the rigidity and the

Osanbashi International Port Terminal, Yokohama, Foreign Office Architecture, 2000



impasses of the allegedly sterilized formal thinking developed in the West in recent centuries. The architecture of deconstruction destroyed the purity of geometric shapes, the rigor of their composition, their metaphysics. It replaced them with the confused lines of the draft drawing and the uncertainty of the layers.

Later on, parametric design started to be increasingly used for generating forms; although many do not look like it, such forms are in fact the product of the strict logic of mathematics and not of some more or less arbitrary decisions of the conventional "creator"—although computer programming probably resorts to as many personal choices as the design of decorative elements in the Beaux Arts buildings. Curved and twisted to this or to that direction, mysterious but legible, contemporary buildings

talk to us about our agony to create something special, something different from the sea of trivial constructions surrounding us, but also something not establishing its identity on the display of humans' superiority
over (the rest of) nature.

One of the most interesting buildings of the new era is the Osanbashi Port Terminal in Yokohama, designed in the mid-nineteen-nineties.
Its architects, Foreign Office Architecture, developed their concept on the
program's requirement to fully separate the movement of departing and
arriving cruise ships passengers, their luggage, staff, and visitors. Passen-

**Quai Branly Museum, Paris, Jean Nouvel & Patrick Blanc, 2004**



gers are led via gently sloping ramps from the entry level to the check-in
level. The visitors taking their stroll—usually people living nearby—without
really noticing their ascent end up on the decked roof where they are offered a unique view of the impressive harbor, while beneath their feet, the
level zero of the wharf is dedicated exclusively to serving ships. The floors,
the walls and the ceilings form a continuum, a radicalization of the baroque
aesthetics when the walls evaporated into the curved ceilings; thus, the
configuration of the building undermines the rigor of the statement that it
is an artifact constructed on clear principles conceived by human mind and
by human hands, and make it appear as born from the ground.

The idea to use plants and earth for building insulation is an old
one. While green roofs have been around since the time of the Hanging

**Waste incineration plant, Hiroshima, Yoshio Taniguchi, 2005**

Gardens of Babylon, green façades are quite a novelty, apart from some grown-over rural buildings. They are found more and more often in our cities; despite their looking quite "natural," they employ advanced technology and specialized know-how. Quai Branly—the museum of African, Asian, Oceanian, and American cultures in Paris—a work by Jean Nouvel from 2005, in which a large vertical garden designed by Patrick Blanc was incorporated, is a prime example of this trend.

Roughly at the same time Quai Branly was being designed, the city of Hiroshima decided to build a waste incineration plant. Its design was assigned to Yoshuo Taniguchi—the architect of a new wing of the New York MoMA—who implemented a radical idea. What distinguishes this plant from others of the same purpose is that it invites the people of Hiroshima to visit it for a walk, and reach the sea in a zone where the city's waterfront is devoted almost exclusively to commercial activities. In doing so, it calls upon us to realize how necessary it is to apply our most advanced knowledge to not destroy the very conditions of our lives; and to reconcile with something that people normally do not want to know about—that we produce waste, and that we must dispose of it properly. It is no longer an option to throw garbage somewhere out of sight as people in the past often had the luxury to do: in the voids of the compact urban fabric in Çatalhöyük 8,000 years ago; out of our window in medieval towns (the repeated threats of punishment for those who did it indicate only that this practice was widespread); in Thames and in the Seine in early nineteenth century; in the air in the twentieth century.

Throughout history, architecture gave shape sometimes to one, sometimes to the other aspect of the complex relationship between humans and their natural environment. Sometimes architecture has expressed vividly our power to modify nature, and sometimes it has attempted to turn our attention to what we lose by doing that—prime examples are the formal French and the English garden respectively. It was relatively recently, though, that it became apparent that the latter was just a visually pleasing manipulated nature that had only some attributes of real nature.

New ideas began to take shape, as demonstrated in the case of New York's old dumping ground at Staten Island. When it reached its capacity in 2001, the city's authorities decided to turn it into a large park. This was not a completely original idea: in Japan the transformation of former dumps into golf courts was common practice. For the design of the new park, the Fresh Kills Park, concepts have been employed that were developed in late twentieth century; the borders between nature and artifact were blurred to a degree never achieved in the English garden. The final form of the park was not predetermined in detail, but would largely result from the dynamic balance that will be reached with the passage of time between carefully selected plant species. The park in itself points out that the global community has to rethink the concept of human "creation" and redefine its limits. The arrogance contained in the attempt to fully subdue our environment to more or less arbitrary mental schemes is dangerous for the future of humanity and a host of other species. The same stands for the attempt to fully control the image of our surroundings, since the result is nothing but a visualization of our intention to alter our environment according to our occasional preferences without respecting the necessities of nature.

**Fresh Kills Park, New York, 2001**

But parks are parks; trees and bushes produce oxygen either meticulously manicured or grown wild. Buildings are buildings; it is still doubtful whether there will ever be a zero-emission edifice from conception to demolishment.

The Osanbashi Terminal Port of the Yokohama harbor, Quai Branly in Paris, or the waste incineration plant in Hiroshima invite us to reconsider the relation between our artifacts and the environment; they will probably need significant improvement in their energy efficiency, though, to meet tomorrow's standards; and their overall ecological footprint (including their construction) is by no means small. Depending on our point of view, we may consider that there is—or that there is not—a mismatch between the quantifiable and measurable characteristics of these buildings and their formal features; that these buildings are actually respecting the environment or that they just pretending to respect it. Depending on where we will shift our focus—to the factual data or, on the contrary, to the power of images to make us think about ourselves and our world and to appeal to our consciousness and imagination to encourage us to maintain a more ecologically responsible attitude—we can conclude that there is (or there is no) mismatch between their identity and their shape; i.e., that their architecture is either an architecture of truth or an architecture of falsehood. Architecture is such a multifaceted activity and its assessment so complex that it can allow this suspicion linger above it, without losing its luster; at least for the time being.

### Notes

1  Plutarch: *Lyc.* 13.
2  Vitruvius: *De Architectura* II.1.2-8. Transl. M. H. Morgan.
3  Vitruvius: *De Architectura* I.2.8.

### Selected Bibliography

Betsky, Aaron/Adigard, Erik: *Architecture Must Burn: A Manifesto for an Architecture Beyond Building.* Thames & Hudson 2000.
Blanc, Patrick: *The Vertical Garden: From Nature to the City.* Norton 2012.
Burgel, Guy: "La ville contemporaine: de la Seconde Guerre mondiale à nos jours." In: J. L. Pinol (ed.): *Histoire de l' Europe Urbaine, II.* Éditions du Seuil 2003.
Giddens, Anthony: *The Politics of Climate Change.* Polity 2009.
Sandercock, Leonie: "Practicing Utopia: Sustaining Cities." In: *DISP,* 148, 2002, 4ff.
Siebel, Walter: "Wesen und Zukunft der europäischen Stadt." In: *DISP,* 141, 2000, 28ff.

© 2014 by jovis Verlag GmbH
Texts by kind permission of the author.
Pictures by kind permission of the photographers/holders of the picture rights.

All rights reserved.

Front cover image by Mabry Campbell

Translation: Michael Iliakis, Athens
Copy-editing: Inez Templeton, Berlin
Design and setting: jovis:
Susanne Rösler and Franziska Fritzsche, Berlin
Lithography: Bild1Druck, Berlin
Printing and binding: graspo CZ a.s., Zlín

Bibliographic information published by the Deutsche Nationalbibliothek
The Deutsche Nationalbibliothek lists this publication in the Deutsche Nationalbibliografie;
detailed bibliographic data are available on the Internet at http://dnb.d-nb.de

jovis Verlag GmbH
Kurfürstenstraße 15/16
10785 Berlin

www.jovis.de

jovis books are available worldwide in selected bookstores. Please contact your nearest
bookseller or visit www.jovis.de for information concerning your local distribution.

ISBN 978-3-86859-315-0